Language and Globalization

Series Editors: **Sue Wright**, University of Portsm
University of Limerick, Ireland.

In the context of current political and social developments, where the national group is not so clearly defined and delineated, the state language not so clearly dominant in every domain, and cross-border flows and transfers affect more than a small elite, new patterns of language use will develop. The series aims to provide a framework for reporting on and analysing the linguistic outcomes of globalization and localization.

Titles include

David Block
MULTILINGUAL IDENTITIES IN A GLOBAL CITY
London Stories

Jenny Carl and Patrick Stevenson (*editors*)
LANGUAGE, DISCOURSE AND IDENTITY IN CENTRAL EUROPE
The German Language in a Multilingual Space

Julian Edge (*editor*)
(RE)LOCATING TESOL IN AN AGE OF EMPIRE

Alexandra Galasinska and Michał Krzyżanowski (*editors*)
DISCOURSES OF TRANSFORMATION IN CENTRAL AND EASTERN EUROPE

Roxy Harris
NEW ETHNICITIES AND LANGUAGE USE

Diarmait Mac Giolla Chríost
LANGUAGE AND THE CITY

Clare Mar-Molinero and Patrick Stevenson (*editors*)
LANGUAGE IDEOLOGIES, POLICIES AND PRACTICES
Language and the Future of Europe

Clare Mar-Molinero and Miranda Stewart (*editors*)
GLOBALIZATION AND LANGUAGE IN THE SPANISH-SPEAKING WORLD
Macro and Micro Perspectives

Ulrike Hanna Meinhof and Dariusz Galasinski
THE LANGUAGE OF BELONGING

Richard C. M. Mole (editor)
DISCURSIVE CONSTRUCTIONS OF IDENTITY IN EUROPEAN POLITICS

Leigh Oakes and Jane Warren
LANGUAGE, CITIZENSHIP AND IDENTITY IN QUEBEC

Colin H. Williams
LINGUISTIC MINORITIES IN DEMOCRATIC CONTEXT

Forthcoming titles

John Edwards
CHALLENGES IN THE SOCIAL LIFE OF LANGUAGE

Helen Kelly-Holmes and Gerlinde Mautner
LANGUAGE AND THE MARKET

Jane Jackson
INTERCULTURALITY IN STUDY AT HOME AND ABROAD

Mario Saraceni
THE RELOCATION OF ENGLISH

Christina Slade and Martina Mollering
FROM MIGRANT TO CITIZEN: TESTING LANGUAGE, TESTING CULTURE

Language and Globalization
Series Standing Order ISBN 978–1–4039–9731–9 Hardback
Series Standing Order ISBN 978–1–4039–9732–6 Paperback
(*outside North America only*)

You can receive future titles in this series as they are published by placing a standing order. Please contact your bookseller or, in case of difficulty, write to us at the address below with your name and address, the title of the series and one of the ISBNs quoted above.

Customer Services Department, Macmillan Distribution Ltd, Houndmills, Basingstoke, Hampshire RG21 6XS, England

New Ethnicities and Language Use

Roxy Harris
King's College London

First published in hardback 2006.
This paperback edition published 2009 by
PALGRAVE MACMILLAN

Palgrave Macmillan in the UK is an imprint of Macmillan Publishers Limited, registered in England, company number 785998, of Houndmills, Basingstoke, Hampshire RG21 6XS.

Palgrave Macmillan in the US is a division of St Martin's Press LLC, 175 Fifth Avenue, New York, NY 10010.

Palgrave Macmillan is the global academic imprint of the above companies and has companies and representatives throughout the world.

Palgrave® and Macmillan® are registered trademarks in the United States, the United Kingdom, Europe and other countries.

ISBN-13: 978-1-4039-9894-1 hardback
ISBN-13: 978-0-230-58007-7 paperback

This book is printed on paper suitable for recycling and made from fully managed and sustained forest sources. Logging, pulping and manufacturing processes are expected to conform to the environmental regulations of the country of origin.

A catalogue record for this book is available from the British Library.

A catalog record for this book is available from the Library of Congress.

10   9   8   7   6   5   4   3   2   1
18   17   16   15   14   13   12   11   10   09

Printed and bound in Great Britain by
CPI Antony Rowe, Chippenham and Eastbourne

*For my mother
and
in memory of John La Rose*

Contents

Acknowledgements

First, I must express my gratitude to the 'Blackhill Youth' who cheerfully and patiently gave up their time to co-operate with my persistent enquiries over an 18-month period. I am also grateful to Rachel, one of their teachers, who generously facilitated my research. I am indebted to Celia Roberts who first created the opportunity for me to embark on this research, which has culminated in *New Ethnicities and Language Use*. She, and my colleagues Ben Rampton, Constant Leung and Brian Street have provided unwavering comradeship, intellectual stimulation and fun, during some very difficult times in the UK higher education system, for which I offer my appreciation. I would like to thank all my family and friends for many different kinds of support. In particular my mother for an example of steadfast spirit forged in Africa and for the kind of encouragement only a mother can give; also, Pat for support earlier on; Roxy jr. and Remi for practical help and a touching overestimation of my powers and abilities; and John and Sarah for showing down the years that anything is possible if you just 'keep on keeping on'. Roger Hewitt exemplified, in his book *White Talk Black Talk* (1986), the value of deploying a certain kind of interdisciplinary perspective in the study of black and brown youth in Britain which has been all too rarely attempted. Together with John Solomos he gave me confidence by suggesting that this book might be possible. Thanks are due to Jill Lake and her team at Palgrave for a trouble free passage through to publication. My greatest debt is owed to Les Back for the inspiration offered by his own work, together with invaluable and wise guidance and an example of how exciting the activity of engaged scholarship can be. Finally, I thank Barbara for an all round support which made the completion of the research and the book far less arduous than it would otherwise have been. None of the above should be held to account for any failings in the finished product – for these, I am entirely responsible.

1
Introduction

This is not a book about religions (Sikh, Hindu, Muslim). Nor is it a book about languages (Panjabi, Gujarati, Hindi, Urdu). It does not claim or aim to give a holistic account of putatively homogeneous 'South Asian' ethnic or racial groupings. Rather, it is a study of the self-representations of their own patterns of language use of a group of 30 adolescents (aged 15) of mainly South Asian descent in West London in the late 1990s.[1] More precisely, the book offers an interpretive analysis of what might be learned, from these representations, about the nature of ethnicity amongst Britain's visible minorities at the turn of the century. The principal argument is that the children and grandchildren of South Asian migrants to the United Kingdom, are living out British identities which go largely unrecognised as dominant voices both inside and outside their communities seek to foreground and hold in place alternative positionings of them as principally either Sikhs, Hindus and Muslims or as Indians, Pakistanis and Bangladeshis or again as Panjabi, Gujarati, Hindi and Urdu speakers. This book argues that amongst these young people a highly significant group, perhaps a majority, while retaining both diasporic and local links with a variety of traditions derived from the Indian subcontinent, are nevertheless fundamentally shaped by an everyday low-key Britishness, albeit a Britishness with new inflections. It is this sensibility which marks them as *Brasians*. The bold use of this term challenges the diffidence of the increasing number of observers and commentators who use binary expressions such as British Asian. Terms like British Asian, in my view, continue an entrenched mindset which envisages two entirely separate, strongly bounded and homogeneous cultures which individuals need to negotiate by jumping from one to the other alternately as if inhabiting first one sealed world and then the other. *Brasian*, on the other hand, suggests a continuous flow of everyday life and cultural practices in which, at any given moment, both British and particular South Asian derived elements are always co-present. For the individual this is an existence in which one or the other cultural element is more or less marked depending on circumstance, occasion or context. Nevertheless, whether *Brasian* or a phrase like British Asian is used, both these kinds of terminology are indicative of profound social forces and changes which have long been visible in popular culture (for instance in *TV*: Goodness Gracious Me, The Kumars at No. 42; *Film*: East is East, Bend it Like Beckham; *Novels*: Anita and Me; *Sport:* 2004 Olympic Silver Medal boxer Amir Khan whose dominant presentation of identity is as a young man from Bolton, Lancashire, despite his family's origins in Pakistan).

I explicitly reject the popular notion that the young people depicted in the book are in any way 'caught between two cultures'. This observation is especially pertinent since the completion of this book, in the summer of 2005, coincides with yet another fervent debate in Britain about the nature of Britishness, occasioned by the lethal bombings and attempted bombings of the London underground and bus systems on the 7 July and 21 July 2005 respectively. The shock of the bombings, in which a number of bombers apparently killed themselves along with their more than fifty victims, was followed by something which seemed to amaze British politicians, media commentators and political analysts. Their early attribution of the bombings to malign outside forces such as Al-Qaeda and a variety of dangerous foreigners, both named and anonymous, was soon overtaken by an emerging reality which seemed to stun them. Several of the alleged bombers came from West Yorkshire and had strong connections with the city of Leeds. In other words, their strongest identifications were as local British, specifically Yorkshire, young men. Some of their families may well have migrated from South Asian roots in Pakistan, but they themselves were Yorkshiremen. They spoke as if they came from Yorkshire, and the overwhelming majority of their everyday cultural practices were unexceptional in this local context in the north of England. Yet the aforementioned leading British politicians and commentators found this difficult to grasp. Certainly they adjusted their early rhetoric about the bombings so as to acknowledge that the suspects were 'British born', and began to refer to them as 'home-grown' terrorists; but always with a tone of astonishment or bemusement. The idea that these young people could live as unremarkable Britons, not standing out against their local landscape, *at the same time as* retaining both affective and concrete links with global diasporas, seemed to strain the imaginative resources of British leaders. Their stance in this respect is curious, since very large numbers of white British people have little difficulty in retaining fierce local British identifications and allegiances alongside continuing affective and concrete links with *their* diasporas in Australia, New Zealand, South Africa, Zimbabwe, the United States of America and Canada, to give just a few examples.

I recognise, of course, that the youth who are the focus of the present book are linked with South Asian diasporas primarily connected, in one way or another, to Indian origins, rather than Pakistani or Bangladeshi ones. As such, notwithstanding the more than 200 million muslims who live in India, they are mostly not influenced by global muslim diasporas, which may well operate in a different way. It must be emphasised, immediately though, that this book is not intended to be a book of political analysis, or about race or ethnic relations. Also, the research on which it is based predates the atmosphere and perspectives following the London bombings of summer 2005 by some eight years. Consequently, the book itself is not in any way offered as a commentary on these very recent events, although it is hoped that the reader will find it illuminative in a number of ways. One thing the book *does* claim is the perhaps unusual approach of opening up its analysis of the ethnicities of a group of young people through their representations of their own patterns of everyday language use and an examination of their actual language use. This reveals that their everyday interactions are navigated through a rich polyphony of London English, community languages like Gujarati and Panjabi, as well as Jamaican and African American English expression. In this ensemble it is the specifically London dimension which is dominantly heard above all others. Sociologists and cultural studies specialists interested in questions of ethnicity and culture have routinely overlooked the importance of the everyday patterns of language use of ordinary people. Conversely, sociolinguists have traditionally studied the language use of ethnic minority groups employing relatively unsophisticated and essentialist notions of ethnicity, culture and community. This book draws on insights from all three disciplines to demonstrate how young people both represent and perform their new ethnicities. The young people in this book, known collectively as the Blackhill Youth[2] are a group of thirty 15- and 16-year-old boys and girls of mainly South Asian descent whom I studied over a period of 18 months in their school environment in West London in the late 1990s.

The research was founded upon a proposition advanced by Stuart Hall concerning the concept of what he calls *Translation* which he argues,

describes those identity formations which cut across and intersect natural frontiers, and which are composed of people who have been dispersed forever from their homelands. Such people retain strong links with their places of origin and their traditions, but they are without the illusion of a return to the past. They are obliged to come to terms with the new cultures they inhabit, without simply assimilating to them and losing their identities completely. They bear upon them the traces of the particular cultures, traditions, languages and histories by which they were shaped. The difference is that they are not and will never be unified in the old sense, because they are irrevocably the product of several interlocking histories and cultures, belong at one and the same time to several "homes" (and to no one particular "home"). People belonging to such cultures of hybridity have had to renounce the dream or ambition of rediscovering any kind of "lost" cultural purity, or ethnic absolutism. They are irrevocably translated ... . They are the products of the new diasporas created by the post-colonial migrations. They must learn to inhabit at least two identities, to speak two cultural languages, to translate and negotiate between them. Cultures of hybridity are one of the distinctly novel types of identity produced in the era of late-modernity, and there are more and more examples of them to be discovered.

(Hall, 1992a: 310)

This book interrogates what these 'cultures of hybridity' and Hall's associated and highly influential theoretical proposition 'new ethnicities' (Hall, 1988), might look like in terms of how they are formed and how they develop in the context of everyday life.

In pursuit of answers to these questions I advance a number of linked arguments. Firstly, I argue that the British Cultural Studies tradition which inspired the research, has tended in its study of youth, including ethnic minority youth, to concentrate on the spectacular. As such its gaze has missed what might be learned from the study of ordinary youth and their routine behaviour. This book shows how the analysis of the everyday prosaic self-representations and behaviour of a group of young people can offer illuminating insights into the nature of one youth social formation looked at in a 'new ethnicities' and 'cultures of hybridity' frame. Secondly, I suggest that the anti-essentialist strand within British Cultural Studies, despite its aspiration to promote the idea of fluidity and the indefinite deferment of closure, has been nevertheless trapped by its concentration on the visual. Consequently, talk of 'new ethnicities' and 'cultures of hybridity' can appear to be chronically undermined by the essential enduring biological fixity of the skin colour of black and brown people in Britain and what this signifies in social, cultural, economic and political life. This book attempts to escape these limitations by showing the richer insights which become possible when the frame of analysis with respect to ethnicity is based on a landscape of sound rather than of vision alone. Thirdly, sound in this context inevitably refers to the everyday language use of ordinary people which has also been startlingly ignored in British Cultural Studies. Thus, I show why focusing on this aspect of cultural life might be important for developing an empirical understanding of the concepts 'new ethnicities' and 'cultures of hybridity'. Finally, the book attempts to show the importance of foregrounding the voices and self-representations of the youth involved in the study in a way that many leading British Cultural Studies theorists have neither successfully managed, nor necessarily wanted to do; preferring, instead, the scope of the sweeping magesterial authorial voice in which individual black and brown Britons appear principally as objects of textual analysis. In developing these perspectives I seek to temper theoretical formulation with the sober groundings of empirical data, and to find a way of reconciling helpful insights available from the cultural studies, sociolinguistic and sociological traditions.

In autobiographical terms the starting point for the research was a perspective developed from my personal positioning in British society. I was born in Britain to black parents who came from West Africa and have overwhelmingly lived my life in Britain, albeit with strong and continuing diasporic connections with West Africa. This background has fashioned in me a deep experience of the nuances of living as part of a collection of visible,[3] black and brown skinned, formerly colonised ethnic minorities, subordinated to a dominant white majority in a strongly racialised society. Populations like these have grown accustomed to an everyday experience in which our representation by the white majority has fluctuated between being ignored, being belittled and being stereotyped. Of particular interest to me has been the distance between those representations of the ethnicity of visible minority groups deployed in public discourses in Britain by dominant forces, and the representations which have salience amongst the minority groups themselves. As Bhabha has commented,

> An important feature of colonial discourse is its dependence on the concept of 'fixity' in the ideological construction of otherness. Fixity, as the sign of cultural/historical/racial difference in the discourse of colonialism, is a paradoxical mode of representation: it connotes rigidity and an unchanging order as well as disorder, degeneracy and

daemonic repetition. Likewise the stereotype, which is its major discursive strategy, is a form of knowledge and identification that vacillates between what is always 'in place', already known, and something that must be anxiously repeated.

(Bhabha, 1994: 66)

In pursuing my interest in minority group self-representation I had previously discovered that the elicitation from informants of accounts of their own patterns of language use was a fertile source for the perception and charting of shifts in ethnicity. The sites I had previously chosen were educational ones in further and adult education where the informants ranged in age from 16 upwards. The research approach had not been intended to 'prove' that informants actually used language in the way they themselves described but to interpret the significance of the fact that they chose to select particular representations when asked. This work yielded two videos – *Afro-Caribbean Language Issues: Some student views* (Harris and Savitzky, 1985), *West African Students, Language and Education* (Harris and Billington, 1987) and two publications – *My Personal Language History* (Harris and Savitzky, 1988) and *Language and Power* (Harris *et al.*, 1990). Central to my concerns was the idea that representations of ethnicity were contestable – not fixed; and furthermore that the agency and conscious experience of research informants was critically important in this process.

It was these antecedents and these interests which led directly in 1996 and 1997 to the research project, at a secondary school site, which forms the empirical basis for this book. Methodologically, a key research problem throughout was how to maintain the primacy of the informants' voices without abrogating the academic's responsibilty to offer analysis and interpretation. Theoretically, the book, as mentioned earlier, was originally inspired by the anti-essentialist current developed from one strand emerging from the British Cultural Studies tradition. A series of writings by Stuart Hall, Paul Gilroy and Kobena Mercer delineating 'ethnic absolutism' (Gilroy, 1987), 'new ethnicities' (Hall, 1988), 'diaspora' and 'hybridity' (Mercer, 1994), for example, provided a theoretical vocabulary with which to work on some of the problems already outlined in this introduction.

The term 'ethnic absolutism' precisely and powerfully describes the tyrannical everyday straitjacket within which most black and brown descendants of the Empire have lived in Britain over the last fifty years and more. It encapsulates the experience of seeing the rich variety of dispositions and behaviours of individuals and groups in family and community settings reduced to crude, supposedly eternal, essences. Ethnic absolutism is, as Gilroy put it,

> a reductive, essentialist understanding of ethnic and national differ-ence which operates through an absolute sense of culture so powerful that it is capable of separating people off from each other and divert-ing them into social and historical locations that are understood to be mutually impermeable and incommensurable.
>
> (Gilroy, 1993b: 65).

It is true, as Gilroy points out, that many black and brown people themselves have used ethnic absolutism as a protective cloak in their defensive fight against racism. This is a manoeuvre which Spivak (1984) has described as strategic essentialism. Being against ethnic absolutism is relatively straightforward, but does not offer a creative framework for the thinking through of questions of ethnicity. Hall's (1988) pluralisation of the concept stimulated possibilities for the loosening and destabilising of ethnicity so that it could be investigated as something capable of temporal and spatial change and emphasising its performativity and not its ascrip-tion. For Hall, globalisation plays a central role in this process because,

> It does have a pluralizing impact on identities, producing a variety of possibilities and new positions of identification, and making identities more positional, more political, more plural and diverse; less fixed, unified or trans-historical.
>
> (Hall, 1992a: 309)

In the British context I had also previously encountered two further phenomena which needed to be sharply theorised. The first concerned the highly significant number of young people in London whose parentage, even within essentialised, binary, analytic frames, involved mixed ethnic-ity. The academic analysis of the 1991 census data offered copious evidence of the complexities suggested. For instance, there was the fact that among ethnic minority males aged 16 to 34, 40 per cent of those des-ignated as Black-Caribbean, 7 per cent of Indians, 6.2 per cent of Pakistanis, 16 per cent of Chinese, 18 per cent of Other-Asian, 19.2 per cent of Black-African and 60 per cent of Black-Other were, 'currently living with a white partner' (Berrington, 1996: 199–200). As Peach (1996 : 24) stated, 'A significant proportion of the ethnic minority population is derived from mixed unions and new ethnic identities are being forged which will be increasingly difficult to capture within the existing census categories ... Indeed, one of the lessons to be derived from the 1991

Census, is that new ethnicities are emerging in Britain'. The other phenomenon which required attention was that many young people (and others) in Britain retained both real and imaginary global African, Asian and Caribbean diasporic affiliations *at the same time as* definite British identities. Here, Mercer (1994) consistently argues that a helpful advance is to be found in a theoretical reconfiguration focusing on the discussion of the concepts of diaspora and hybridity. Mercer (2000) acknowledges that the lineage of this opening can be traced to the writings of Stuart Hall as far back as the 1960s and 1970s. Elsewhere, Mercer states boldly,

> I suggest that the emerging *cultures of hybridity* [emphasis in the original], forged among the overlapping African, Asian and Caribbean diasporas, that constitute our common home, must be seen as crucial and vital efforts to answer the "possibility and necessity of creating a new culture": *so that you can live.* [emphasis in the original] ... In a world in which everyone's identity has been thrown into question, the mixing and fusing of disparate elements to create new, hybridized identities point to ways of surviving, and thriving, in conditions of crisis and transition.
>
> (Mercer, 1994: 3–5)

and further asks in relation to the ' "younger generation" of hyperactive, hybrid overachievers' (*ibid.*: 5),

> what exactly was it about the condition of England, as compared to other European countries or to the United States, that made it such a fertile site for the flourishing of diasporic outlooks and identities in the 1980's?
>
> (*ibid.*: 5)

To sum up, Hall, Gilroy and Mercer, working within British Cultural Studies, have all written extensively on new ethnicities, diaspora and hybridity, identifying and opening a theoretical space with which this book engages and which it develops with the assistance of grounded empirical investigation. The site for this empirical investigation was a mixed comprehensive secondary school with more than 1400 pupils in the western suburbs of London, which stated that more than 78 per cent of its pupils were what it described as 'bilingual'.

Chapter 2 traces the importance of the British Cultural Studies tradition of characterising the study of class, youth, gender and eventually 'race' and ethnicity as integral to any serious consideration of culture. All of these dimensions are important aspects in the study of the Blackhill youth. Nevertheless, this chapter identifies and addresses areas where this tradition is relatively weak. Firstly, as noted earlier, there is its concentration on the spectacular cultural practices of a minority of youth at the expense of the, so to speak, 'silent majority' of youth including the ethnic minority youth. Secondly, there is its attempt to discuss the culture of ordinary people without considering their everyday use of language. Linked with this and also already mentioned earlier, is the tendency to constrain analyses of ethnicity within parameters marked by visual appearance. Given these limitations, Chapter 2 pursues the question of how then might everyday language use, ethnicities and culture be researched in an empirically grounded way, which also foregrounds the voices and self-representations of the young people being researched. The chosen approach was organised around the elicitation of data in the form of four acts of representation drawn from the Blackhill youth. The first was an extensive survey of language use, which in a sense broadly maps the terrain under consideration. It was based on a replication of the Linguistic Minorities Project's Secondary Pupils' Survey.[4] Secondly, I elicited from the young people 30 written accounts on the theme of *Language use in my life*. The third source of data was audio recordings made by 23 of the young people representing patterns of language use in their everyday lives. Finally, I conducted intensive, but open-ended interviews with each of the 30 young people. These were recorded and transcribed and provided a source of self-report data on their language use, but also on their naturally occurring speech, which served an important function in the analyses of ethnic positioning that the book provides. These data are, for instance, the source of the insights I gained into the ways in which the Britishness and other unconscious identifications of the Blackhill youth were embodied. Taken together, these approaches to data gathering constitute an attempt to deal with the problem of how to effectively centralise informants' voices; to listen to and interpret the significance of some of their low key everyday utterances and self-representations. Chapter 3 draws on data obtained from the Language Survey Questionnaire to present a kind of mapping of the terrain of language use and ethnicity which the Blackhill youth inhabit. This is important because with respect to the children and grandchildren of migrants of South Asian descent in Britain, one of the ways in they are discursively confined, whether inside or outside educational contexts, is through the ascription of a 'romantic bilingualism'. This term refers to 'the widespread practice, in British schools and other educational contexts, based on little or no analysis or enquiry, of attributing to pupils drawn from visible ethnic minority groups an expertise in and allegiance to any community languages with which they have some acquaintance' (Harris, 1997 : 14). Chapter 3 challenges these dominant discourses. What emerges is a picture of a group of young people who began their lives speaking languages other than English, then made the transition by their teens to an English language dominance. However, this did not mean that they left their original community languages behind. Their use was retained in limited form in a variety of complex ways in specific contexts and with specific people; with varying degrees of proficiency but limited literacy, and linked with an even wider range of linguistic influences through their diaspora families. Among the notable behaviours reported by the youth was a distinct and particular use of community languages with their grandparents alongside a marked and dominant use of English with their siblings. It is acknowledged that although the elicitation of this kind of evidence is broadly and usefully informative it cannot shed light on the how and why questions related to the description and analysis of cultural processes. This task is accomplished in Chapters 4, 5, 6, 7 and 8.

Chapter 4 attempts to express what the theoretical notion of 'new ethnicities' might be like when presented as lived experience. Although, theoretically, 'new ethnicities' has been enormously influential and suggestive, it has rarely been realised empirically. This chapter, therefore, offers new ethnicities in the form of a kind of relatively unmediated 'thick description'. In order to convey this effect the chapter consists of a series of portraits of individuals keeping as close as possible to their own representations in their own voices and muting, as far as possible, the mediation of the authorial voice. These portraits also question the implication of the 'new' in 'new ethnicities' which might suggest that young people like the Blackhill youth forge new ethnicities by casting off the 'old' as represented by their inheritance from their grandparents and parents. The chapter shows, rather, that the everyday lives of the young people are characterised by the co-presence of the old *and* the new – the traditional and the contemporary. One boy, Amaljeet, who claims a Sikh inheritance, both supports traditional cultural forms like his dhol drumming band related to Bhangra music and simultaneously subverts it in his choice of stage outfit. At the same time he declares some of his favourite music to be reggae music. He is strongly affiliated to Panjabi language but claims a strong affiliation to Jamaican Creole too. Yet at the same time when he talks he sounds like a Londoner. A girl, Diya, who also speaks with a markedly London accent, says that she belongs to a fairly religious Hindu family, shows an awareness of caste and takes part in a range of Hindu festivals and cultural practices. However, she expresses little interest in other aspects of the maintenance of cultural traditions such as learning Gujarati language. Despite her participation in Hindu rituals, according to her, her knowledge of their meaning is wafer thin, while her understanding of the meanings of the everyday cultural practices of her British teenage life is very deep. In both these instances significance is attached to how Amaljeet and Diya sound when they talk and the implications this might have for their identities. This perspective receives an expanded treatment in Chapter 5.

Chapter 5 concentrates on how the Blackhill youth talk. Using examples drawn from their naturally occurring speech the chapter demonstrates how their identities are embodied. A broad sociolinguistic analysis reveals that in their routine utterances they embody a fundamental Britishness. This is inscribed as a specific Londonness which is marked phonologically, grammatically and lexically. But this inescapable and dominant marker of identity does not stand in isolation. It is interwoven in complex ways with other linguistic markers of identity and affiliation. These markers are connected with two broad cultural influences – the traditional and the emergent contemporary. The traditional is seen in residual linguistic markers in their speech connected with languages like Panjabi, Gujarati and Hindi. The emergent contemporary linguistic markers in the speech of the Blackhill youth take a variety of forms. Sometimes the influence appears to be locally acquired through contact with other ethnic formations (Jamaican language). At other times the influence is global and apparently encountered through popular culture (African American Vernacular English, Upspeak or Australian questioning intonation). The latter in particular, signals a global teenage affiliation which has not been inherited. This kind of configuration is difficult for many people to grasp as was seen in 2001 when the then British Home Secretary David Blunkett struggling to account for rioting by youth of South Asian descent in northern English cities such as Bradford, Burnley and Oldham, partly blamed the lack of English being spoken in what he called their 'Asian' homes. This despite the plainly Yorkshire and Lancashire Englishes and accents in which they explained their activities on national radio and television. The difficulty in readily perceiving these phenomena is exacerbated by the habit of allowing the visual rather than the aural to dominate in considerations of ethnicity. Chapter 5 proposes instead, the suggestion that we should 'think with the ears rather than think with the eyes'.[5]

Chapter 6 shows that it is not possible to understand the 'new ethnicities' and 'cultures of hybridity' of the Blackhill youth, and others like them, without understanding the ways in which their everyday cultural practices are constructed in dense patterns of inheritance, expertise and affiliation operating both locally and globally. These behaviours can be most clearly perceived in terms of their relationship to communities and practices. Rather than belonging to any one community, the Blackhill youth simultaneously inhabit a number of ethnic and cultural subcommunities whose practices articulate together drawing both on residual traditional elements informed by diasporic influences, and on emergent local elements with different emphases dominant at contingent moments. Membership of these subcommunities requires participants to manoeuvre and negotiate their way through everyday practices connected to community language use, interaction with adolescent peers, religious practices, and diaspora connections and continuities. This is all accomplished with little or no overt sign of crisis or serious discomfort. In this intricate mosaic, what is dominant is at most times heavily marked by cultural behaviour typical of contemporary British customs, practices and sensibilities among young people in general, regardless of their nominal ethnic positioning. These developments are emphatically the product not of spectacular incidents, moments or behaviours, but of countless exchanges, experiences and observations accumulated in the routine intercourse of daily life. Again, as throughout the book, issues of language play a significant role. The prominent themes in the chapter are illuminated by striking empirical illustrations. These shed light on questions such as why the youth claim allegiance to Hindu, Sikh and Muslim religions while being weakly committed to their observances and knowing little about their central tenets; why they claim a community language as their own while having very limited proficiency in it and no practical interest in rectifying this state of affairs; why they proudly claim their global diasporic links while explictly comparing their grandparental and parental homelands unfavourably with Britain; and how the boys reconcile their self-characterisation as *Asians* with their strong affiliation to black masculinities heavily dominated by African American and Jamaican influences.

Chapter 7 challenges the familiar view that the popular cultural tastes of young people of South Asian descent in Britain are essentially dominated by an attachment to 'exotic' cultural forms such as Bhangra music and Bollywood films. The empirical evidence, drawn from the Blackhill youth themselves, shows that they are more likely to declare allegiance to a wide variety of Anglo-American popular music and to *Hollywood* films. In the shaping and positioning of their tastes, questions of language are conspicuously influential. Their tastes comprise a synthesis between the typically British adolescent and the markedly South Asian, but with the British inflection dominant. As in other areas of their lives this represents no simple struggle between the old and the new, the traditional and the modern. Rather, all these elements are potentially available to the Blackhill youth at all times. In other words, in their popular cultural tastes they are very similar to other British youth, except that they live with a constant sonic and visual backdrop not normally as readily available to other formations of British youth. This sonic and visual backdrop is provided by those elements of music, film, TV and radio which connect with the circulating migrations and cultural flows of the global South Asian diasporas; all linked intimately with languages other than English. The arguments in the chapter are supported throughout by vivid examples of, for instance, a). the ways in which the eclectic 'pop' music affiliations of the girls co-exist with their empathy for Bollywood movie aesthetics or b). the attachment of the boys to a wide range of 'hard' black music styles together with an avid identification with the aesthetics of Hollywood movies and strong disavowal of the aesthetics of Bollywood movies. In an unexpected twist, evidence is provided of the surprisingly strong vein of indifference amongst perhaps the 'silent majority' of Blackhill youth to all these popular cultural currents.

Finally, Chapter 8 argues that the empirical realisation of 'new ethnicities' and 'cultures of hybridity' leads to the uncovering of emergent configurations of identity. It suggests that one such identity formation is that of the *Brasian*. It is emphatically recognised that there are indeed significant specificities connected to Sikh, Hindu and Muslim ethnicities and cultural spaces; and recognised particularities related to East African, Indian, Pakistani, Bangladeshi, Singaporean and Mauritian experiences; and also distinctive flavours associated with Panjabi, Gujarati, Hindi, and Urdu linguistic environments. Nevertheless, a distinctive emergent *Brasian* identity developed from collections of ethnicities and cultures of hybridity is clearly discernible in contemporary Britain. The fused term *Brasian* overcomes the implied essentialising dichotomies of increasingly popular terms such as 'British Asian'. *Brasian* is certainly not intended to be just another homogenising term, nor does it imply assimilation. Instead, it captures the rich and elaborate interwoven enactment of ethnicities in the interstitial textures of everyday life. It is a formulation embracing openness, variability and unpredictability. It also identifies the ways in which, for the majority of young people of South Asian descent in Britain, Britishness is always there, deeply rooted, especially in its embodied and therefore inescapable form as everyday language use. The *Brasian* formulation is also supported in this final chapter with references to a range of indicative phenomena visible in many other aspects of contemporary British life. It is in no way suggested that the *Brasian* is the only way in which South Asian heritage identities can be imagined and demonstrated. But I speculate that it is the dominant perceptible formation amongst young people of South Asian descent in Britain, and that similar forces are at work amongst the youth in the communities of other ethnic minority migrant groups in global cities like London.

A note on textual devices

1. In block quotations of the direct speech of informants certain features of the speech are regularly and deliberately marked within square brackets [ ]. This is especially used as a device to emphasise their local Londonness and to remind the reader of this at all times. The marker most often used in this respect is the phonetic marker of T–glottalling [ʔ] which is historically a classic symbol of working class London speech. This is intended to act as a counterweight to the overwhelming distracting significance customarily accorded to visual appearance and other surface indicators such as nomenclature, style of dress, and religious affliation as the key markers of ethnicity. Occasionally, an enclosure within square brackets in a block quotation of speech is an author's insertion to assist reader comprehension.
2. In direct quotations of informants' speech 'ums', 'ers', and other hesitation phenomena such as restarts (I- I- I-) are included. This is intended to give a flavour of *how* the young people responded to certain questions and their relative ease or difficulty in reaching for their statements of position.
3. ... indicates omission of a section of text
4. (.) indicates a significant pause
5. = indicates latched speech in which the speaker's utterance joins directly onto their interlocutor's previous turn with no discernible gap between the two utterances.
6. // shows overlapping speech in which the speaker begins an utterance while their interlocutor is still engaged in speaking.
7. Where there are block quotations taken from informants' written accounts these are presented within inverted commas ' '.
8. Sometimes in the middle of a block quotation a word is bracketed ( ). This indicates that the enclosed word was difficult to decipher during the transcription process. The enclosure represents my guess at what the speaker said.

2
Researching Ethnicities and Cultures

Introduction

Researching ethnicities and cultures using an ethnographic perspective is not an easy matter. In the first place, there is the question as to whether the researcher should investigate ethnic and cultural formations as an in-group or out-group member. In the former guise there is the well-known risk of missing what is strange about the familiar. The latter stance lays the researcher open to accusations of inauthenticity and of fundamentally misunderstanding, patronising or misrepresenting the group under study. This problem is particularly marked where the group concerned has historically suffered severe forms of domination, racism and stereotyping. Linked to these difficulties, are those concerning ways in which research data can be elicited in the least exploitative fashion and judging what degree of prominence should be given to the direct expression of the world view of the research informants. Despite these potential impediments, this chapter sets out (i) why it is nevertheless important to carry out such research in Britain (ii) some of the difficulties involved (iii) how my research addresses these problems.

The need for research on black and brown speaking subjects

The introduction to this book made clear its indebtedness to the British Cultural Studies (CCCS) tradition.[1] This tradition's approach to the study of class (Clarke *et al.*, 1979; Willis, 1977/1980; Cohen, 1997), youth (Hall and Jefferson, 1976), gender (Women's Studies Group, 1978; McRobbie, 1980; Carby, 1982/1992; Parmar, 1982/1992) and 'race', (CCCS, 1982/1992; Gilroy, 1987; Hall *et al.*, 1978; Hall, 1988, 1991, 1992a), in Britain has been pioneering and inspirational. The importance of these interventions, with respect to the analysis of questions of 'race' and ethnicity lies in two directions. Firstly, they reflect the treatment of culture within the frame of Williams' type (ii) definition of the term. That is, culture in the sense of 'a particular way of life, whether of a people, a period or a group' (Williams, 1976: 80). On the one hand British Cultural Studies has offered a stimulating vision of what might be possible in the study of the ways of life of black and brown Britons. On the other hand it has all too rarely been able to carry out itself or stimulate an abundance of such studies rooted in ethnographically informed detail. Nevertheless, the tradition has been important in another way. It opposed the dominant representation of people of Caribbean and South Asian descent in British society which has been essentialist and one dimensional, with a confused mix of the racial and the ethnic to the fore. However, this essentialism has been only weakly challenged by detailed academic studies of the ways of life of these groups in Britain. To be sure there have been some youth oriented studies of some of the communities, and also some gendered studies, but rarely studies where these communities have been depicted as also classed or inter-generationally connected in ways not characterised by relations of crisis. In the present book I have tried to link together the possibilities related to class, gender, youth, 'race' and ethnicity opened up by the CCCS tradition. For instance, I have taken care to record, where available, information locating the Blackhill youth in socio-economic terms (see Appendix B). So they are not just any group of young people of South Asian descent, behaving just as they please free of any such constraints of class. I have also taken issues of gender into account and boys and girls are given broadly equal prominence. However, there are certain weaknesses in the CCCS tradition, and indeed more widely, with regard to black and brown youth that I have set out to redress. First of all, even when it had overcome its early relative lack of interest in this youth (Hall and Jefferson, 1976), British Cultural Studies could be critiqued (Harris, 1996) for concentrating, as far as ethnic minority youth was concerned, only on the spectacular cultural practices of black working class male youth of Caribbean descent (e.g. Hebdige, 1979, 1987/1990). Paying attention to females as demanded by McRobbie & Garber (1976) and McRobbie (1980/1991) did not solve the problem since black and brown females were then marginalised (Carby, 1982b/1992; Parmar, 1982/1992). In addition to the overall concentration on youth, this approach presented youth as a somewhat hermetically sealed social category with little sign of its broadly consensual interaction with its parental generation. An important problem here was one that had been apparent in the CCCS work in general not simply in the work on 'race' and ethnicity; that is a tendency to treat those on whom it was commenting as objects of textual analysis rather than as agentive speaking subjects. Angela McRobbie has succinctly summarised the issues at stake,

> [T]he problem in cultural studies today ... is the absence of reference to real existing identities in the ethnographic sense. The identities being discussed ... are textual or discursive identities. The site of identity formation in cultural studies remains implicitly in and through cultural commodities and texts rather than in and through the cultural practices of everyday life.
>
> (McRobbie, 1992: 730)

continuing in similar vein she concluded with,

> [a] plea for carrying out interactive research on groups and individuals who are more than just audiences for texts ... it is necessary that we somehow move away from the binary opposition which still haunts cultural studies, that is, the distinction between text and lived experience, between media and reality, between culture and society. What is now required is a methodology, a new paradigm for conceptualising identity-in-culture, an ethnographic approach which takes as its starting point the relational interactive quality of everyday life and which brings a renewed rigor to this kind of work by integrating into it a keen sense of history and contingency.
>
> (*ibid.*: 730)

McRobbie's challenge to researchers is one taken up by the research approach presented in this book. An ethnographic sensibility has been brought to bear in order to depict identity formation in and through the representation of the cultural practices of everyday life. I have endeavoured to show how these myriad practices are interrelated rather than atomised, and how they are imbued at all times with the marks of both the historical and the contemporarily contingent. It is, though, fair to say, that since British Cultural Studies took an anti-essentialist turn on questions of 'race' and ethnicity as epitomised by Stuart Hall's 'new ethnicities' theoretical frame, a number of empirical studies influenced by it have at least partially met McRobbie's criticisms.

Back (1996), is straightforward about its intellectual antecedents and is one of very few texts to unambiguously claim the phrase 'new ethnicities'.[2] It makes clear its indebtedness to Cultural Studies in general and the work of Hall, Gilroy and Mercer in particular, in attempting to construct a measured countering of cultural absolutism and essentialism. The sociolinguistic study produced by Rampton (1995) makes extensive reference to the influence of Gilroy's work on ethnic absolutism and the cultural inadequacy of unitary notions of Britishness. Gillespie (1995) refers heavily to the aspect of Hall's theoretical work which pluralises terms like identity and ethnicity. She also makes it clear that she finds the thinking of Mercer and Gilroy helpful as she incorporates concepts such as diaspora and hybridity into the interpretive frame of her research. Alexander (1996) and Alexander (2000), are studies of British youth of African Caribbean and South Asian descent respectively, which *do* draw substantially on these traditions of theory. The former boasts a foreword by Stuart Hall who acknowledges,

> Much of the debate that flows from the questions identified above [relating to 'black' identity in the British urban context] has been pursued on a very broad and general canvas – one that is too wide to capture the complex and subject interweaving of practices and meanings which now constitute the taking-on of this identity among young British 'black' people. Claire Alexander, however, has gone back to the detailed 'micro-physics' of power and meaning which alone offers a sufficiently fine-grained analysis to show the mechanisms of identity construction and 'performance' at work in all the rich detail we require if these more abstract theoretical questions are to be adequately addressed.
>
> (Hall, 1996: vi)

In her later text (Alexander, 2000), Alexander states her intention to 'challenge monodimensional, essentialist accounts of Asian youth identities' (Alexander, 2000: 23). Sewell (1997) in his study of boys of African Caribbean descent does mention this theoretical perspective of Hall and others, but is hesitant and in the end not entirely clear as to the extent to which he embraces its relevance to his concerns. A more recent author who is explicit in trying to make the anti-esentialist 'new ethnicities' theory of Hall and Gilroy work empirically is Tate (2005), albeit like Rampton (1995) drawing on sociolinguistics for her analysis. While this list is not exhaustive, these studies represent most of what is available in the United Kingdom, notwithstanding additional signs in unpublished work (see Pang, 1999; Desai, 2000 and Dudrah, 2001 for examples). Nevertheless, these texts would appear to represent offerings which are both relatively meagre and late given a mass presence in Britain of black and brown citizens which now spans a period of over half a century.

Researching ethnicity through language use

Given this background the research in this book had a number of interlocking objectives. The prime focus of these was the desire to place ordinary young male and female people of South Asian descent at the centre, with a particular commitment to listening closely to their voices in a number of different ways. The question arose how, in research terms, to best accomplish these tasks. The most obvious approach was one which was more or less ethnographic. However, as Back puts it, 'There is little in the cultural studies literature that attempts to describe the cultural dynamics of new ethnicities at the level of everyday life' (Back, 1996: 4). A number of empirical studies have attempted such descriptions using methodological approaches resting on ethnographic warrants of some kind. Bloome and Green (1996) draw a useful tripartite distinction between (1) 'doing ethnography', (2) 'adopting an ethnographic perspective' and (3) 'using ethnographic tools'. I will expand on these distinctions later and show their relevance to the research in the present book. Authors like Hewitt, 1986; Rampton, 1995; Back, 1996; Gillespie, 1995; Baumann, 1996; Alexander, 1996, 2000; Hall, 2002, are among those who have pursued the study of parts of the everyday life of visible ethnic minority peoples in Britain and have done so based on strong ethnographic claims. This approach, which emphasises prolonged contact and intimacy with selected informants who have been closely observed, attempts to offer, in textual form, direct, naturalistic, emic representations of the informants' lived realities. Other studies have schools as their primary focus (Mac and Ghaill, 1988; Mirza, 1992; Sewell, 1997; Anwar, 1998; Bhatti, 1999), whether or not their claims to ethnographic insights are all equally justified. Whereas all the studies just mentioned have been realised as published books, it is also worth mentioning a cluster of unpublished studies, some also with stronger ethnographic claims than others, which have been carried out by researchers who additionally make some claim to be relative ethnic insiders. In addition to the already cited studies by Pang (1999), Desai (2000), and Dudrah (2001), there are others by Raj (1997), Huq (1999) and Lakhani (2000).

My study, unlike many of those mentioned, does not overtly claim to be an ethnography. I do not place an especially heavy emphasis on the value of my participant observation nor on the particular efficacy of my field notes. I did not see my informants in social situations outside the school research site. I did not 'hang out' with them. I did not visit their homes. They did not visit mine. I did not attempt to learn and deploy languages such as Panjabi and Gujarati or atttend community events such as birthday parties or weddings. On the other hand, in different ways the methods I used clearly overlapped with those employed by those calling themselves ethnographers. Bloome and Green (1996), as indicated earlier, have usefully drawn a distinction between (a) doing ethnography (meeting the full criteria for ethnography as laid down by a discipline such as anthropology or sociology), (b) adopting an ethnographic perspective (using the disciplinary criteria to guide the research without meeting the full requirements) and (c) using ethnographic tools (using methods and techniques associated with fieldwork). For them 'doing ethnography' implies an in-depth, long-term (perhaps lasting a number of years) study of a social and cultural group using participant observation. It also implies working and/or living with a particular group of people and thus experiencing their lives across a complete range of their social, cultural and employment practices. By contrast Bloome and Green state that 'adopting an ethnographic perspective' does not imply the same stringency in terms of length, depth and scope. Such studies particularly aim to concentrate on a small number of specific aspects of the everyday life and social practices of a group of people. Finally, 'using ethnographic tools' refers simply to the use of techniques like participant observation, open-ended interviews, the elicitiation of oral life histories and the utilisation of field notes. It seems to me that, by these definitions, my own research is perhaps best characterised as a piece of qualitative research which employs ethnographic tools in an attempt to work towards an ethnographic perspective. It is within these parameters that my encounters with the Blackhill youth occurred.

Encounters with the Blackhill youth

My interactions with the Blackhill youth took place at their school – a secondary school called Blackhill[3] in the Western suburbs of London, close to the area, Southall, ethnographically researched by Baumann (1996) and Gillespie (1995).[4] This was an area in which many of the Blackhill youth lived. Blackhill, at the time of the research fieldwork in 1996–97 was a Grant Maintained school[5] with more than 1400 pupils. The School's own 1996 analysis claimed that 20 per cent of the students were white and that 78 per cent were of 'Asian origin'. In addition, 'only 19 per cent of students stated that English was the principle (sic) language used at home' and 'Asian languages are the most predominant, with almost 50 per cent of our intake using both Punjabi and English in conversation everyday'. (Blackhill School unpublished document, 1997). In addition the school attempted to characterise itself in terms of the socio-economic status of the students and their parents, stating that in national comparisons,

> Our catchment area has lower than average numbers of students coming from households in which adults have higher education and are deemed of 'high social class'. We have above average numbers of pupils on free school meals ... Over double the average number of children living in overcrowded households.
> (Blackhill School Development Plan for 1997. July 1998: 3)

This information is taken from a Performance and Assessment Report of a type which was produced for all secondary schools in England, by a variety of official educational bodies. There are obvious weaknesses with it and it begs many questions. However, it is useful as a general guide to the rough socio-economic positioning of the Blackhill youth. As such it should be read together with the approximate accounts that the Blackhill youth gave, during their interviews, of what they understood their mother and father's occupations to be (see Appendix B).

The research was conducted over two extended periods. Firstly, during the spring term 1996. Secondly, from December 1996 to July 1997. The data outcome of the first period was 19 written accounts from a group of year 9 pupils, about their personal language histories which I used as a guide to potentially salient issues, concerns and methodologies, on which the research reported in this book might be based.

During the second period, the main research was conducted with a year 10 class at Blackhill in 1997 (about a third of whom had been members of the year 9 class which had featured in the 1996 research). Data was collected during approximately 40 visits to the school at times when the Blackhill informants were timetabled to be studying GCSE English. There were 31 students in the class, (reduced to 30 when one boy left the school at the end of the spring term 1997), 17 girls and 14 boys. This is the group that has already been identified as the Blackhill youth. All but four members of the class had strong connections with a South Asian ethnicity, in many cases combined with an East African one. 16 claimed to have used Panjabi language with their families before they first attended school, nine claimed Gujarati, one Kurdish, one Mauritian French Creole, one Swahili, one Urdu. Only two students in the group claimed to have spoken nothing but English with their families before they first attended school. None of the students was white. Initiating research on language, ethnicities and culture in contexts like these is a difficult and sensitive process, which I approached in the following way.

I adopted four main research stances. Firstly, as *participant/observer* in the classroom. This occurred in two ways. (i) when I taught a short unit (3 lessons) on linguistic diversity and followed this by conducting a language survey with the Blackhill youth; eliciting from them a set of written accounts entitled 'Language use in my life'; also eliciting from them a set of self-made audio recordings on the same topic (ii) occasions when students called on me for assistance with individual or small group work when their class teacher was busy with other students, or when the class teacher had to leave the classroom to pursue other duties. Secondly, as *observer/participant* in the classroom which occurred in the many lessons when I watched and listened and took notes, commenting briefly when occasionally invited to do so by the class teacher. Thirdly, as *general observer* during my regular visits to the school when I also took notes on what I regarded as significant events. Fourthly, as *ethnographic interviewer* when I conducted individual recorded conversational interviews with all 30 students.[6]

The Blackhill youth and the representation of self

It is important to emphasise, here, that the data obtained was treated, not as naturalistic accounts of 'reality', but as *Acts of Representation* offered by the Blackhill youth in response to my extended enquiries concerning their own assessments of the nature of the patterns of language use in their lives. The first of these *Acts* was obtained by a pupil language survey questionnaire.

Act of Representation One: Pupil Language Survey Questionnaire

Undoubtedly, one of the weaknesses of surveys are that they involve self-report on the part of respondents which in turn introduces obvious problems of validity. However, the research reported in this book deliberately sought the self-reports or self-representations of informants because of an explicit interest in interrogating these. Linguistic diversity surveys have in the past decades been a fairly regular feature of the British educational context in geographical areas containing significant numbers of 'visible' ethnic minority pupils. Most have been routine exercises and localised at the level of individual Local Education Authorities and schools. A few have been of major wider significance and carried out by professional academics. These include the fairly recent (Baker and Eversley, 2000), those carried out by the Inner London

Education Authority until its abolition in 1990, Rosen and Burgess (1980), and the Linguistic Minorities Project (1983). However, the latter remains, to date the most substantial such survey and one of its questionnaires is the one used for the first part of the data collection in the present research.

All 31 of the Blackhill youth completed a modified version of the 60-question Linguistic Minorities Project's Secondary Pupils Survey of linguistic diversity with very slight modifications (Linguistic Minorities Project, 1983: 64). However, my survey retained virtually word for word the 60 survey questions of the original. Nicholas (1994) has usefully summarised some of the weaknesses of the linguistic diversity survey as a research instrument within educational establishments. Apart from the specific problems of the self-report in relation to language use, there is the problem of the teacher as the elicitor of the data since teachers are typically both authority figures and elicitors of 'correct' information. At the same time, when 'visible' ethnic minority students respond to such questionnaire surveys in their school or college in the United Kingdom they are often doing so in an ideological environment which has typically seen their 'other' languages as a serious obstacle to the pursuit of Standard English as medium of instruction, language for literacy and principal instrument of educational success. Also, historically, these students have frequently been asked to offer their survey answers alongside peers who are relatively monolingual in English and who express hostility to them on grounds of both ethnicity and language. In addition, language diversity surveys have found it difficult to cope with the ambiguities surrounding language use. These include status boundaries concerning the labelling of language use as 'language' or 'dialect'-related; the handling of languages without a written tradition, and the eliciting of data from plurilingual respondents using instruments with a monolingual research design perspective. I think I partly overcame the problem of the teacher as elicitor by carrying out the survey without being the class teacher and by showing a consistent non-hostile interest in linguistic diversity at the research site for over a year before administering the questionnaire. This also helped me to overcome the problem of data elicitation in ideologically adverse environments. I was helped in this, too, by the fact that I and all the respondents were ourselves members of 'visible' minority groups and they knew that I had grown up in a bi/multilingual home. Finally, I believe that the unit of three lessons on linguistic diversity which I taught before the questionnaires were issued, created an atmosphere favourable to their enthusiastic completion. The typical UK classroom approach to linguistic diversity has been to directly plunge into facing pupils with leading questions about the 'exotic' languages they speak (see Harris, 1997), and I would argue this is part of what leads to the kind of respondent defensiveness alluded to above by both Nicholas and the LMP researchers.[7] In the end, though, my reason for using the language questionnaire survey as my first method of significant data elicitation was to map the territory which I would later be able to follow-up with intensive qualitative research methods including interviews. I also calculated that it was the least threatening opening research move I could make towards the informants. The survey is a relatively hands-off data gathering instrument with each question requiring minimal, largely one-word, responses, and in this case responses were provided individually and privately in writing. My overriding aim was to evoke from my informants, acts of representation concerning their patterns of language use, and through this perhaps a glimpse of their own representations of their ethnic positionings. Their responses to the language questionnaire constituted the first such act of representation.

Act of Representation Two: Written accounts of patterns of language use

After the language survey and the short taught unit (3 lessons) on language diversity in Britain, I asked the Blackhill youth to work on a two part project entitled *Language Use in My Life* to be completed during the Easter holidays 1997 and handed in immediately afterwards. The first part involved them producing an open-ended piece of writing entitled *Language Use in my Life*. All 30 of them completed the task and handed their texts to me. My purpose here was to elicit a second act of representation but one which gave the informants an opportunity to be expansive, to transcend the limitations of the questionnaire format and to begin to deal with some of the complexities involved in describing patterns of language use. I deliberately asked them to engage with the project over the holidays in the hope that they might draw some members of their families into the task. As suggested earlier I was concerned, unlike many other studies of youth, to depict the everyday cultural practices of my young research informants in interrelationship with their elders, rather than simply with their adolescent peers. In the event many of the informants made explicit reference to helpful confirmatory consultations they had sought with their parents, and others. While emphasising an awareness of the limitations of self-report as a means of obtaining accounts of human social behaviour, my confidence in the value of what could be learned from information obtained in this way, had been generated by earlier work in classrooms across London (Harris and Savitzky, 1988).

Nevertheless, the limitations implicit in this kind of data elicitation was offset by the data obtained from the third act of representation of the Blackhill youth – their preparation of self-made audio recordings on language use in their lives.

Act of Representation Three: Self-made audio recordings

Twenty three of the Blackhill youth compiled recordings on typical patterns of language use in their everyday lives. In the field of sociolinguistics the proposed solution to the limitations of self-report has been the collection and analysis of what has been called *naturally occurring speech data*. However, the problems, ethical and otherwise, of achieving this have been well recognised (Wardhaugh, 1992: 150–2; Fasold, 1987: 192–3). The technique chosen here followed Sebba (1993: 11) who found, 'a number of people, in their late teens and early twenties, who were willing to take a tape recorder home with them and make recordings of themselves, their families and their friends in conversation'. In my research, too, informants were encouraged to consult their parents or other relatives if they so wished in completing these tasks, and indeed parental support was forthcoming in the making of the recordings as well as in some of the written accounts in the second act of representation as described above. Some of the informants, particularly girls, told me that they had asked for help from their mothers in constructing representations of, for instance, Gujarati script. Several informants both male and female told me that they had enlisted the help of older family members in producing taped representations of spoken Panjabi, Gujarati and other languages. In addition to the 23 informants who made recordings, a further six produced written reconstructions of what they said were typical examples of conversational exchanges which occurred in their lives. Nevertheless, the attempted acquisition of naturally occurring speech data is always a problematic activity and the resultant interpretations need to be both multi-layered and provisional. However, the data obtained through these recordings, taken together with that gathered in the other ways indicated, offers openings to glimpses of some of the community, family and peer influences in language use experienced by the informants. These recordings contained some intimations of new, hybrid, diasporic ethnicities and, in their approximation to some kinds of naturally occurring speech events, move beyond the purely representational into the realm of the 'real'. All of this data was augmented by data obtained by the final act of representation which was elicited through a series of extensive interviews.

Act of Representation Four: Individual conversational interviews

I interviewed all 30 of the Blackhill youth individually for between approximately 30 and 60 minutes each. The interviews were recorded. The tenor of the interviews was shaped by the fact that I was someone whom at least a third of the informants had seen in their English classes and around the school during the Spring Term of 1996. Additionally, all of them had seen and interacted with me inside and outside these classes intensively from December 1996 until the period of the interviews between May and July 1997. They were quite clear that I was someone who was interested in their patterns of language use. The starting point for each interview was that I had been interested in what they had said about their language use in their survey questionnaire responses, written accounts and self-made audio recordings, but accepted that all these sources of information were intrinsically limiting and wanted to give them a chance to expand on some of the points they had made there. In these senses then, the individual recorded interviews had an ethnographic quality. I was very familiar to the informants, and conducted the interviews in a conversational style formulating my questions and prompts in an open-ended way which made it clear that I was there to listen to their perceptions rather than to 'get answers' to set questions. The term *interview* is, in this respect, a little misleading in that typically the encounters had a quality which was more like a discussion. These interviews with the Blackhill youth could be described as conversational interviews. However, although this book places great emphasis on the value and importance of the data obtained from these interviews, it is careful not to do so naively. Hammersley (2003) has drawn attention to 'the radical critique of interviews' which,

> focuses on what is regarded as increasing over-dependence among qualitative researchers on interview data, and above all their use of such data as a window on the world and/or on the minds of informants.
>
> (*ibid.*: 119)

He refers to authors, (Dingwall, 1997; Silverman, 1997; Atkinson and Coffey, 2002), who criticise,

> what they refer to as the 'romantic impulse' which treats open-ended interviews as capturing the 'genuine voices' of interviewees. Instead it is argued that any 'voice' is 'not an experientially authentic truth.

It is in itself a methodically constructed social product that emerges from its reflexive communicative practices'.

(Gubrium and Holstein, 2002, p. 11 cited in Hammersley, 2003: 119)

It is my awareness of these caveats and the associated dangers that led me to treat the interview data as constituting one of four acts of representation rather than as true, or naive indicators of some putative reality. This data is convincing only to the extent that it yields patterns of repetition worthy of commentary and analysis, and to the extent that the reader is persuaded by the ensuing interpretive argument.

'Blacks' v. 'Asians': 'Insiders' v. 'Outsiders'

There were a number of potential asymmetries relating to ethnicity, language and gender associated with the process of interviewing. In the first place, of the original 31 informants all but four claimed a South Asian ethnic descent. This meant that I had to consider seriously the effect on my interactions with them of the historical conflict in Africa, the Caribbean and Britain between people of African descent and people of Indian subcontinental descent. This conflict had its origins in the British Empire's deliberate movement of Indian labour to locations in Africa and the Caribbean as competition for existing African labour between the mid nineteenth century and the First World War.[8] Elements from both these subordinated groups have in the past 40 to 50 years migrated to the United Kingdom and settled here in significant numbers. In UK conditions this conflict has been muted but it has been there.[9] Consequently, when it came to the analysis of interview data, consideration needed to be given as to in what ways, if any, informants' interview responses might be shaped by the echoes of historic African-South Asian tensions when they could see that I was visibly African. According to Egharevba (2001: 225), 'There is a dearth of discussion on the methodological dilemmas faced by minority ethnic researchers who research minority ethnic communities of which they are a part'. Describing herself as a 'British-born first generation Nigerian woman [who] came to conduct research on a group of South Asian women' (*ibid.*: 226), she concludes,

while factors such as gender, class, establishing credibility and rapport, language, religion, and culture are important, a shared minority status and understanding of racism between the researched and the researcher may affect the research relationship most significantly in relation to the type and level of information shared by the researched.

(*ibid.*: 226)

The parallels with my own biographical trajectory and research inform-ants are obvious, as indicated in the Introduction, and I came to much the same conclusions as Egharevba. The second consideration concerns lan-guage. There were occasions when informants hesitated when explaining certain things to me and I felt that the hesitation was because they felt that there was something that as an 'outsider' I might not understand; also, perhaps that this something might have been linguistic. In other words, they refrained from saying something in Panjabi or Gujarati because they knew that I did not understand these languages. There were, indeed, a few occasions when I actively encouraged them to set aside their hesitations and they proceeded to say something in these languages. On the other hand, there were other occasions when their hesitations were due to their uncertainty as to whether it was legitimate for them to swear when narrating an anecdote representing themselves, friends, family, or other characters. Third, there was one issue of gender which needed reflexive attention. Before I began interviewing I had concerns about whether my status as a middle-aged black male might interfere with my capacity to initiate individual interviews with adolescent female inform-ants of South Asian descent. Specifically, I was anxious in case these females should decline to be interviewed alone by me or show a marked reticence about becoming involved in the research. In the worst case sce-nario I feared that either before or after any such interviews there might be an incident involving strong objections by parents about their daugh-ters becoming involved in such a situation. These anxieties proved to be unfounded. Here, I, myself, may have too easily absorbed the ethnic stereotype suggesting that all families of South Asian origin engage in the fierce, vigilant and slightly paranoid policing of every aspect of the lives of their female members. Finally, one other factor in the interview process which needs to be taken into account, was the possible effects and limita-tions arising from the age divide between me and the informants, taken together with my adult potential authority figure, quasi-teacher position operating within the precincts of a school.

Conclusion

Having set out, briefly, a number of limitations and reservations about the research process, this chapter has also outlined why research on black and brown Britons as agentive speaking subjects is both important and all too rare. The research means by which this might be effectively achieved has been summarised with a full recognition that while precision and rigour is important, art as opposed to science is also involved. As Bourdieu has commented,

> I do not believe that it is useful to turn to the innumerable so-called "methodological" writings on interview techniques. Useful as these may be when they describe the various effects that the interviewer can produce without knowing it, they almost always miss the point, not least because they remain faithful to old methodological principles which, like the ideal of the standardised procedures, often derived from the desire to imitate the external signs of the rigor of the most established scientific disciplines. At any rate it does not seem to me that they do justice to what has always been done – and known – by researchers who have the most respect for their object and who are the most attentive to the almost infinitely subtle strategies that social agents deploy in the ordinary conduct of their lives.
>
> (Bourdieu, 1999: 607)

Before, beginning to turn to an analysis of these subtle strategies in Chapter 4, the next chapter broadly maps the patterns of language use of the Blackhill youth as a group.

3
Language Use and Ethnicity: Mapping the Terrain

Introduction

This chapter offers a broad sketch of how the Blackhill youth position themselves in the multilingual environment which they inhabit. This is achieved by developing an analytic commentary on, and summary of, the data collected in the language survey questionnaire. In this analysis the terrain is divided into two open dimensions – their patterns of language use at home and within the family and the patterns outside the home in interaction with others in the wider community. The foundations of this scene are the languages the Blackhill youth said that they used at home with their families before they ever went to school. Here three languages stood out. Of the 31 respondents, 13 listed Panjabi,[1] eight named English and seven mentioned Gujarati. It should be noted, though, that while all the young people showed a strong awareness of their linguistic inheritance by being able to name the native sources of the languages other than English which they used at home pre-school, they were much less sure when it came to markers of any contemporary expertise such as deploying up-to-date spellings and terminologies for the languages in question. For example, respondents were much less likely to use the standard modern spellings 'Panjabi' and 'Gujarati' than spellings such as 'Punjabi' or 'Gujerati' and 'Gujrati'.[2]

Charting the terrain

The weaknesses and limitations of the language survey questionnaire as an investigative tool have already been discussed, however the patterns of answers it stimulates can be used as the basis for a tentative series of speculative inferences, about the nature of the intricate interrelationships between language and ethnicity across the generations. This approach is worthwhile in two different ways. Firstly, as has already been seen, the theoretical current of cultural theory commentating on the construction of identities and ethnicities,[3] which substantially informs this book, has been remarkably silent on the part that everyday routine patterns of language use might play in shaping the very core of these ethnicities and identities. A person's patterns of language use constitute, along with their physical appearance, styles of dress and decoration, their history and ancestry, as well as their religious practices, central components of their ethnicity and identity. What the language survey questionnaire clarified was the broad and definable framework within which the routine linguistic and cultural practices of the Blackhill youth were executed. The following sections briefly map the nature of the terrain involved.

Pre-school language use

The first significant element worthy of comment is that most of the informants first used a language other than English at home in the first five years of their lives before they first went to school. This is one respect in which they are significantly different from the overwhelming majority of British under fives during the early to mid-1980s and still so today. This kind of distinctive linguistic identity was, for the Blackhill youth, heavily dominated by Panjabi and Gujarati speaking identities. But this is immediately complicated and qualified by the fact that almost a quarter of the group claimed that English was the first language they used at home pre-school, thus nominally aligning them with the early years experience of the majority of people in the United Kingdom. In fact two students claimed that they used *only* English with their families at home before they first attended school, while only one student claimed to have used only a language other than English (Gujarati) at home prior to school. Finally, the overwhelming majority of respondents who did not claim English as the first language that they used with their families pre-school, certainly claimed English as a second language that they used in that context. To make sense of the reported experience of the respondents one has to envisage identities which can be characterised, in the early years of their lives, as multilingual identities. A number of languages are present and in the prosaic encounters of everyday life their use can be negotiated in a variety of patterns.

The overwhelming majority of the Blackhill youth claimed to be still able to understand quite well the languages they first used at home pre-school. This is not at all surprising where that language is English. However, for this also to be the case for languages other than English is highly significant. None said that they now had no understanding at all of the first languages they had used at home prior to school. So although English was reported as being a pre-school language whose use had progressively increased, at the same time respondents claimed that they also, simultaneously, retained a strong understanding of languages other than English. This suggests a complex aspect of ethnicity and identity comprising both English and other languages in the formation of a distinct kind of linguistic ecology. While most said that they could still speak their pre-school languages quite well, a significant minority said that they could now speak the languages other than English, only a little or not at all. In addition, very few of those claiming to have spoken pre-school languages other than English claimed to be able to write them at all well and in fact most said that they could not write them at all. This, of course, contrasted strongly with their evident literacy skills in English. In other words, the insistent literacy practices in English which come as a naturalised part of schooling in Britain acted to secure a particular place for English in their linguistic ecology while simultaneously displacing languages other than English from these spaces – especially, as I have suggested, spaces involving literacy. Overall, these young people depicted themselves as individuals who, in adolescence, could still understand to a significant extent, a language other than English which had not been studied compulsorily as a secondary school subject. In positioning themselves in this way they are clearly marking themselves as distinctly atypical in linguistic behaviour in comparison with the generality of the British population which has a tendency to be resolutely unilingual in principle and practice (CILT, 2001; Nuffield Foundation, 2000). Yet, nevertheless, for the Blackhill youth, too, English remained dominant, albeit in distinctive ways.

The ubiquity of English

While a substantial minority recorded a language other than English as the main language they used with family and friends, of those who claimed English to be the dominant language mainly used with family and friends, English was the *only* language they used to any significant extent with family and friends. These findings are highly pertinent in the light of the political atmosphere in Britain in the early years of the new millenium where, as already indicated, elements in the British government depicted 'Asian' youth and their families as problematic citizens because of their supposed failure to use English, particularly in family domains. In addition, the British State has legislated in the *Nationality, Immigration and Asylum Act* (2002), to make English language competence a compulsory requirement for the obtaining of British citizenship.

As has so far been suggested, it is not enough to seek to constrain the informants within a binary of either using or not using a language other than English. An even finer-grained distinction needs to be drawn between an aural dimension (listening and understanding), an oral dimension (speaking), and a literacy dimension (reading and writing), and the particular mix evident in a contingent situation in a specific domain. When the questionnaire respondents were asked what language they usually spoke to their fathers and mothers (oral dimension), a clear majority said that they usually spoke to them in English and there was a strong indication that a majority wanted to represent themselves as speaking nothing but English to them. But simultaneously one must take account of the fact that a substantial minority represented themselves as usually speaking a language other than English (Gujarati or Panjabi for instance) to their parents. Of these a small number portrayed their usual speech to their parents as being a hybrid of English and a language other than English. It is in these kinds of practice that it is possible to perceive potential identity formations which trouble binary conceptualisations.

With respect to the languages that informants claimed to usually speak to their siblings, an overwhelmingly decisive majority of those who had brothers or sisters said that they usually spoke English and only English to them, notwithstanding a small number who said that they did indeed usually speak a language other than English, or a mixture of English and a language other than English, with their brother or sister. So, overall, whether or not other languages appear in a particular context, as far as the Blackhill youth are concerned, English is everywhere.

English use with multilingual interruptions

The responses for patterns of speech usually used with siblings appear to be reversed when respondents indicated what language they usually speak to their grandparents. Here the overwhelming majority stated that they usually spoke a language other than English to their grandparents and never or very rarely spoke English to them. Consequently, what can be observed in the oral dimension is the emergence of at least three sharply differentiated dominant patterns. One with parents, one with siblings and one with grandparents.

When one switches to the aural dimension the patterns change again. Just over half of the respondents said that their fathers usually spoke to them in English and just under half said that their mothers usually did so. Further, there was a definite and perhaps significant tendency to claim that their mothers were more likely to speak to them in a language other than English than were their fathers. In addition the responses provided evidence that none of the respondents claimed that their mothers usually spoke more than one language to them whereas a substantial minority (just under a third) claimed that their fathers regularly also spoke a second language to them and in one case a third. All kinds of ethnically absolute speculations and inferences linked to gender-based positionings within families of South Asian descent are tempting in accounting for these variations, but a richer more nuanced interpretation will be presented later in the book and more specifically in Chapters 4 and 6. This applies, too, to the finding that an overwhelming majority of respondents claimed that their grandparents usually spoke to them in languages other than English.

Nearly all respondents claimed that their siblings usually spoke in English to them and there appears to be nothing surprising in this as this pattern closely matches the pattern of speech they said they in turn used for speaking to these same siblings. One might reasonably speculate that the reciprocal patterns of dominant English speech that respondents shared with their siblings might be replicated in the patterns of speech shared with their peers during school breaks; and this in fact proved to be the case at first sight. But a closer look appears to reveal that talk with peers during school breaks occurs in a much more complex multilingual environment. For one individual, for instance, Panjabi was the language usually spoken. For another one Gujarati was sometimes spoken in these contexts. Two other components of this multilingual environment were particularly noteworthy. Firstly, a number of respondents said that German was a language that they sometimes spoke with their peers during school breaks. German was the key language studied by students in the school as an examinable school subject. Why they should speak it to each other outside classroom contexts is something which will be briefly considered later. However, it represents a linguistic practice that I'm not aware is customary amongst the generality of British adolescents in those moments in the school day when they escape the confines of the classroom. The second phenomenon was references made by two respondents, to their involvement, with interlocutors, in what they termed 'Rasta talk'.[4] It was not evident from the questionnaire responses whether the conversations concerned typically occurred between peers of Caribbean descent or of South Asian descent, or both, or between peers from a variety of ethnic lineages. Nevertheless, when these reported linguistic exchanges are taken together with those reported above connected with Panjabi, Gujarati and the dominant English, there are clearly grounds for speculating as to whether it is possible to see here the raw materials to flesh out one of Roger Hewitt's theoretical propositions. Hewitt postulated the existence among urban British youth, of a, 'local multi-ethnic vernacular' or a, 'community English' which he speculated may well constitute, 'the primary medium of communication in the adolescent peer group in multi-ethnic areas' (Hewitt, 1992: 32).

The relative clarity of the findings so far, mask somewhat the ways in which the language survey questionnaire with its inevitable quest for succinct either / or answers can be inherently misleading and induce the making of dangerously premature inferences. Two examples illustrate the point. For instance, when they were asked to cite any additional languages which they understood, respondents identified, without being able to elaborate in the space available, languages such as Arabic, Malay and Sign Language. Another instance relates to patterns of language interaction within a more widely drawn family circle, namely one encompassing uncles, aunts and cousins. In these circumstances languages such as Hindi and Swahili rose to much greater prominence and languages like Portuguese, Spanish and Chinese emerged in the listing. Indeed all of the Blackhill youth stated that they had family members who grew up speaking a language other than English, and in this context languages like Marathi, Pashto, Italian and Turkish appeared. More precisely and markedly they linked many of their uncles and aunts to a Swahili language usage suggesting a diasporic connection to East African and Indian ethnicities. In sum, mapping the terrain of familial language use by questionnaire responses allowed the Blackhill youth to paint a broad picture without textural depth. In this general sweep, however, it is quite clear that their older relatives were people who had experienced multilingual childhoods featuring one, two, or even three languages or more, in addition to English.

Thus, their familial environments were highly multilingual both in terms of the quantity of languages spoken and the depth of the multilingualism. Yet what is striking once the aural dimension is considered is the marked way in which the informants indicated that when these languages are spoken in the family they either understand only some of what is said, only a few words of what is said, or nothing at all. So an element of their identity formation appears to involve saturation in a variety of multilingual environments, including the family, while their own direct participation is intermittent, fragmentary and partial. At the same time when they are at school they are immersed in a classroom environment peopled by multilingual peers and can mostly name a significant number of the languages extant there. Similarly, the great majority of them are highly aware of living in multilingual neighbourhoods and can name a variety of languages used by their neighbours. Many of them are also acutely aware of inhabiting neighbourhoods where signs, notices and symbols pertaining to languages other than English and religions other than Christianity are prominent; and they can name them.

One example of the chronic, but fragmentary, linguistic engagement with languages other than English is seen in the way in which the Blackhill youth represent their encounters with the learning of languages other than English in community language classes. On the one hand a majority of them said that they had attended such classes, predominantly to learn Panjabi or Gujarati, at the instigation of their parents or other older relatives. On the other hand almost a third said that they had not attended community language classes. Significantly, of those who *had* attended none was still doing so. So, in this scenario, while their parents and older relatives were eager that they should attend out of school classes to reinforce the maintenance of specific ethnic traditions and practices embracing language, religion, history, music and dance, they themselves adopted a stance which in a variety of ways resisted these efforts. Certainly, most of the Blackhill youth had made significant efforts to learn a language other than English outside school, either in community language classes, from relatives, from trips to ancestral homelands or on their own. Yet, to summarise, in the aural, oral and literacy dimensions of their linguistic ecology, we find a repetition of shifting indefinite patterns of expertise and affiliation. For instance in the oral dimension, while a majority claimed to still be able to speak quite well the languages they had tried to learn, a significant minority said that they could now speak them only a little, and some said that they could now not speak them at all. Meanwhile in the literacy dimension well over half claimed that they could not write the languages they had once been learning, a small number said that they could write them only a little, and only a few said that they felt they could write them quite well; this pattern was closely followed when it came to reading. This is one way in which the limitations of a research approach which seeks to perceive an ethnic formation on the basis of either / or questions like 'does X speak or not speak Y language?' and 'does X identify with Y language and culture?', becomes readily visible. There are further complications related to the question of linguistic expertise. Most of the Blackhill youth were studying German at school as a curriculum subject. As a result, whereas they felt a lack of productive expertise in their nominal family/community languages, they felt far more confident about their speaking, reading and writing expertise in German. Whether this is because they were in fact applying different standards or measures of expertise to the different types of languages, or whether their expertise in German was indeed greater because they were in fact receiving many hours of tuition each week in aural, oral and literacy skills in German is not clear. What is clear is that factors like this disrupt attempts to construct straightforward representations of ethnicity and identity around a variety of simple measures of affiliation and expertise related to language use.

Ethnic affiliations in a British context

One apparently simple measure of affiliation to which the informants responded concerned their religious affiliations. Several patterns immediately became clear. Firstly, the dominant affiliations were related to religions strongly associated with South Asian contexts, that is Sikh, Hindu, and Muslim, in that order of prominence. These taken together accounted for all but three of the respondents. Secondly, Sikhs and Hindus were almost evenly balanced numerically and made up over three quarters of the total. Those identifying themselves as Christians were a tiny minority. These listings give no more than a vague imagining of a kind of ambience that might exist, but this imagining inevitably rests on pre-existing essentialised notions developed as part of ethnically absolute dominant discourses concerning visible minority groups of South Asian migrant descent in Britain since 1945. As has been emphasised previously in this analysis, the language survey questionnaire is an inadequate instrument for capturing subtle and complex characterisations of ethnicity and identity. Nevertheless, it is possible to make at least one strong and confident statement. This is that, whichever way this language data is interpreted, the Blackhill youth live ethnicities and identities which are at their core British ones. All but three of them were British born and brought up. Of the remaining three, one had been in Britain for eight months but the other two had lived in Britain for 11 years, and almost eight years respectively. Before closing it is worth glancing very briefly at what one of the most authoritative and contemporaneous surveys of British ethnic minority ethnicities and identities (Modood *et al.*, 1997) had to say on the question of language with regard to people of South Asian descent. Broadly, its findings fit closely with those of my own survey, albeit mine is much more tightly focused and detailed. Modood and colleagues found, for instance that,

> within each ethnic group, a language other than English is more likely to be used when speaking to family members older than oneself rather than younger than oneself. This suggests the latter cannot comfortably speak that language or prefer to use English.
>
> (Modood *et al.*, 1997: 310)

Modood's team also reported that with regard to languages other than English the dominant relationship among people of South Asian descent is one of occasional rather than routine participation – a tendency which is more marked amongst the youth since, 'despite the fact that nearly all South Asians have facility in at least one South Asian language, the use of such languages is experiencing some generational decline' (*ibid.*: 332).

Conclusion

The utilisation of the language survey questionnaire as a data collection device was an important part of my research strategy in a number of ways. Firstly it afforded me a degree of ethnographic comfort. That is, as a researcher in the field, I felt more comfortable in attempting to elicit personal information from a large group of people whom I did not know very well as individuals, in not asking them for this information directly. The individual questionnaires were, therefore, a relatively unthreatening and indirect way to acquire initial data. Another way in which the questionnaire was valuable was as a building block in a progressively more intimate data collection strategy. Thus the written accounts were more intimate and sensitive than the questionnaires, the self-made audio recordings more intimate than the written accounts, and the individual conversational interviews more than the self-made audio recordings. The other main importance of the questionnaire as I have already indicated in the present chapter was as an aid to charting the linguistic and ethnic terrain inhabited by the Blackhill youth. It was by this means that I was able to get the first intimations of a group of young people who began their lives with languages other than English, then made the transition to English language dominance by their teens, but retained community language use in a variety of complex ways in specific contexts with specific people, with varying degrees of proficiency, but limited literacy; and who were linked with a wider range of linguistic influences through their diaspora families. Certainly, the language survey questionnaire has severe limitations as a tool for enabling delicate analysis and interpretation. As the Linguistic Minorities Project has observed,

> it is not enough just to say that bilingual children learn different languages. We must also realise that they come to perceive and use the languages in different ways, and that this gives their languages different meanings in their eyes. And the way children come to use them is not just a product of the linguistic skills of family members or the norms set by their elders, but of how their local network of social relationships is structured. The networks within which children interact need to be better known before we can understand fully their patterns of use – why they use a language or variety.
>
> (Linguistic Minorities Project, 1985: 278–279)

Nevertheless, the broad sketch in the current chapter, has attempted to build from the respondents' answers, an intense sense of how they choose to place their identities and ethnicities along pre-prepared aural, oral and literacy dimensions. The next chapter begins the process of coming to a more subtle understanding of how these local networks of social relationships operate and how they relate to the selected patterns of language use.

4
New Ethnicities as Lived Experience

What speaks to us, seemingly, is always the big event, the untoward, the extra-ordinary; the front-page splash, the banner headlines ... Behind the event there has to be a scandal, a fissure, a danger, as if life reveals itself only by way of the spectacular, as if what speaks, what is significant, is always abnormal: natural cataclysms or historical upheavals, social unrest, political scandals ... How should we take account of, question, describe what happens every day and recurs every day: the banal, the quotidian, the obvious, the common, the ordinary, the infra-ordinary, the background noise, the habitual? ... To question the habitual. But that's just it, we're habituated to it. We don't question it, it doesn't question us, it doesn't seem to pose a problem, we live it without thinking, as if it carried within it neither questions nor answers, as if it weren't the bearer of any information ... How are we to speak of these 'common things', how to track them down rather, flush them out, wrest them from the dross in which they remain mired, how to give them a meaning, a tongue, to let them, finally speak of what is, of what we are ... Not the exotic any more, but the endotic.

(Perec, 1999: 209–10)

Introduction

One key concern in this book is the question of how to effectively centralise informants' voices; to listen to and interpret the significance of some of their low key everyday utterances and self-representations. This consideration indicated a desire to depart from the tradition, in British Cultural studies of youth, of concentrating on the spectacular and the subcultural. One way of addressing the problem of how to simultaneously capture a sense of individual agency and a sense of social structure is offered by approaches developed by Georges Perec which, Howard Becker states, attempted to, 'characterize a culture and way of life, both the relevant beliefs and their coordinate activities by the accumulation of formally unanalyzed detail' (Becker, 2001: 72). Perec's declarations at the head of this chapter provide an apt articulation of the nub of the issue. What follows is an attempt to realise the effect of a cumulative sense of both individual agency and the spatial and temporal ecology of a specific social and cultural formation. To achieve this effect and to emphasise the unspectacular, commonplace, everyday nature of the informants' self-representations, I deliberately defer to later chapters detailed interpretation or analysis of their accounts. At this juncture the reader is instead invited to *feel* new ethnicities in construction as the selected individuals represent their patterns of language use. I have already suggested that since Stuart Hall coined the term 'new ethnicities' in the late 1980s, it has endured as an influential, heavily cited, point of theoretical reference far more than any utility it has had as a framework for the precise description of the lived experience of specific individuals or groups. This chapter provides one such collection of specific descriptions, before proceeding in subsequent chapters to show how the intricate specificities attaching to named individuals broaden out into the more generalisable identification of a nascent social and cultural formation. The following portraits have been constructed from the representations which the Blackhill youth produced in a variety of ways. These are presented, here, as dense narratives sticking as exactly as possible to the informants own words and expressions and in this sense approximate to some kinds of actually lived experience.[1] In the construction of the portraits, the choice of typical individuals was a difficult one to make. An examination of the informants' representations yielded, in each case, complex and often unexpected, particularities such that no individual could be said to be 'typical' of any ethnic group or sub-group. In the end two girls and three boys were chosen; a boy and a girl describing themselves as Sikhs; a boy and a girl describing themselves as Hindus; and one boy describing himself as a Muslim. These choices reflected the representation of these groups in the data as a whole and attempted to reflect, too, their range of languages.

Portrait one: Amaljeet's everyday ethnicity

Amaljeet describes himself as 'half cast' because, 'my mother is sikh and my father is muslim'. After he was born his father left him and his mother, and Amaljeet has since lived with his mother and her parents. Although his father is based in the USA he often stays with the family when he visits Britain. Amaljeet's parents and grandparents were brought up in India and he thinks this is why he himself knows Panjabi language very well. When he was growing up he spoke Panjabi at home because his grandparents could not speak English. Even though his mother could speak English he spent most of his time with his grandparents because she was out at work. His grandparents had a shop in the middle of Southall and,

> 'In Southall they (sic) are not many English people so therefore I used to speak Punjabi all day with everybody. I used to speak Punjabi at the shop and at home'.

Amaljeet labels the kind of Panjabi he speaks at home as 'standard casual punjabi'. He had sometimes tried to speak Hindi at home to his grandfather's lunch and dinner guests when he was younger but had usually made many mistakes requiring constant correction. But he also learned a lot of Hindi through attending a religious mandal (group) with his grandparents. Before he first attended school Amaljeet mainly spoke Panjabi and had low exposure to English, a pattern which continued at his infants school,

> infants' school I went to it was mostly Indians there as well so we used to speak we never used to take notice of we just used to do what we used to do in class and that talk Panjabi with friends.

It was not until he attended his junior and middle schools that English began to impose itself on his life because his peers were mainly white British,

> but when I came to junior school I learnt more cos most of the population there were white people cos it was a- in Northolt so I just that's when I properly got to speak English

Amaljeet has recently changed his name (aged 15) at the behest of his mother to a Sikh name having hitherto had a name with muslim associations. Panjabi language is important to him. He remarks that if he couldn't speak Panjabi, people in the community would think, 'he's not really interested in his culture ... he's not like right'. Conversely, People would consider that his display of competence in Panjabi language showed that his grandparents and parents had brought him up in the right way. He has often worked in his uncle's restaurant in Southall to earn some money and this experience has exposed him to a variety of languages such as Hindi, Urdu and Gujarati as he has listened to the customers speaking them with his uncle – especially Gujarati.

Amaljeet is strongly aware of caste distinctions among Sikhs. He says that he belongs to the Jat caste which, according to him, is a high class group of farmers and landowners in India. He says that there are lower class groups that he knows as Churey and Turkhan who traditionally work for the Jats,

> they're the ones that do the work for a living but we like we do we have big farms like our last generation gave us and we just work them up we get a lot of money out of that and uhm so that we make the low class do the work for us

He draws some distinction between community practices in India and those in London but,

> In the British situation um it's not that sort of thing it's not much round here ... like in er in India you you don't get married to a low class as well cos otherwise then your parents kick you out

However, he talks about one of his male cousins who he describes as loving a Turkhan woman with whom he has been going out for a long time, but whom he is not allowed to marry. He says that his cousin's mother has forbidden the marriage and his cousin does not wish to go against his mother's wishes. Nevertheless, Amaljeet is aware that community conflicts between castes have more drastic consequences in India than in Britain:

> in India there's a lot of fights a lot of fights happen and like round here there's a fight just a little punch up know what I mean but there it's it's a serious thing

It is his mother and his grandmother who educated him about the influence and significance of caste. Indeed, his grandmother can tell him the castes that his friends belong to, based on hearing their surnames. He gives one example of a friend whose surname is Bhogal which he describes as a Turkhan name.

In addition to speaking Panjabi well Amaljeet had attended community language classes to learn to read and write it. He had attended these classes on and off on Sundays for about two or three months. He found it difficult to retain what he had learned and soon stopped going. He found it particularly difficult to master the script used for writing Panjabi especially when compared with the script which he used for writing English and which he had already learned at school. He feels more confident about writing Panjabi using the Roman script he uses to write English and is very ready to do this as the following example written by him shows:

' "Tu alright ha".'

This is a typical sentence that would be said by a learner in Punjabi. It means are you okay (alright), it's not said in respect. A person who knows and understands Punjabi very well would say.

'Tusi cikh ho' meaning are you alright

… This conversation is one that I saw in a Punjabi film.

Binder: Kidha, tikhay
Rupi: Tikhaye
Binder: Hor das paaren dey aira
Rupi: Kid dasan.

Translated in English

Binder: Alright hows it going
Rupi: I'm alright
Binder: Anything going on (and he swears at his sister)
Rupi: Nothing's going on.

Jatt's have such ability to switch when they speak to a elderly person they use words which show respect e.g. Tusi. 'English does not have these sort of words'.

Amaljeet says that when he stopped going to the community language classes it did not bother him. Although other children who attended the classes with him seemed to learn to read and write Panjabi very well he doesn't know why he found it so hard, 'I just didn't catch on to it'. However, neither his mother nor his grandmother could write Panjabi so he did not feel it was all that important and says that his grandparents did not mind,

they didn't mind me leaving Panjabi school they weren't really worried about it I thought … I can't get into it then what's the worth

Amaljeet has always experienced many different aspects of Sikh religion in his everyday life but whenever he has attended the Gurdwara he has found it very difficult to read or follow the kind of Panjabi used there. His family participates in religious rituals, often very lengthy ones lasting a number of days, sometimes in the home and involving a Giani,[2] and centred on the Guru Granth Sahib.[3] These rituals can be concerned with major events like weddings or with pleas for good fortune in achieving pregnancy and successful childbirth or for luck with exams. He is conscious of a large number of practices representing observances which he thinks Sikhs are supposed to follow; including not eating meat, not drinking alcohol and not smoking. However, he himself does not observe any of these, except for smoking which he tried but avoids because it is particularly important to his family that he shouldn't. Additionally, he often makes reference to the ways in which his grandfather transgresses some of these ideal Sikh practices, especially through his heavy drinking, 'my granddad he's a strong drinker, dad drinks, everyone eats meat'. Amaljeet's references to his grandfather are approving and admiring, 'he's my sort of role model as well I take after him and he drinks a lot'. He says that one of his grandfather's other transgressions is swearing:

> grandad he's he's gold medallist in swearing he knows all the swear words and my dad he he swears bu[?] they just say it like in a conversation they don't, they don't mean it

As to other visible signs of being a Sikh, such as not cutting hair, wearing a turban and carrying a kirpan,[4] Amaljeet does not observe them, although he had long hair and a turban when he was a very young child, until either his mother or grandmother had had it cut off when he was two or three years old. When his grandfather came to Britain in the 1950s he had been forced to remove his own turban and cut his hair because of stipulations laid down by the factory in which he found work, although he had subsequently been able to restore them. Amaljeet disagrees with people who sport the visible signs of Sikhism while transgressing the ritual requirements of the religion. He declares, for instance, that he takes seriously Amrit Pahul, a Sikh initiation ceremony, involving the ritual drinking of water regarded as purified, 'you drink that you're purified you don't do nothing wrong after that'. In sum, Amaljeet regards his mother's side of the family as being not particularly religious in contrast to his father's side, who are Muslim.

Amaljeet says that he speaks a lot of Panjabi with his peers at school especially at breaks and at lunchtime, and that he speaks more Panjabi than English to his friends in class. He says that in year 9 he taught a white British friend to speak some Panjabi.[5] He also speaks some Gujarati to Gujarati-speaking friends at school.

Apart from this, he and many of his friends speak Jamaican language, which he calls 'rasta talk', to each other:

> once you get into (.) that department you you can't get out of it really so they've got into the rasta man talk and all that they can't come back to Panjabi like I know V. in our year he's he's Panjabi but he speaks rasta and all that he he doesn't he doesn't I don't think he knows a lot about his religion

This use of Jamaican language comes from inter-ethnic friendships forged both in school and community, 'we don't say hello so we say "wha gwan" and all that we say it like that we don't talk English'. The consequence is that some people, 'think you're weird because you're Indian why are you speaking like that?'.

Amaljeet was born in Britain, but has visited India twice; once when he was about five and the second time when he was about eleven. He enjoyed it and learned a lot. He absorbed a tremendous amount, for example, about drumming. But he did not find the Panjabi he heard there easy to understand, 'when I go to India I get very confused because they speak very weird Panjabi. In India they pronounce words differently'.

Music plays a major part in Amaljeet's life. He is a leading member of a traditional Panjabi dhol[6] drumming band, and often performs in school on important occasions, when pupils from different ethnic groups contribute essentialised presentations of their traditional cultures. However, when asked if his band ever wear the associated traditional dress from the Punjab, he is emphatic that for them this denotes the practices of an older generation. His band in fact wear Ralph Lauren designer clothes and black Kicker shoes:

> [the] older time ones yeah they wear their Indian clothes yeah the proper bhangra so like ... we're the Dholis of the new generation yeah so we wear Ralph Lauren clothes and all that we like we got our Ralph Lauren suits ... stripey trousers with blue shirts ... we wear um black Kickers.

Nevertheless, three of the seven members of the band wear Sikh turbans, although Amaljeet himself does not do so, nor does he display other visible signs of his Sikh ethnic affiliation. His band have designed a logo based on a Yves St Laurent motif. Through his dhol band he maintains direct contact with the Indian diaspora in major shows in London in which he has played alongside well known bhangra artists from India, and alongside Indian (Bollywood) film stars. The band also plays at private functions and student dances as well as at community festivals. However, Amaljeet is perturbed by the attitude of his parents who he says strongly oppose the idea that he should ever consider making his living from playing in his dhol band. They regard this as something that lower class people do. At times he partly acquiesces with this view but he remains strongly committed to and absorbed by all his activities with the band. These include regular practising; designing, printing and distributing band publicity; rehearsing choreographed stage moves; and creating a stage costume 'look'.

Amaljeet is very proud of some of his older cousins who he says are among the biggest and best known professional DJs in the South Asian communities in the West of London. He started working with yet another sound system run by other cousins when he was about 12, before he became involved in his dhol drumming activities. He comments that his cousins mix bhangra music with what he describes as 'English' tracks. Apart from Bhangra music he likes reggae, swing beat, soul and jungle but not hip hop. He is especially fond of reggae music and mentions Bob Marley, Freddie McGregor and Jah Shaka as particular favourites.

Amaljeet's speech includes local elements of London English pronunciation,

> yeah like it's you they show car[ʔ]oons dancing to that there are car[ʔ]oons dancing

and Caribbean and London pronunciations together with London English grammar,

> and um [d]at we organised it we [done] the posters and every[f]ing and then we er organised the DJs it was a bit hard to get the price but because they charge 450 a par[ʔ]y 450 pounds

London English grammar,

> our family [ain't] too religious

and traces of lexical items directly linked with Indian forms of English,

> with your uncle you jus speak with respect when I'm talking to my brother [cousin brother] you just use swear words swear and curse and whatever but they don't mind.

Amaljeet's account of his own ethnic and cultural formation demonstrates how fluid and open these categories can be once an enabling discursive framework allowing such accounts to be constructed and carefully listened to, is offered. His account in its unpredictability, complexity and subtlety gives a strong sense of what the empirical realisation of the 'new ethnicities' and 'cultures of hybridity' theoretical formulations might look like and feel like. In Amaljeet's case, he both supports traditional cultural forms like the dhol drumming band related to Bhangra music and simultaneously subverts it in his choice of stage outfit. At the same time he declares some of his favourite music as reggae. He is strongly affiliated to Panjabi language but claims a strong affiliation to Jamaican Creole too. Yet at the same time when he talks he sounds like a Londoner. The question of linguistic sound and style will be taken up more fully in Chapter 5, and issues of musical taste will be discussed more extensively in Chapter 7.

*   *   *

Portrait two: Gurleetaa's everyday ethnicity

Gurleetaa says that in her life, 'Punjabi was the first language I came into contact with', but adds that,

> in my house there are only two languages which are spoken English and Punjabi. Punjabi gets spoken by the older generation of the house and English more by the younger generation of the house.

Although her early life prominently featured the use of Panjabi, her entry to school signalled a major shift leading to the increased and rapidly dominant use of English. But she did not find this shift problematic because on the one hand most of her classmates when she went to school were also Panjabi speakers and also because of a white British teacher who spoke a little to her in Panjabi although, 'with a sort of British accent so that sounded kind of um bizarre'. On the other hand her mother, who had once planned to be an English teacher at home in India, having been taught English there herself, helped her to learn to read and write in English,

RH: How did you deal with Panjabi say in your younger days?
Gurleetaa: erm that was probably the only language that was talked
             to me and yeah English was probably there but erm it was

probably mainly dominated by Panjabi so I spoke that for
the first five or six years and then you know English and
Panjabi became mixed together

Although Gurleetaa uses both English and Panjabi at home, she sees
English as clearly dominant in her practice while having certain aspira-
tions towards developing her usage of Panjabi. Her use of English is so
habitual that, 'if my mum talks to me in Panjabi I'll answer back in
English'. Four years previously her father had had a stroke which had
physically disabled him on his right side and severely restricted his
speech. Even in these circumstances Gurleetaa does not feel constrained
to speak Panjabi

RH:	so how do you deal with him then do you speak to him in English and hopefully
Gurleetaa:	yeah we do all sort of speak to him in English he does understand it and he worked, he worked you know, and it's sor[?] of like we can speak to him in Panjabi but we tend not to because of force of habit and you know we do talk to him in English

Gurleetaa's 'we' in this context, probably refers specifically to herself
and her two brothers, one older (aged 20), the other younger (aged 11).
They usually speak English reflecting the relative failure of her mother,
despite strenuous teaching efforts, to increase her and her brothers'
expertise in, and use of, Panjabi. She cannot explain why she and her
brothers are so resistant to developing their Panjabi further.

RH:	right mm mm so you were saying earlier on that your mum had actually tried to teach you Panjabi
Gurleetaa:	yeah =
RH:	= a bit
Gurleetaa:	yeah yeah she tried to get us to learn our um alphabet in Panjabi I can do a little bit, I can do like **ooraa airaa eeree sassa kakaa khakhaa gaggaa** (u/o/a/e/s/k/Kh/g) and then that's where I stopped and then ...
RH:	so why didn't it work then, I mean you said she was a sort of teacher type person
Gurleetaa:	I don't know I have no idea I just think that we just didn't want to learn or something.
RH:	mm

Gurleetaa: because she tried really really hard to teach my older brother how to do it and I just remember her trying to teach him it and it wouldn't work and we–we all know li[ʔ]le bits of it you know (inaudible)like a joke you know.

RH: yes

Gurleetaa: er it's sor[ʔ] of like that we all tried but it never sort of worked.

Gurleetaa cannot read or write Panjabi. Although she can speak Panjabi to some extent she cannot speak it fluently because she does not use it enough. She cannot conduct lengthy conversations in Panjabi but can communicate about what she calls 'basic things', in Panjabi. One of these 'basic things' is her practice of addressing her relatives by their Panjabi labels:

Gurleetaa: they're just um the words I can say you know a few things I can say with relatives you know in India you have different names for different relatives like your mum's er your mum's sister is a marsi and her husband is a marsa and your dad's sister is bhua and her husband is a puppar and so you know I can do things like tha[ʔ] I can say um three types er um I can speak a li[ʔ]le bi[ʔ] but it's not great detail

RH: sure sure

Gurleetaa: when I just have to ...

Gurleetaa: er well what you do if there is someone older than you and they're your cousin you call them bhenji you know, it comes as a respect or if it was her brother then you would say bhaji bu[ʔ] um we don't normally say tha[ʔ] we just them call them by their names or by nicknames within the family but to certain er to all we should do really do as a sort of sign of respect call them by their names like we have to call my mum's dad biddaji and we have to call our dad's brothers jufjir and their wives jufdi and we have to call our mum's mum mufdi her brother's mumme and their wives mumya

The act of showing respect is a major motivation for making such conversational moves in Panjabi. Gurleetaa reports that what also encourages her to use Panjabi with her grandfather is that this usage is linked to a wider web of community related ethnic practices. She feels compelled to speak Panjabi to her grandparents not only to show them ready and willing respect but also to protect her parents from family and community accusations that in not producing Panjabi-speaking children they have failed in their duty as parents. She indicates that this influence reaches her from across distant diaspora locations.

Gurleetaa:	Yeah. It's like if I don't talk to my grandfather in Panjabi or to my grandmother or whatever it's sort of like you know they sort of look down onto my mother or to my father thinking that you know they haven't raised their children like they should be because they all really you know sort of India they have to stay like that
RH:	mm
Gurleetaa:	and so that would be a particular reason why I'd speak it.
RH:	yeah sure.
Gurleetaa:	because I wouldn't want my mum to have like a bad reputation within the family so I try my hardest to do that although my mum's dad is in India so I haven't seen him for like what 7–8 years and my dad's er mum she doesn't live with us so you know

Gurleetaa consciously tries to improve and increase her use of Panjabi to please her mother because by so doing she will be able to present herself as a worthy future candidate for marriage into a 'good' family. She suggests that in this context speaking Panjabi is just one of a number of attributes on which a prospective wife would be judged by potential in-laws:

Gurleetaa:	more recently I've made the effort to you know respond to her speaking Panjabi so that you know I practise my skills because um there's always that thing because erm a few months ago my cousin sister you know it was an arranged marriage
RH:	mm
Gurleetaa:	and like you know they take a whole delegation of people from one side of the family to the other family
RH:	mm
Gurleetaa:	and one of the questions asked in the interview was you know 'can you speak Panjabi?' to the bloke she was getting married to and my mum you know she looks after us and she wants us to get married into a good family so she doesn't suffer the problem so that WE don't suffer the problems that she did

RH:	mm
Gurleetaa:	er so you know if I don't meet up with the recommenda-
	tions that brings then you know it makes her feel bad and
	then you know it just sort of works like that so I can
	understand it perfectly from her point of view and I
	would like to be able to speak it as well

According to Gurleetaa the ability to speak Panjabi is sometimes linked with a number of other skills, like being able to cook well, that after marriage she would have to continuously demonstrate to sceptical in-laws, and particularly to a faintly, or actually, hostile mother-in-law. Gurleetaa refers to a time, early in her mother's own marriage when she was living in a house with a very large number of her in-laws and had to look after them all, had found her position problematic, and did not want Gurleetaa to suffer in the same way. As she puts it,

Gurleetaa:	not er not like you know she obviously she'd learned to
	speak Panjabi but it's sort of like yeah if fam- if the other
	side of the family if my mum didn't let's just say she
	couldn't cook, yeah, then my grandma would you know
	she would be upset at tha[ʔ] and then she would be spiteful
	to my mother so if I weren't able to speak Panjabi properly
	my future mother-in-law might =
RH:	= I see =
Gurleetaa:	= you know
RH:	Yes. I see what you mean. I see what you mean.

Gurleetaa can't point to any practical steps that she actually takes to give effect to her apparent concern to improve her Panjabi, such as for instance attending community language classes. She has never attended such classes.

She describes herself and her family as Sikhs but says, 'my family isn't particularly religious ... I think that there's being religious and there's being too religious ... and too religious is just sor[ʔ] of doing whatever the Guru Granth Sahib says.' On the other hand she observes one of the 5 ks by wearing kaccha (shorts). However, she rarely attends the Gurdwara, her previous visit having occurred more than a year previously. She says that this is because she does not have time to attend. At the same time, though, she says that she prays. Despite her claim that her family is not religious consternation was caused in the family when her brothers took the relatively transgressive act in Sikhism of cutting their hair.

> *Gurleetaa:*   yeah I mean my brothers they cut their hair and that just caused a whole uproar thing in our family and when I went with my younger brother when he got his hair cut, just before he came to this school and I was absolutely I was so close to tears that you know he had this you know he had really nice hair as well and they just took it and they cut it and I had to walk out of the shop because I was so upset like it took him 11 years to grow that and that now it's just cu- it as it were and so you know that affects me as well it's alright now I feel

It is not clear from her comments whether Gurleetaa's concerns about her brothers' hair is aesthetic or religious; though she can draw readily on religious resources if she feels needs to, such as in one instance when she recited in Panjabi a Sikh prayer at a theme park before boarding a terrifying roller coaster ride.

Gurleetaa's interactions with her peers are conducted in English rather than Panjabi because their Panjabi is not fluent enough for extended conversations, although she considers that her own Panjabi is the best in her friendship group. She and her friends allot Panjabi a ludic function, 'er we do we do it in a sort of fun way, sort of we just say i[?] just to be fun just to make a joke', while leaving the discussion of what she regards as serious topics like racism to English:

> *Gurleetaa:*   or I'll go **buna** you know mean a vest it wouldn't be funny
> *RH:*   mm
> *Gurleetaa:*   but if I say it in Panjabi it's more humorous.

Gurleetaa also identifies her interactions with her peers as moments where she uses slang and she makes a point of identifying the use of slang with London phonological speech tokens such as pronouncing /th/ as /f/ and says that it is something that she consciously tries to move away from even to the extent of 'correcting' its use by her younger brother. She associates this speech feature with characters in the popular British TV soap opera Eastenders, but it is the only token of London speech that she is conscious of using herself. She also associates the use of slang with her relationships with her friends and their joint general consumption of popular culture; particularly TV and films.

She links the use of outgroup language to influences from (especially American) TV and film:

> An example of this travelling would be the word 'diss', meaning to insult verbally. Within my own year at school, I have heard 'diss' many times and I have also used this word. The word originates from America and the greatest influence on the younger generation to say this word is probably black American TV shows.

One specific example named by Gurleetaa concerns a fictional pro-gramme called Moesha[7] about a black girl in the United States of America, in which she heard 'diss' and other words such as 'homies'. She also identified the film Pulp Fiction as the source from which she learned expressions such as 'big cahooner'. With regard to her taste in films, TV and music Gurleetaa does not say that she identifies with the characters in these cultural sources or that she feels any sense of strong affiliation with them. Nor does she cite 'black' musical styles as an interest or influence. On the other hand she explicitly declares her dislike of Hindi language films and the music associated with them. She grudgingly admits to quite liking one Bally Sagoo hit and talks of being 'lumbered' with one his CDs by her older brother. She has one Bon Jovi CD, but says that she particularly likes the band Kula Shaker partly because they have eastern influences in their music, though she is extremely vague about these.

Gurleetaa:	... er Kula Shaker they've sort of taken um eastern wha-eastern influences and put it into their music which I think is really good and they've um released a song called Govinder and it's written in Sanskrit and sung in Sanskrit and erm my mother says it's sort of like um something, saying something praise to the god and you know that would be you know something
RH:	something you like?
Gurleetaa:	yeah yeah

Other influences in her language practices include German which she sometimes uses even outside her German lessons at school. This usually takes the form of inserting German phrases like sehr interessant (very interesting) or sehr langweilig (very boring) into everyday contexts when with her friends. She also sometimes tunes into German satellite

TV stations when she is at home and tries to watch German films. Her satellite TV system also allows her to listen to German radio stations which play what she calls 'English music' and which feature German DJs talking to their audiences about the music in German.

Typically, when Gurleetaa speaks she sounds as if she comes from London. This is marked, for instance in her pronunciation, by her t–glottalling, and in her grammar by the London-marked use of the verbal token 'done'.

> *Gurleetaa:*   they've got two older er children, a boy and a girl, and they [done] BTECs and they [done] GNVQs and they were kind of jealous that my brother sor[?] of broke away from that trend and he cut his hair and so it was sor[?] of like you know
>
> *RH:*   mm
>
> *Gurleetaa:*   they're jealous and I think it's really pe[?]y to argue over something like that

Apart from when she is speaking Panjabi or using Panjabi cultural and religious lexical items when she is speaking English, Gurleetaa also uses expressions which are specific to an Indian form of English. These include the use of terms like 'cousin sister' for female cousin, and the expression, 'she gives it' where local Englishes in England typically use the narrative device, 'she goes' for 'she said', in animated speech. Gurleetaa also shows signs in her speech of patterns which are typical of contemporary patterns of general British youth usage and which are perhaps connected with wider international influences. These patterns include upspeaking,[8] 'one thing I do remember is once my mum forgot me (rising tone, upspeaking) at school'; and the contemporary youth usage of 'like',

> … you get people that you're housing for twenty years come back round your house twenny years later and they're like 'oh hello we used to be in your pind'.

Gurleetaa has visited India twice, once when she was about six months old and once when she was about nine years old, when she stayed for about seven weeks. She remembers having to do far more household chores than she ever does at home in Britain, and under more difficult conditions such as having to pump water to wash dishes in the absence of taps. The visit she remembers was to the Punjab region where her mother's parents and the rest of her mother's family live. She enjoyed some aspects of her trip such as being taught how to make chapatis, but actively disliked the conditions of life in her father's family's pind?[9] She is strongly aware of the existence of her family diaspora but is extremely hazy about the precise details of its historical formation. She thinks that her father's family moved from India to East Africa (Kenya), where she thinks he may have been born. She thinks that his immediate family subsequently returned to India before eventually moving to Britain.

Gurleetaa's account gives a sensation of a differently constituted, but equally complex and interwoven set of ethnic and cultural elements, as Amaljeet's. On the one hand she appears to be living as a contemporary London girl as part of a family which is disinclined to be too religious with respect to the Sikh religion. On the other hand she seems to be strongly aware of the potential future influence on her life of the global reach of traditional diasporic strictures regarding proper behaviour for women and suitable wives. Yet, conversely, her potential responsiveness to the residual demands of traditional cultural practices at first sight seems to represent incompatibilities with the side of her cultural life in which her favourite music is produced by white Anglo-American rock bands. Some of the everyday cultural negotiations between the individual, and local and global diasporic community demands, like those represented in Gurleetaa's account will be more fully analysed in Chapter 6. The ways in which musical tastes position many of the Blackhill youth as typical British teenagers will be demonstrated in Chapter 7.

* * *

Karwan's everyday ethnicity

According to Karwan's account the leading language in his home is Kurdish.[10] However, he is clear that English plays a regular auxiliary role:

> When we are at home we tend to use Kurdish but if we need to use different languages to help us talk and get our point across we do use the next best language, English

To be more precise, he suggests that in his home English has a useful mediating function as a recourse at moments when the limits of his receptive competence in Kurdish and his father's productive competence in English are reached:

> If my father explains a program to me he talks in Kurdish, but if I have problems understanding he explains in English, and if I still

don't understand he hands the problem to my brother, because we both talk the same type of English

There is a hint here, too, of the highly significant place of English in the home as a mode of communication between Karwan and his brother regardlesss of the general use of languages other than English, with his parents or other older relatives. On the other hand, and at the same time, Karwan is emphatic that he makes a special effort to speak a community language, rather than English, with older relatives. Specifically, Karwan says that his motivation for doing so had something to do with respect:

> If my parents have visitors it would be disrespectful to talk to them or among ourselfs (sic) in English or in any other language, [but Kurdish] for many reasons. One reason is that we must not grow up not knowing our language and another is, we set/show a bad example and a lack of self respect

Another component of Karwan's everyday multilingualism in the home appears to be connected to visits from his wider diasporic family residing abroad or to family members marrying outside their ethnic group and consequently acquiring the languages of their partners which then become a presence during family visits and gatherings of various kinds. In Karwan's case French and Portuguese are sometimes heard in domestic environments because one of his uncles is married to a French woman and one of his aunts is married to a Portuguese man. The evidence does not suggest that Karwan regards these moments as 'spectacular' but part of a low-key reciprocal exchange in which the French and Portuguese relatives in turn have learned and use Kurdish.

Karwan:	it's um my uncle he he's he he's married to a a a French lady
RH:	mm
Karwan:	my aun[ʔ]y:: is married to a erm Portuguese man
RH:	right
Karwan:	an' an' his language you know it's just taught
RH:	so so do you hear them speaking French and Portuguese
Karwan:	yes sometimes I do
RH:	yeah
Karwan:	bu[ʔ] er funnily enough my my er my aunty's husband he learnt sp– er to speak Kurdish and my uncle's wife has learned has learned as well

Karwan's parents are enormously encouraging about, and committed to, the maintenance of Kurdish language in the home, even though they can also speak English well. However, in addition, he also attended community language classes for the maintenance of his parents' ethnically identifying language. He continued his attendance for nine years. This appears to be partly because his mother was a teacher in such classes. His attendance ended when he was 12 years old. Karwan suggests that his initial attendance at the classes at a very young age was governed by pragmatic concerns – 'I used to go you know because because there was no one at home to look after me'.

Activities concerning the muslim religion were prominent at his community language Saturday school – 'i[?] was basically how how the Kurdish go[?] go[?] in – introduced to the m-muslim religion'. But while Karwan is equivocal about his own level of personal religious commitment he is much more sure that the levels of both religious commitment and transgression in his family are gendered. When asked how religious he thinks he is, he seems somewhat uncertain:

RH: so how do you think where do you place yourself
Karwan: I – I //[11]
RH: //religious not religious?
Karwan: I um I'm more I'm in the middle but more or less to the religious side
RH: right
Karwan: because I- I truly believe tha[?] that one day the world gonna end and and we're all going to be summoned
RH: yeah
Karwan: you know we- we're all gonna to ge[?] (.)[12] you know questioned by God

However, his firm view is that it is the females in his family who are serious about religious observance.

RH: uh so I mean how how religious are you are you and your family?
Karwan: well my mum she's she's very religious
RH: yeah
Karwan: all my aunties and all my cousins well that's that's the female side
RH: yeah =[13]
Karwan: =you count to er-every female in my family are religious the males and the other fathers they're they're they slack a bi[?]

At the same time he depicts the males in his family (and by implication himself) as being transgressive in their practices with regard to religion.

> *RH:*   =what do you mean by slack what (inaudible)=
> *Karwan:* =well in in in our religion we're not allowed to drink bu[?] (chuckles) all my uncles and all my parents I mean er my dad they all drink
> *RH:*   right
> *Karwan:* erm certain things we can't do you you know w- w- we have to wear erm religious hats and pray and all tha[?] all the females do tha[?] bu[?] the males nah

One illustration of Karwan's stance on religion relates to his explanation as to why he only occasionally attends Mosque on Friday afternoons. An initial embarrassed diffidence eventually gives way to the admission that on Friday afternoons he prefers to mess about and play football with his friends.

Along with other aspects of his linguistic world Karwan professes a strong affiliation to Jamaican language:

> *RH:*   when you're doing the mc'ing what kind of language do you use ...
> *Karwan:* its its not proper English its not proper English some some- things you say are not even words its just you you just try and make make every[f]ing that you say rhyme ... and and and if there's no word to rhyme with what you've just said you just make up a a sound
> *RH:*   mm but I mean when you say its not proper English then what is it what what=
> *Karwan:* = its its more or less slang slang different words an'
> *RH:*   associated with what kind of people though I mean where does it come from
> *Karwan:* where does it come from to to tell the truth it's more yardie talk ... i- it's all MC's prefer yardie talk cos a I I dunno it's just easier to talk like that
> *RH:*   do you think that I mean do you know what country's associated with it in yardie talk
> *Karwan:* er Jamaica and [de][14] Caribbean
> *... RH:* so I mean and and you found that easy to do
> *Karwan:* yeah I f- I find it easy to do because who the friends I hang around with Amaljeet an' Vijay an' do nine out of ten times

	when when we talk we're talking like that anyway ... it's just it's just a way of life now
RH:	mm so I mean how did you get into talking in a Jamaican kind of way then
Karwan:	it was like Brixton was where I started learning things cos er where I lived was nine out of ten people were were Jamaican or or black ... an' I just go[?] it from them
RH:	so how lo- how how many years did you live there
Karwan:	er :: rr[15] about six years yeah
RH:	from what age to what age
Karwan:	from about five to eleven
	[...]
RH:	can you remember the first phrase you heard in Jamaican
Karwan:	ye::h yeh the f- I can remember you know um the Desmonds[16] show ... it Porkpie 'yeh ma::n!' [Jamaican exclamatory intonation]
	[...]
RH:	mm so could you give me an example of that [speaking Jamaican]
Karwan:	erm (.) like we say 'wha a gwan'
RH:	mm
Karwan:	tha[?] means ... what's happenin' if you say to Ms W [teacher] 'wha a gwan' she'll probably [f]ink wha[?]'s tha[?] but if you if if I say that to Amaljeet now I say 'wha a gwan' he'll say 'yeh man coo every[f]inks coo[17]
Karwan:	ou[?] of all the accents I must admit I I love the Jamaican accent I love the way they talk it's just I w- I wanna learn every par[?] of i[?] every word because I I just I just enjoy talkin' i[?]

Karwan seems to link his original use of Jamaican language with the development of a particular inter-ethnic friendship he had when he was very young, as well as with TV programmes and music which have caught his imagination. He does not mention any current friendships with other young people of Jamaican descent, but claims that Jamaican language is important to him.

He is beginning to be involved in musical presentation and perform-ance. He has older siblings and cousins who are well known professional DJs serving their local ethnic minority communities, is heavily influenced by these relatives and aspires to be like them. Specifically he wants to be an MC, and a number of his peers have remarked that he is beginning to be noticed as someone with talent in this field. For Karwan, his DJ relatives, and other contemporaries there appear to be two key questions in styling their performances. *One*: how to incorporate Jamaican and other black-influenced language and styles. *Two*: how to symbolically incorporate linguistically a closely felt specific community ethnicity. In Karwan and his DJ relatives' case – the latter meant Kurdish.

What is striking about Karwan's representation of his cultural and ethnic self, is the discordant disruption it inserts into routine British discourses about Kurds being simply refugee victims. These discourses typically do not allow for a Kurdish refugee to be imagined as a young man who is firmly proud of Kurdish language and traditions while professing proficiency in, and love for, Jamaican language; or a burning ambition to be a sound system MC. What emerges from paying close attention to Karwan's agency is a striking demonstration of the fertility of the empirical pursuit of the idea of 'new ethnicities'. Some of the ways in which individual agency leads to the development of particular ethnic and cultural affiliations will be explored more analytically in both Chapters 6 and 7.

*   *   *

Diya's everyday ethnicity

The first language that Diya encountered in her life was Gujarati but she also began to speak English during the early development of her speech in her pre-school years. Although Gujarati came first in her life she cannot speak it as fluently as she can speak English. The two languages are woven intricately through her everyday experience and not a day passes when she speaks only one language:

> The language I use changes 24 hours a day depending on the people I am with. I don't think there has been a day where I have only spoke (sic) one language.

Diya's father is a fluent English and Gujarati speaker, but she speaks to him only in English. She does, however, speak Gujarati to him on occasions when the family are at home and her mother asks her to call him, or sometimes when she is speaking to her father and her mother cannot understand what they are saying, or again when the family has visitors who don't understand English very well. She writes,

> Another time I speak Gujerati with my dad is when my mum doesn't understand what we are saying and when we have guests over. All the

guests that usually come to my house are all Gujerati so when I want to ask my dad something I ask him in Gujerati so the guests don't find it rude, because sometimes they don't understand English and they will be thinking to themselves 'are they talking about me'.

While Diya's mother speaks many languages such as Gujarati, Hindi, Panjabi and Urdu, she speaks only a little English. Consequently, Diya feels compelled to mostly speak to her in Gujarati. Her own limitations in speaking Gujarati means that the Gujarati she speaks to her mother is always laced with English as she explains in the following written account:

When there is a time when I am talking to my mum in Gujerati I always mix English into it. I think I do this because I can't speak Gujerati properly and I am used to always speaking English. So when I ask her for a newspaper I would say,
'Mum newspaper apis'
When I really should be saying,
'Mum chapu apis'

Diya speaks English with her brother; but while speaking English is also a marked feature of the language use of the older *male* members of her family, the use of Gujarati is a marked feature of the language use of the older *female* members of her family. She attributes this contrast to the greater participation of the males in working environments outside the home.

oh um I just usually speak it when I'm talking to u- elders people who are older than me apart from the men cos all the men they work and they can speak English so I usually speak English to them whereas the ladies they're usually at home and they don't know much English so I have to speak Gujara[ʔ]i with them

Diya: (.) um cos like I think they're all work yeah and um we used to have our own shop so they used to talk English and um so when they're like usually at home and my dad usually talks to me in English and so you talk back in English and you're used to that cos if I'm just talking to my dad in English I'll just talk in English=

RH: =mm

Diya: =and um (.) so when I'm with my uncles sometimes like they talk to me in Gujara[ʔ]i yeah bu[ʔ] I always talk English with

them unless when its sometimes when we're in front of
everyone=

RH: =mm

Diya: =it's just th- they're just used to us talking to English to
them=

RH: =mm

Diya: =whereas all the ladies um they hardly hear us speak English
in front of them so it's like we have to talk to Gujara[?]i with
them cos they hardly don't understand anything we say

RH: right in English

Diya: yeah

Diya thinks that her father who was born in Uganda came to Britain
during his teens whereas her mother's whole upbringing was in India
and her arrival in Britain coincided with her marriage. Diya sometimes
hears Swahili during family gatherings when her grandmother who was
born in Uganda speaks it with one of Diya's uncles purely in order to
teasingly check whether Diya and others can understand it.

Diya is linguistically influenced by her immediate community environment which she depicts as being routinely multilingual and multiethnic.

My Neighbours are all Muslim, Hindu or Panjabi (Sikh) so when I hear
them talking I usually understand them and I pick upon what they say
so I can remember it. I can still not speak any of the languages like
Panjabi or Urdu but I think I can speak some Hindi.

She remarks that these attempts to speak Hindi are the product of
commonplace interactions:

you know our neighbourhood it's like friendly and stuff so we're like
we'll all talk to each and stuff and sometimes when like we have to go
somewh- to our next neighbour's house to give them something it's
like I usually end up talking in their language

Diya maintains that when she was about ten years old she had
attended community language classes to learn Gujarati, particularly to
learn how to read and write it. However, she only attended two classes
before she stopped going. She had joined the classes midstream, the
other children were ahead of her, and she found she couldn't understand
the teacher's questions. In addition, she had found the script in which
Gujarati is written particularly difficult to cope with, both to read and to

reproduce. Diya says that she feels no need to learn to read and write Gujarati as her mother and others don't require her to. She can't explain why but, 'well I don't really wanna learn it'. She contrasts this feeling with her experiences with languages like English and German. When it comes to German as compared with Gujarati she confirms her reason for finding it easier to learn:

> *RH:* =to get (.) so I mean if you compared say your Gujarati with when you started German (inaudible)=
>
> *Diya:* =but the probl- the thing is you know with German you use the actual English alphabet=

Diya sums up her experience by writing,

> When I was really young I went to learn Gujerati. I only went for a few weeks, then I left because I couldn't get it in my head. I learnt how to write and say the ABCs in Gujerati and soon I forgot it. Whereas anything I learn in English I remember it

Diya describes herself as a Hindu. She is aware that Gujarati Hindus are divided into castes and that her surname identifies her as belonging to the Lohana (business caste). She takes part in many major Hindu festivals, ceremonies and rituals encouraged by her grandmother who is the key instigator of the family's religious involvements. She particularly enjoys participating in festivals like Divali,[18] Navaratri[19] and Jaya Parvati,[20] which tend to involve family gatherings and celebrations, attendance at temple and a variety of fasting rituals.

> *Diya:* ...[21] my gran she's really religious so every time a religious events come we either fast we celebra[ʔ]e i[ʔ] and um we go to the temple when like stuff like Divali and stuff=
>
> *RH:* =yeah=
>
> *Diya:* =comes and we celebra[ʔ]e all tha[ʔ]
>
> *RH:* mm and then I me- I mean do you take an active part (or anything)
>
> *Diya:* yeah
>
> *RH:* yeah do you pray or
>
> *Diya:* yeah um (.) do you know that festival thing I told you about it lasts nine days
>
> *RH:* yeah what's it called
>
> *Diya:* um (.) Navaratri

RH: Navaratri
Diya: yeah and um for nine days everyone comes round to my
        house and we pray to God and like I'll just sit up there and
        watch and um so we just take part in tha[?] we take part in
        Divali and there's this um kind of fasting you do.

Though Diya can describe the kind of fasting she does including the
foods she eats and those that she doesn't, her participation in these
events and activities does not necessarily mean that she is either very
knowledgeable or very committed to their religious nature.

you can't ea? all that kind of stuff so you have to eat all this Indian
food without salt and it doesn't taste very nice

Diya: ... the last time when I went to India that was the time when
        I had to do this fast so it was alright cos I was around all these
        other girls who were doing it and stuff so that's easier bu[?]
        round here's qui[?]e cos not a lo[?] of people are really into it
        all that religion kinda stuff bu[?] i[?]s cause of my gran inni[?]
RH: mm
Diya: um I think I'll probably do it nex- start my one [special fasting
        ritual] next year
RH: mm what y- m- right through till you get married
Diya: yeah
RH: so wh- what what what's that one called
Diya: mm (.) ah I can't remember (slightly apologetic, embarrassed)
RH: uh huh huh (chuckles) can't remember
Diya: Jaya Parvati
RH: Jaya Parvati (inaudible)
Diya: yeah

Diya mostly speaks in English with her peers when she is at school. She
describes the English she speaks with them as slang and contrasts this
with Standard English although she cannot define clearly the difference
between these two varieties of language. She also sometimes inadvertently
includes slang in her attempts to write Standard English for her English
teacher:

Diya: =I didn't really think it was slang I just thought it was just
        normal English so I just wro[?]e i[?] but when I found ou[?]
        and Miss went to my work I realised tha[?] after she told me

what all of that i[?] was slang bu[?] erm if I went to do i[?]
myself I don't think I would have realised=

RH: =yeah=

Diya: that I use slang

Diya sometimes speaks Gujarati at school with one of her close
friends. They do this when they want to talk to each other without other
people understanding what they are saying. This strategy often fails to
work since many of their peers understand Gujarati, and on these occasions she and her friend resort to elaborate measures such as deliberately
saying the opposite of what they mean to disguise their purposes.

One of Diya's grandmothers was born and brought up in Uganda and
now lives in London. The other one lives in India and Diya and her family
stay with her, in the Gujerat region, when they visit the country. Diya
herself has visited India three times, the last occasion being when she
was 13 when she stayed for about two months. Her visits there have made
her more aware of the limitations of her Gujarati. These limitations are
exposed whenever she is forced to use English words for Gujarati words
she does not know and finds she is not understood, or when she is faced
with the challenge of relatives and others who understand no English at
all, or again when these locals use Gujarati words that she has never
heard before.

Diya's mother sometimes visits Tanzania, where the family has relatives,
bringing back gifts like t-shirts bearing dual language Swahili/English
slogans. Her Tanzanian relatives are a reflection of an even wider diaspora
of which she is a part.

Diya: so we've got no one in Uganda any more we've got in
        Tanzania and India=

RH: =mm=

Diya: =and we've go[?] relatives all over the place we've got some in
        Germany France

Diya describes how she is further exposed to this diaspora at religious
events in London:

Diya: yeah um when we like have um we have religious events and
        we all get together in like a hall all the like in our religion we
        have castes so everyone's a different caste and like the one
        caste they all get together in some h- in a hall and then they
        sing and dance and everything and when we go there um it's

like we get to know all these people that we never knew and
find out they were par[?] they're like in on like our s- side of
the family=

RH: =mm=

Diya: =and like my surname's like Chotai and um (.) round here
London and everywhere there there are so many Chotais and
I never ever knew that

More routinely, Diya says that most weekends her family gets together
with her father's four brothers, their wives and all their children. This
means that she is thrown together on an almost weekly basis with about
twenty of her cousins.

When her father and one of her uncles are together they watch BBC
programmes while the older females in her family usually watch Zee TV.[22]
They watch mainly Hindi language soaps and films. They sometimes
watch programmes shown on British TV, like *Eastenders* and *Neighbours*
but this tends to be because others in the family are watching. Her
grandmother likes watching the latter programmes but because she
doesn't understand English, she often asks Diya, in Gujarati, what is
going on. Sometimes Diya and other younger family members escape
their elders to watch TV upstairs rather than in the main sitting room.
She watches *Neighbours* and *Home and Away* everyday as well as
Eastenders.[23] She also lists *ER* and *X–Files* as programmes which she
watches dedicatedly, watching one and taping the other for later viewing
whenever they clash.[24] She stores taped programmes for viewing on
Wednesday evenings when she has nothing else to watch. If she has to
choose between watching a televised football match and one of her
favourite regular programmes she chooses the football because it is a
one-off event and she can easily catch-up with her other programmes.

She also very regularly watches Hindi language films whose content
she understands very well. These are films that the girls in her family
watch far more than the boys but she does not know why this is the
case, although she thinks it might possibly be because of what she
describes as the 'unrealistic' and highly predictable format of these
films. She listens to the Hindi language music accompanying these films
but is not prepared to say that she actively likes it. She stresses, rather,
that she much prefers to listen to what she describes as 'English' music
rather than to either Hindi film music or to Bhangra music, although
she does like listening to Hindi remix music (Hindi film music mixed
with Anglo-American musical styles and beats). Although she is aware that
Zee TV has its own Hindi Top Ten programme she pays more attention

to radio. Sunrise Radio[25] is always playing in the kitchen in her home where it is listened to by her father and others, but she doesn't listen to it herself. In her own room she listens to Capital Radio,[26] Radio One[27] and Kiss FM.[28]

When Diya talks she has a noticeably London accent, represented, for instance, in her t-glottalling. At the same time she uses lexical items such as 'cousin sister' associated with a specifically Indian form of English; and also Gujarati and Hindi language lexical items, often in contexts associated with religious and cultural rituals.

Diya's presentation of self provides a number of cautions about the importance of not reaching premature judgements when researching 'new ethnicities'. At first sight she appears to be framed in relation to residual elements of traditional culture in that she belongs to a fairly religious family and, shows an awareness of caste and takes part in a range of Hindu festivals and cultural practices. However, the dominant strand in her everyday practices reveals her as someone with little interest in other aspects of the maintenance of cultural traditions such as learning Gujarati language. Furthermore, despite her participation in Hindu rituals her knowledge of their meaning is wafer thin, while her understanding of the meanings of the everyday cultural practices of her British teenage life is very deep. Diya's portrait raises wider issues concerning how the Blackhill youth manage interactions with community and family religions which will be studied in Chapter 6, while the comparison between the Blackhill youth and unspectacular British teenage popular cultural con-sumption and tastes will be discussed in Chapter 7.

* * *

Amod's everyday ethnicity

Both Amod's parents were born in East Africa. He is unsure whether his father was born in Uganda or Kenya, but knows for sure that his mother was born in Nairobi, Kenya. He thinks that she came to Britain when she was about nine years old after the death of her mother, and attended a local school not far from the school Amod now attends. His father also had a significant amount of his schooling and other education in Britain. One of the reasons why Amod's family returned to Britain after living elsewhere, was that neither his grandfather nor his parents liked the schools in Kenya when compared to those in Britain. Amod himself, was born in London and taken as a baby to live in Kenya returning to live in London when he was seven years old. His memories of his early childhood in Kenya embrace a family life which included servants. These servants spoke Swahili which was the language his grandparents used to converse with them and at that stage of his life Amod learned Swahili too. While he can still understand quite a lot of Swahili he can no longer speak it very well. These days his parents no longer speak Swahili to each other except when the family has visitors from Kenya when the language is used for greetings and initial conversation.

In Amod's home Gujarati and English are the two languages in constant use. He judges that Gujarati is the most used language in his house because his grandmother does not speak English, and Gujarati, 'is the only language she can speak which the whole family can understand'. Nevertheless, the use of English in his home is extremely extensive, with him, his parents, his brother and grandfather all speaking English fluently. Family members speak English when they have guests who don't speak Gujarati, and, when guests are Gujarati speakers, both English and Gujarati are used. Although Amod always speaks Gujarati to his grand-mother, and either English or Gujarati with his parents and particular aunts or uncles, he prefers to speak English, 'because I find it largely easier to talk to people'. He rarely speaks Gujarati with his brother because they feel more comfortable speaking English to each other. This is partly due to his brother's limitations in speaking Gujarati. At the same time neither he nor his brother can understand Hindi and Panjabi when his parents and grandparents sometimes speak it to visitors who are not Gujarati speakers.

Apart from learning Gujarati directly from his family, Amod attended a Gujarati community school for three years from the age of nine. As well as Gujarati language, the school concentrated a lot on teaching a variety of cultural practices including folk-dancing and the playing of tabla drums. He even bought tabla drums, but once he left the school at the age of 12 he stopped playing. He is not too clear about why he stopped going to the Gujarati community classes. One reason he offers is that the classes took place on Saturdays when his friends would meet up to go out and pursue a variety of other activities as part of their leisure time. He does add, though, that he particularly disliked the folk-dancing, partly because of the attitude and methods of the teacher.

Amod:	the Gujara[ʔ]i classes were okay but I didn't like I didn't like the folk-dancing things like tha[ʔ] but it was alrigh[ʔ] otherwise
RH:	wh- what did you think about the folk-dancing
Amod:	pff yeah it was alright but the teacher we had he was a bit of he wasn't that good

RH: how did he sort of fall down?

Amod: he used to get angry too easily if you didn't if you messed up but I was always at the back we had a mixed class and it was like the sports hall and it was a class that size I was always at the back so anyone near him he used to just shout if they got anything wrong

The dropping of these classes did not signal an end to Amod's endeavours to learn Gujarati in a formal way, since his mother hired a private home tutor to teach him, his brother and two cousins in pairs at separate times. This tuition helped him to learn how to form and sound the Gujarati language script and left him able to read Gujarati a little and to write it a little too:

I can write as well I still remember all the alphabets and all tha[ʔ] and I can still wri- wri[ʔ]e things like my name and common things.

Although he feels quite confident in his ability to understand and speak Gujarati there are moments and contexts when there are serious limitations to his capacity to understand it. This is particularly so in relation to religious events. Amod identifies himself and his family as Hindus and by way of illustration describes a week long ritual which occurs when a family member dies. The ritual is lead by a Pandit[29] who, 'reads out the story of the Gi[ʔ]a'.[30] But,

it goes through the whole week and he um he says do i[ʔ] in the memory of all the people who die and he it's s- it's read in all Gujara[ʔ]i and tha[ʔ] so I have to ask qui[ʔ]e a lo[ʔ] um

RH: mm

Amod: because there's some words tha[ʔ] I don't know.

Certainly he participates in such prayer rituals but depicts himself as an uncomprehending semi-detached participant:

Amod: I don't think I'm really tha[ʔ] into religion cos um (.) don[ʔ] know really um (.) I think I jus- I just go cos it's there basically er so I know the meaning to some of them like to Divali[31] and all tha[ʔ] and um but there are some things tha[ʔ] I don't qui[ʔ]e understand like birthdays of gods and all tha[ʔ] I don't understand why we celebrate i[ʔ] cos (.) I don't believe

that there are that many gods that we say there are I reckon
it's just one person so (.) ... don't go to the temple that often
I don- I don't (.) I've been to the new that the new that's
open in Neasden but I don't//

RH: //(I've seen that it's amazing)

Amod: yeah that's amazing but I don't hardly ever kind of actually I
haven't been in the last year.

His feeling of involvement in religion and prayers is fundamentally
affected by what he sees as his limitations in Gujarati language:

Amod: yeah praying um praying I don't always understand i[ʔ]
that's difficul[ʔ] I find that difficul[ʔ] to understand because
the words are different

RH: mm

Amod: they're not usually used.

Weddings too, are occasions when Gujarati language and cultural
practices are prominent but where, again, he feels relatively detached
and uncomprehending:

Amod: ... there's certain things if it's like if it's erm my erm mum's
brother w- w- wedding then I h- then there's some spe- certain
thing I have to do I can't remember what it's called bu[ʔ] I am
one of the boys who has to take some things in to i[ʔ] and
I have to be I have to be there to do tha[ʔ]

RH: yeah

Amod: and then they g- they give me money for doing tha[ʔ].

In contrast Amod feels comfortable speaking English, making it clear that
with his peers as well as his brother and cousins, this is the dominant
form of communication – a language of ease.

I don't know um with with my cousin she's she's the same age as me
um I I speak Gujaraʔi with them sometimes but most of the time it's
English er er I just find I just feel more comfortable speaking English
with people my age.

and,

and um with my friends it's I don[ʔ] I don[ʔ] know how to explain i[ʔ]
bu[ʔ] it's just I just feel more comfortable speaking English with them.

When speaking with his peers the form of English which dominates is what he calls slang, and which he associates with the use of specific linguistic tokens and the specific location of Southall:

> RH: so wh- when you say slang what are talking about what does
>   slang mean
> Amod: right things like words like um 'inni[?]' and (.) 'innit an
>   tha[?] and er it's all Southall language.

Although Amod associates himself with the use of this form of language, he slightly distances himself from the strongest affiliation to it by adding that his own usage is slightly different since he lives in Ruislip rather than Southall.[32] He also links the use of slang with the practice of cussing in which he and his peers heavily engage. Cussing is something that his Panjabi-speaking peers do in Panjabi. When they do so he only really understands bits of what they are saying but is familiar with what they are saying because so many of his peers at school are from what he calls Panjabi backgrounds. He also associates the word slang with popular music which he talks about using the broad label 'English songs', and he talks about Rap music in particular. He listens to Rap music but not nearly as much as many of his peers. His own musical tastes are centred on 'top 10 music' and Michael Jackson is a favourite. His interest in popular music is, though, not fervent and is just in, 'anything that r–really sounds good to me'. He likes the 'background tunes' in the Hindi movies that he watches but does not like the 'Indian songs' in them because he doesn't understand the words:

> Amod: like I like the background tunes bu[?] because I don't under-
>   stand the words I never understand the words in Indian
>   songs erm so that's why that's why I don't like the songs
> RH: are they in Hindi though
> Amod: yeah they're in Hindi but erm it's just I don't know erm it's
>   the way they see them I listen to the background music but I
>   never listen to the words cos I won't understand them.

Broadly, however, he is much happier with jungle or club remixes of Hindi film music since

> I don't listen to the words that much so um that's why I like the er
> remixes.

On the other hand Amod understands the Hindi dialogue as opposed to the Hindi song lyrics in Hindi movies, and he even sometimes goes to the cinema to watch them. He is critical of what he sees as the far-fetched non-naturalistic comic book style of these films which he contrasts unfavourably with the naturalistic and realistic style of 'English' films. As he sees it, in the 'Indian' films 'they punch one person and he flies abou[ʔ] 100 metres' so that,

Amod: in English films most of it is reali[ʔ]y in Indian films hardly
RH: yeah
Amod: or say the good guy in one gets sho[ʔ] a hundred times he won't die but if the Eng- the bad guy gets sho[ʔ] once he'll die.

Nevertheless, he does enjoy Hindi films and when there are Panjabi language passages in them he asks any Panjabi friends who might be watching with him for a translation. He attributes his acquisition of some Hindi language understanding to his repeated watching on TV and video when he was younger of the Hindu epics the Mahabharata and the Ramayana. He was aided greatly in developing his understanding of the Hindi, by the accompanying English subtitles. This is a pattern which has subsequently been replicated by his younger brother.

When Amod speaks he sounds locally London in his pronunciation (bu[ʔ]) (any[f]ing), and sometimes in his grammar (I done bad), and occasionally Caribbean in his pronuciation too ([d]em),

Amod: and the thing about German is is it's like i[ʔ]'s like i[ʔ]'s like learning facts you see y- you le- learn you learn the lines and and you remember [d]em and I am good at tha[ʔ]
RH: mm
Amod: so tha[ʔ]'s tha[ʔ]'s why I [done] well in i[ʔ] but um I didn't concentrate on my spellings so that's why I [done] bad that's why I didn't get proper good marks well I did get good marks bu[ʔ] I didn't I lost all my marks on spellings I didn't lose any[f]ing on reading or writing I just lost it on spellings.

To add to this linguistic mosaic, Amod mentions German language which he is studying as a school subject, saying that he and his friends rarely use the language outside classes except for occasionally greeting each other in German and more frequently swearing at each other in German. He also refers to occasions on which he watches parts of German language films on satellite TV.

Apart from spending most of his first seven years of life in Kenya and having relatives there still, he has visited Kenya on about six further occasions; more or less every year unless it was a year when his Kenyan relatives were visiting Britain. On the other hand he is emphatic that although his mother told him that he had visited India once when he was a one year old baby he had no desire to go there again, though he concedes, 'I know I'll be going there sometime I'll have to go there sometime'. He feels like this even though he has large numbers of relatives in India. His attitude has been shaped by TV images of Indian life and by the reports of his peers who have visited India,

Amod:	no I've never been India er I know my mum said I b- I went when I was one bu[ʔ] I don[ʔ] really want to go there
RH:	why not
Amod:	I don't know (.) I haven't got a good impression of it (moment)
RH:	so what is it you're worrying about it
Amod:	er erm o- overcrowding (.) a bit poor and (inaudible) I just don't think I don't want to go there
RH:	and is there relatives there=
Amod:	=yeah yeah loads
RH:	mm and wh- where did you get these images from about (overcrowding) and
Amod:	er that poor is um this is a lot of street people and I don't know I just don't like things like tha[ʔ] cos I don't know erm (.) see things on TV and some some people say when it comes back 'oh it smells there a lot' and 'the toilets are in the ground and everywh-' I don't like things like tha[ʔ] I know my relatives haven't got i[ʔ] they've got proper houses and but still it's just (.) I don't really want to go there (light laugh).

Amod's linguistic and ethnic profile, like others in this series of portraits, conveys a strong sense of how any single relatively unmediated investigation of any given individual's agency would yield a portrait defying easy definition. He was born in Britain but has spent a significant proportion of his life in East Africa which he still visits on a very regular basis. Yet when it comes to another part of his diaspora family, those in India, he assumes the ethnic identification of the squeamish Briton abroad dismayed at the poverty, foul smells and deficient toilet facilities available there. Reconciling these seeming contradictions in a theoretically and empirically and coherent way is one of the central tasks of this book and will be taken up further, especially in Chapters 6 and 7. But the sense of unpredictability and apparent contradiction in all five of the portraits presented here, is characterisitc of what 'new ethnicities' means, as lived experience.

Interpreting new ethnicities and cultures of hybridity

It has been suggested that the best interpretivist approaches to human inquiry are those which 'share the goal of understanding the complex world of lived experience from the point of view of those who live it' (Schwandt, 1998: 221). The five individual portraits in this chapter have attempted this through dense, relatively unmediated description, foregrounding the voices of the individual Blackhill youth selected. Yet a further problem remains. How might one move beyond such particular evocative description towards a broader interpretive frame, something more indicative of the kind of structured social formation or phenomenon suggested by the terms 'new ethnicities' and 'cultures of hybridity'? Here I propose a number of ways in which these contrasting perspectives – the specifically detailed and the more widely significant might be productively accommodated. Certain formulations by Raymond Williams, E.P. Thompson and Alfred Schutz are extremely useful for demonstrating the importance of giving full rein to individual voices and representations while simultaneously insisting that the consistent repetitions of these voices and representations in a specific milieu at a specific historical moment is itself constitutive of structured social meaning. The concepts 'new ethnicities' and 'cultures of hybridity' might be taken in different ways to imply an unruly myriad of individual differences in social and cultural practices. While ideologically sympathetic to this perspective, I also argue that these individual experiences are not merely artefacts of voluntarist free will but can also be read as patterned and structured. Some aspects of the work of Williams and Schutz justify the argument that the accumulation of significant quantities of contingent individual experience is indicative of the presence of significantly structured cultural and social formations. At the same time, aspects of Thompson's work show why prior respectful attention to the specifics of individual agency is equally important, and I will return to this point later. First, though, I'll begin to outline some of the ways in which aspects of Raymond Williams' theory of culture assists these endeavours.

Williams and the Definition of Culture

It is a characteristic of Williams' work to attempt to construct multi-faceted definitions of the term culture (Williams, 1976/1983). Here just one of these will be examined – his persistent reference to culture as being to do with a whole way of life,

> But in theory and practice I came to believe that I had to give up, or at least to leave aside, what I knew as the Marxist tradition: to attempt to develop a different kind of theory of social totality; to see the study of culture as the study of relations between elements in a whole way of life.
> (Williams, 1980: 20)

The attempt to identify and describe specific 'cultures of hybridity' bene-fits from this kind of definition. This is particularly so when the study of the structure of 'the whole way of life' is built on the foundations of a close analysis of the behaviours, practices and statements of individuals,

> I shall try to do this by examining, not a series of abstracted problems, but a series of statements by individuals. It is not only that, by tem-perament and training, I find more meaning in this kind of personally verified statement than in a system of significant abstractions. It is also that, in a theme of this kind, I feel myself committed to the study of actual language: that is to say, to the words and sequences of words which particular men and women have used in trying to give meaning to their experience.
> (Williams, 1958: p. xix)

This chapter has focused strongly on the statements of individuals as a principal methodological practice in the task of identifying particular social and cultural formations. Williams (1980) defends the value of this kind of approach to the analysis of cultural groups, even though he is aware of the critique which suggests that small cultural groups are not worth studying since what can be said about them is commonly nuanced, ambiguous and enigmatic and not susceptible to strong statements of certainty based on statistical analysis. Williams, though, does not abandon the search to say, at one and the same time, something of value about larger social and cultural structures in society. This search leads him repeatedly in his writings to make reference to one device which he pro-poses as a way of realising these dual ambitions. The device is the notion he refers to as 'Structures of Feeling', or 'A Structure of Feeling'.

Williams' structures of feeling

Stuart Hall (1989: 62), finds Williams' concept of a structure of feeling 'quite unsatisfactory' stating that it 'continues to have disabling theoretical effects'. I find the reverse. I argue, rather, that it is just one useful way of imagining and analysing the dialectical relationship between the contingent representations of specifically located individuals and the wider social forces which constrain them and which they at the same time help to construct. For Williams a 'structure of feeling' is at bottom an expression of temporality, 'this structure of feeling is the culture of a period' (Williams, 1992: 48). Instead of an anxious rush to say something general and definitive about a putative universal class of young people of South Asian descent in the United Kingdom, the present book endeavours to collect a variety of representations of specific individuals, in a specific geographical location, at a particular temporal moment in a specific institutional setting. If certain representations occur repeatedly in the separate accounts of named individuals who share the social space just described, it becomes possible to suggest tentatively that their representations might indicate a collective way in which a particular encounter with the world is being experienced in a contingent social context. In other words it might be possible to name and describe a 'structure of feeling'. As Williams puts it,

> I do not mean that the structure of feeling, any more than the social character, is possessed in the same way by the many individuals in the community. But I think it is a very deep and very wide possession, in all actual communities, precisely because it is on it that communication depends. And what is particularly interesting is that it does not seem to be, in any formal sense, learned. One generation may train its successor, with reasonable success, in the social character or the general cultural pattern, but the new generation will have its own structure of feeling, which will not appear to have come 'from' anywhere. For here, most distinctly, the changing organization is enacted in the organism: the new generation responds in its own ways to the unique world it is inheriting, taking up many continuities, that can be traced, and reproducing many aspects of the organization, which can be separately described, yet feeling its whole life in certain ways differently, and shaping its creative response into a new structure of feeling.
>
> (*ibid.*: 48–9)

Williams' elaboration is especially helpful in justifying the methodological procedure of basing this book on the collection of such a large data set of individual representations. It also begins to offer a glimpse of a way of interpreting some otherwise elusive tensions apparent in this data. One such example is the fact that most of the informants suggest, throughout their representations, that their grandparents and parents have made considerable explicit efforts to train them in the supposed social and cultural contours of their ethnic group. Yet evident in their own representations is an overriding sense that these efforts are being replaced by different responses to the world which appear to work more comfortably for them; that is, they are arguably experiencing a new structure of feeling. The question of language use represents just one dimension of a potential structure of feeling. Inviting individuals to articulate representations of their patterns of language use is a telling means of appreciating something of the way in which specific 'new ethnicities' and 'cultures of hybridity' might be formed. Again, the collective and the structural can be revealed by starting from the specific and the individual. There is endorsement for this in Williams' further elaboration of the meaning of structure of feeling,

> In spite of substantial and at some levels decisive continuities in grammar and vocabulary, no generation speaks quite the same language as its predecessors. The difference can be defined in terms of additions, deletions, and modifications, but these do not exhaust it. What really changes is something quite general, over a wide range, and the description that often fits the change best is the literary term "style"... For what we are defining is a particular quality of social experience and relationship, historically distinct from other particular qualities, which gives the sense of a generation or of a period.
>
> (Williams, 1977: 131)

When the Blackhill youth discuss their patterns of language use and other aspects of their ethnicity a certain tension is apparent. They often appear to be struggling, simultaneously, to both claim and disavow affiliation to family and community patterns of language use and cultural practices. So, for instance, at one moment they might disclaim expertise in family and community language use or religious practices; at the next moment they deploy personal pronouns ('my religion', 'our language') to reclaim allegiance. Here, too, Williams theorises in a useful way when he suggests that any analysis of culture must struggle to identify elements which are dominant, residual and emergent. These in turn are constitutive aspects of structures of feeling and will be examined more fully later in this chapter, after a brief analysis of what parts of the work of Thompson and Schutz can add to the perspectives of Williams.

Thompson and the importance of agency

Stuart Hall once stated that there were two paradigms in cultural studies (Hall, 1981). These were the culturalist paradigm and the structuralist paradigm. For Hall, the former linked Williams' approach to cultural analysis to that of E.P. Thompson and Richard Hoggart. What was noteworthy in the culturalist paradigm was that,

> The *experiential pull* in this paradigm, and the emphasis on the creative and on historical agency, constitute the two key elements in the *humanism* of the position outlined. Each, consequently accords "experience" an authenticating position in any cultural analysis. It is, ultimately, where and how people experience their conditions of life, define them and respond to them, which, for Thompson defines why every mode of production is also a culture, and every struggle between classes is always also a struggle between cultural modalities; and which, for Williams, is what a "cultural analysis", in the final instance should deliver.
>
> (*ibid.*: 26)

Thompson attaches prime importance in social and cultural analysis to the idea that human beings act consciously, individually and collectively, to advance what they take to be their own interests, and have the capacity to affect the course of their own history. In other words they have agency. As he neatly puts it in relation to the English working class, 'The working class did not rise like the sun at an appointed time. It was present at its own making' (Thompson, 1968: 9). I do not believe that it is possible to get close to a worthwhile understanding of how a specific social or cultural formation might be constituted without proceeding methodologically on these assumptions, and Thompson is severe on sociologists who think otherwise:

> Sociologists who have stopped the time-machine and, with a good deal of conceptual huffing and puffing, have gone down to the engine-room to look, tell us that nowhere at all have they been able to locate and classify a class. They can only find a multitude of people with different occupations, incomes, status-hierarchies, and the rest. Of course they are right, since class is not this or that part of the machine, but *the way the machine works* once it is set in motion – not this and that interest, but the *friction* of interests – the movement itself, the heat, the thundering noise. Class is a social and cultural formation (often finding institutional expression) which cannot be

defined abstractly, or in isolation, but only in terms of relationship with other classes; and, ultimately, the definition can only be made in the medium of *time* – that is, action and reaction, change and conflict. When we speak of *a* class we are thinking of a very loosely defined body of people who share the same congeries of interests, social experiences, traditions and value-system, who have a *disposition* to *behave* as a class, to define themselves in their actions and in their consciousness in relation to other groups of people in class ways. But class itself is not a thing, it is a happening.

(*ibid.*: 939)

Now read the passage again substituting 'ethnicity' or 'ethnic group' wherever the word class appears, in order to arrive at an understanding of some of the methodological assumptions guiding this book. In his coruscating attack on the way in which Althusserian structuralism contemptuously discounts these perspectives (Thompson, 1978), Thompson insists that the excavation of the category which might be broadly termed 'human experience' is an essential element in developing an understanding of what a particular social or cultural formation is and how it came to be what it is.

And we find that, with "experience" and "culture" we are at a junction-point of another kind. For people do not only experience their own experience as ideas, within thought and its procedures, or (as some theoretical practitioners suppose) as proletarian instinct, etc. They also experience their own experience as *feeling*, and they handle their feelings within their culture, as norms, familial and kinship obligations and reciprocities, as values or (through more elaborated forms) within art or religious beliefs. This half of culture (and it is a full one-half) may be described as affective and moral consciousness.

(Thompson, 1978: 363)

The idea that the respectful and rigorous analysis of agentive acts, statements and representations precedes and guides the search for structural frames of analysis and not vice-versa, clearly has powerful methodological salience in this book. In this chapter's portraits, culture is doubly depicted. Individuals express in words both the nature of their experience and how they feel about that experience. A structured collective cultural experience emerges when numbers of individuals, in a specific location at a particular historical juncture, articulate similar experiences and have similar feelings about those experiences. The quest to find convincing ways of linking individual agency and experience with identifiable social structure can also be assisted by aspects of what has been described as the phenomenological sociology of Alfred Schutz.

Alfred Schutz, the life-world and the stock of knowledge

A number of notions in Schutz's work can assist in answering the question of what wider value can be placed on the representational utterances, texts and performances of individual social actors. Schutz is greatly interested in the world of everyday life which he calls the 'life-world'.

> This is an intersubjective world in which people both create social reality and are constrained by the preexisting social and cultural structures created by our predecessors. While much of the life-world is shared, there are also private (biographically articulated) aspects of that world ... Overall, Schutz was concerned with the dialectical relationship between the way people construct social reality and the obdurate social and cultural reality that they inherit from those who preceded them in the social world.
>
> (Ritzer, 1992: 217)

This captures something of the dialectical method I have employed in the interpretation of my research data. Useful, too, in this respect is Schutz's concept of the stock of knowledge.

According to Schutz, when individuals offer an interpretation of their everyday world they do so on the basis of 'a stock of previous experiences of it, our own experiences and those handed down to us by our parents and teachers, which in the form of "knowledge at hand" function as a scheme of reference' (Schutz, 1970: 72). This sense of the collective reflected through the individual, helps to build apparently singular and subjective representations into structured forms. But Schutz is emphatic that the stock of knowledge is not static but is 'in a continual flux' (*ibid.*: 75).

At the same time members of a specific social or cultural group continually seek stability by taking recourse to ready made recipes in the form of schemes of expression for making sense of their world in a routinised fashion derived both from their ancestors and contemporary community authorities. Schutz argues that when specific groups share what appears to be a common social heritage,

> the subjective meaning the group has for its members consists in their knowledge of a common situation and with it of a common system

of typifications and relevances. This situation has its history in which
the individual members' biographies participate ... This acceptance of
a common system of relevances leads the members of the group to
a homogeneous self-typification.

(ibid.: 82)

The significance of these perspectives is clear. If the Blackhill youth,
who share a definable social space both in and away from the research
site, offer self-typifications which are replicated on a significant scale,
then there are strong grounds for inferring that a distinctive socio-cultural
structure has been identified. Borrowing the concept of Verstehen (understanding and interpretation of the acts, utterances, motivations, and
world experiences of individual social actors) from Weber and others,
Schutz summarises the position succinctly,

> The observational field of the social scientist, however, namely the
> social reality, has a specific meaning and relevance structure for the
> human beings living, acting, and thinking therein. By a series of
> common-sense constructs they have pre-selected and pre-interpreted
> this world which they experience as the reality of their daily lives. It
> is these thought objects of theirs which determine their behaviour by
> motivating it. The thought objects constructed by the social scientist,
> in order to grasp this social reality, have to be founded upon the
> thought objects constructed by the common-sense thinking of men,
> living their daily life within their social world. Thus, the constructs of
> the social sciences are, so to speak, constructs of the second degree,
> namely constructs of the constructs made by the actors on the social
> scene, whose behaviour the social scientist has to observe and to
> explain in accordance with the procedural rules of his science.
>   Thus, the exploration of the general principles according to which
> man in daily life organizes his experiences, and especially those of the
> social world, is the first task of the methodology of the social sciences.

(ibid.: 272–3)

Schutz proposes, as we have seen, that there exist socially constructed
commonsense stocks of knowledge which individuals bring to bear on
their everyday experience to make it meaningful. This constitutes a device
for characterising the foundations on which the Blackhill youth's representational accounts rest. In other words, Schutz's concept makes possible
the contention that each young person of South Asian descent, is drawing
on at least three major strands of commonsense stocks of knowledge.

The first is the commonsense stock of knowledge which defines what Sikh culture, or Panjabi language culture, or Hindu, or Gujarati language culture are. In the research data there are countless examples of instances where the informants make explicit references to such notions, which they attempt to use as frames through which they might interpret their everyday experiences and make them meaningful. One of the interesting features of these attempts is the extent to which most of them exhibit considerable tensions when they attempt to make their life worlds meaningful in this way. An example of this difficulty is the frequent occurrence, of, say, an informant from a Sikh family background having disavowed expertise in Panjabi language or any particular allegiance to Sikh religion or to the visible artefacts of Sikhism, nevertheless feeling it necessary to makes countless anxious references to 'my religion' or 'my culture'.

The second commonsense stock of knowledge on which they appear to be drawing is the one defining in what guises an adolescent of South Asian descent in West London in the late 1990s should inhabit the world. This is the stock of knowledge which allows one female informant to identify her preferred music as the white grunge band Nirvana rather than Hindi film music, or numerous female informants to express excited allegiance to the Black British R&B act Damage. Similarly, a significant number of male informants expressed and performed allegiance to African American and/or Jamaican macho ways of being. The key point is that in behaving in these ways these informants seemed to be drawing on stocks of knowledge which appeared to them to be locally unexceptional, but nevertheless important, ways of making sense of the world.

A third, and equally important stock of knowledge on which the Blackhill youth appeared to be drawing was that connected with the way in which official institutions such as their school, depict and define them. This stock of knowledge is of long standing, is deep and has spawned its own complex but well understood routinised common sense discourses. There are a variety of poles of origin of this stock of knowledge. One origin would be official British depictions and common sense knowledges of the peoples of India formed during the Raj.[33] Onto this would be added the stock of knowledge concerning the sections of these peoples who participated in a mass migration to Britain from the 1960s onwards and entered the society as unwelcome immigrants with supposedly no right to be in the country. After this the stock of knowledge developed further, during an era which began in the mid 1970s, with The Race Relations Act 1976, and which is still extant – the era dominated by official equal opportunities discourses in Britain. It is arguable that in this period, according to the prevailing official stock of knowledge, the Indians have become 'a nation of shopkeepers'; successful migrants with stable families and cultures – an example to all.[34] But more specifically a distinctive educational stock of knowledge has developed in Britain during this period. This stock of knowledge has circumscribed pupils of South Asian descent, amongst others, as people with strange languages and cultures which should be ignored (Commonwealth Immigrants Advisory Committee, 1964), tolerated (Bullock Report, 1975) and even funded (Swann Report, 1985). Some specific special funding, once known as Section 11 funding,[35] has historically been set aside to overcome the problems that these languages and cultures have been said to cause in the British educational system. In order to justify the additional funding, schools and other educational institutions have been required to construct monitoring systems in which students are described in numerical aggregates of ethnic, linguistic and religious groups. Once described in these ways a commonsense stock of knowledge has developed concerning the properties and behaviours of such groups. Indeed schools have been required to institute policies and practices based on this stock of knowledge, and related to the raising of educational achievement, to satisfy central government, Ofsted[36] inspectors and school governors. When I, as a researcher, investigated my informants on a British school site I was aware that the accounts that they supplied to me were at least partly shaped by the three stocks of knowledge which I have just identified. Holstein and Gubrium (1998) draw attention to Mary Douglas' (1986: 96) comments on Durkheim's observations on collective representations which she says he regarded as 'publicly standardized ideas [that] constitute social order'. For Holstein and Gubrium,

> Interpretive practice can be understood to involve the articulation of publicly recognized structures, categories, or images with aspects of experience in ways that accountably produce broadly recognizable instances of the objects or events so categorized.
>
> (1998: 147)

My view is, precisely, that the Blackhill youth, both in institutional and community settings have been the, at least partial, prisoners of collective representations. One element in this process is what Holstein and Gubrium refer to as the rhetorics of everyday life and collective representation, which in contemporary society is fuelled by,

> the large-scale and mass-media rhetoric or "publicity" (Gubrium, 1993) that promotes "images of issues" (Best, 1989) that may be applied to categorize experience.
>
> (Holstein and Gubrium, 1998: 148)

One of the purposes of the research reported in this book was to uncover and explore alternative participatory representations which transcend or perhaps contest media, community and institutional representations. In this respect I concur entirely with Holstein and Gubrium's (1998: 150) observation that,

> Practitioners of everyday life are not "organisational dopes", mere extensions of organizational thinking. They exercise interpretive discretion, mediated by complex layerings of interpretive influence. They also carry with them the biographical basis for resistance, personal and interpersonal histories that compete with organizational categories as means for interpreting experience.

Despite the power of aspects of Schutz's approach a small word of caution is nevertheless necessary. There is, in the concept of stocks of knowledge, a hint that the researcher need not be particularly concerned about how well founded they are. Yet it is important to make it emphatically clear that concrete historical and contemporary events in the world *do* have certain structural effects on the perceptions and behaviours of individuals. In short, political, economic, social and cultural power and domination exists and has real effects. The social researcher has a responsibility not to give the impression that in focusing hard on the local and the individual he/she is implying that such effects can be voluntaristically transcended.

One other interpretive consideration emerges from the present chapter. In all the portraits it is possible to perceive a tension between what might appear to be different competing elements between the new and the traditional in cultural practice. However, the interpretive frame proposed for this chapter and the remaining chapters in the book proposes that the new in cultural practice, rather than replacing the traditional, co-exists with it. In other words describing what is new in the ethnic and cultural practices of the Blackhill youth, is in no way intended to imply that they have abandoned or wish to abandon entirely their inherited traditions. Their portraits and accounts should be read as an extended exploration and demonstration of some of the ways in which intricate dialectical relationships in culture are realised at the level of the routine, habitual, unspectacular practices of everyday life. One way of resolving the interpretive problems in these scenarios is to utilise a theoretical formulation, drawn from the work of Raymond Williams, which suggests that culture should be perceived in terms of the articulation of the residual with the dominant and the emergent.

The dominant, residual and emergent, in culture

Williams urges that the cultural analyst must both identify the dominant, residual and emergent in culture as separate elements, and yet understand, too, that in lived experience they operate syncretically. This might be seen in the research reported in this book, at the intersection of linguistic and religious practices. For instance, with respect to the Blackhill youth, Panjabi language use and Sikh religious observances which were dominant in their families in their grandparents' generation may have been significantly replaced by emergent radically new practices. At the same time, however, the former practices live on for them with a specific residual salience. These young people continue to attend the Gurdwara, and they greet their grandparents in Panjabi on a daily basis to show respect. As Williams views it,

> The residual, by definition, has been effectively formed in the past, but it is still active in the cultural process, not only and often not at all as an element of the past, but as an effective element of the present. Thus certain experiences, meanings, and values which cannot be expressed or substantially verified in terms of the dominant culture, are nevertheless lived and practised on the basis of the residue–cultural as well as social—of some previous social and cultural institution or formation. It is crucial to distinguish this aspect of the residual, which may have an alternative or even oppositional relation to the dominant-culture, from that active manifestation of the residual (this being its distinction from the archaic) which has been wholly or largely incorporated into the dominant culture.
>
> (Williams, 1977: 122)

Williams states additionally,

> By "emergent" I mean, first, that new meanings and values, new practices, new relationships and kinds of relationship are continually being created. But it is exceptionally difficult to distinguish between those which are really elements of some new phase of the dominant culture (and in this sense "species specific") and those which are substantially alternative or oppositional to it: emergent in the strict sense, rather than merely novel.
>
> (*ibid.*: 123)

In a sense the Blackhill youth are negotiating doubly dominant, doubly residual and doubly emergent elements in culture. For them the dominant has operated both at the level of the Anglo elements of the dominant cultures of the British nation state and in the dominant strands of the relatively ethnically exclusive cultural practices of the generations of their grandparents and parents in their localities; the residual elements from both traditions are encountered and lived daily; they experience the emergent in the broader cultural arena as British born teenagers of the 1990s at the same time as experiencing the emergent in their narrower more ethnically exclusive environments. When they appear to oscillate between advocacy of emergent elements and the reclamation of previously discarded residual elements they are reflecting the need for defences against the penalties consequent upon black and brown Britishness,

> In the subsequent default of a particular phase of a dominant culture there is then a reaching back to those meanings and values which were created in actual societies and actual situations in the past, and which still seem to have significance because they represent areas of human experience, aspiration, and achievement which the dominant culture neglects, undervalues, opposes, represses, or even cannot recognize.
>
> (*ibid.*: 123–4)

Perhaps, too, intimations of uncertainty and caution, evident both in the Blackhill youth's embracing of the emergent and in my own attempts to name the cultural phenomena which my investigations have identified, can be better understood in the light of the following observation:

> What matters, finally, in understanding emergent culture, as distinct from both the dominant and the residual, is that it is never only a matter of immediate practice; indeed it depends crucially on finding new forms or adaptations of form. Again and again what we have to observe is in effect a pre-emergence, active and pressing but not yet fully articulated, rather than the evident emergence which could be more confidently named.
>
> (*ibid.*: 126)

This struggle to construct an adequate language of description, analysis and interpretation linking the identification of 'new ethnicities' and 'cultures of hybridity' is well served by these fertile observations, especially those drawn from Williams' work. In all these ways, the individual portraits can be construed as part of a structured whole. The Blackhill youth have creatively developed new ways or adaptations of ways of being 'South Asian' – Panjabi Sikhs, Gujarati Hindus and so on. Although many people have a more or less vague apprehension of these processes, they treat them for the most part as if they were a 'pre-emergence, active and pressing but not yet fully articulated'. My treatment, by contrast, seeks to identify, 'the evident emergence which [can] be more confidently named'. This emergence is the one I named as *Brasian* in Chapter 1, and which I will describe more fully in Chapter 8.

Conclusion

This chapter has attempted two main tasks. Firstly, to saturate the reader with a cumulative evocation of new ethnicities located in time, place and with respect to age, mediated through representations of patterns of everyday language use and multilingualism; and secondly to demonstrate how these patterns are characteristic of a group and not just of a series of isolated individuals. Here the sense of the everyday has been deliberately presented in a low key manner and with 'the accumulation of formally unanalyzed detail'. The chapter's central focus has been on how to grapple productively with a key problematic for anyone interested in the representation of everyday cultural practice.

> If ... everyday life is not simply a quantifiable, transparent, palpable actuality to be straightforwardly mined for information, then the question of how to register it needs to be posed. But this is not simply a methodological question about how to eke out information from a shadowy and recalcitrant realm, it is also (and necessarily) a question of how to present and articulate the daily (how to write it, picture it and so on). Indeed the question of how to register the everyday might insist that issues of method take place simultaneously at the level of our attention to the everyday and in our representation of it ... The "coherent narrative" and the "rigorous argument" have been the dominant forms encouraged by social science approaches, but whether these forms of presentation fit the material world of the everyday life is ... in need of questioning. This is to place the question of *form* at the forefront of everyday life theory. If it is not going continually to miss what it seeks, then everyday life studies will need to consider both the form of the everyday and the forms most adequate or productive for registering it.
>
> (Highmore, 2002: 19)

It was argued at the beginning of the book that it was particularly important to pay close attention to the 'voices' representing the everyday unspectacular cultural practices of visible ethnic minority populations in Britain, particularly the youth. It was argued that in order to do this convincingly it is necessary as far as possible to limit and defer the mediating voice of the academic analyst. This approach was carried through in the portraits presented in the first part of the chapter, and it is rare in British contexts for this amount of concentrated attention to be paid in academic environments to the representational agency of brown or black ethnic minority youth. One of the vehicles for these representations, is the voices of the Blackhill youth in the form of their *spoken* voices. Accordingly, the next chapter demonstrates what can be learned about the constitution of their ethnicities from their speech alone.

5
How You Talk Is Who You Are

Introduction

The title of this chapter is an overstatement; deliberately so. Analysts of ethnicity and culture working in the fields of Cultural studies and Sociology in Britain have tended to understate or ignore the role played by people's prosaic patterns of language use; that is, scant attention has been paid to one of the central constituent components of human existence – the fact that in most waking moments and during most everyday activities human beings either speak, or listen to the speech of others. Moreover, how people talk in routine unselfconscious speech is a remarkably tenacious marker of place, particularly in the dimension of pronunciation. It is an index of identity which belies the symbolic pull of the racial phenotype and transcends rhetorical tokens of allegiance to languages, religions and cultural practices emblematic of distant places. Paying attention to the way in which people use language, and to their perceptions of how they and their peers use language, is fundamental to developing an understanding of how cultures and ethnicities are constituted and enacted. What follows sketches some of the repeated patterns in the interactions of the Blackhill youth within their local environment, and gives some idea of the structures of the kind of linguistic ecology which they inhabit. Doing this, though, involves a conceptual shift of focus from the visual to the aural as a key signifier of ethnicity. Many theorists of culture and ethnicity such as Hall, Gilroy and others, while disavowing the tenets of notions of biological 'race' as merely the artefacts of a variety of social constructions, nevertheless have their attention fixed predominantly on the visual – that is the struggles surrounding the presence in British, European and North American societies of sizeable minority populations distinguished by their possession of skin colouring ranging from black through various shades of brown, in contrast to the majority populations of these societies whose colouring ranges from a kind of white to a kind of pink. Certainly, in Britain the relevant debates have substantially been about 'race' meaning skin colour and physical appearance. While purportedly being about culture and ethnicity, these debates have never been about the arrival in Britain since World War Two of migrants deemed 'white', such as Poles, Lithuanians, Italians, Cypriots, Australians, Americans, New Zealanders and so on. Gilroy has recently (Gilroy, 2001), attempted to move beyond these constraints denouncing them as elements of ways of thinking, analysing and acting which he calls 'raciology'.

Certainly, skin colour together with other physical characteristics, has been, and still is, in social discourses globally, a signifier of enormous consequence; but it is a fixed signifier in the sense that it is something that no given individual or group can change. What people are born with in this dimension they carry till they die. This then causes difficulties for anti-essentialist theorists in the British Cultural Studies tradition. However much they depict ethnicity as a category which is open, fluid inherently unstable and not fixed, for as long as the discussion is conducted in terms referring principally, for instance, to *black* people, the ensuing analysis is trapped within a fixed frame. By contrast the social and cultural category of everyday language use, which is customarily left unconsidered, is available as a category capable of considerable change and movement from one generation to another; that is to say, it is a category which is open, fluid, inherently unstable and not fixed from one generation to another. Consequently, a fruitful way of escaping existing confinements is to move to an analytical frame which shifts from a landscape dominated by the salience of the visual to one where the salience of the aural is brought into play. In other words, what can be said and imagined about cultures and ethnicities might appear very different when apprehended on the basis of a landscape of sound; a soundscape. This approach can usefully be construed as an invitation to 'think with the ears rather than think with the eyes'.[1] Such a move broadens the sociological imagination enabling the clearer perception of registers operating across communities, institutions, media and diasporas and ranging linguistically from the local London vernacular, to the globally diasporic South Asian, and to the globally teenage.

This chapter argues that the patterns of language use of the Blackhill youth as a whole, are an essential ingredient of their 'new cultures of hybridity' and of their 'new ethnicities'. These are inscribed in their bodies, not only in the familiar form of their outward physical appearance, but also in how they sound when they speak. In this vocal dimension one can find traces of the local in terms of their London speech and the global in terms of their evident and concurrent production of, and interaction with, a range of the world's languages, particularly Panjabi, Gujarati and Hindi and sometimes Caribbean derived Creole language, as well as African American Vernacular English. Thus, with respect to these young people there are two linked processes. Firstly, in the formation of their ethnicities the local is emphatically dominant. Secondly, and consequently, their ethnicities are unambiguously dominated by Britishness.[2] The evidence supporting these propositions is presented at two ontological levels. On the one hand specific phonological and some grammatical features of the speech of the Blackhill youth during interviews are both involuntary and 'real'. By way of contrast the contents of data obtained from their written and oral accounts are offered as *representations* of reality, in so far as they constitute self-reports on how language operates in their daily lives.[3] It should be emphasised that the evidence presented is not intended to be an exact sociolinguistic treatment in the variationist tradition, but rather a sociolinguistically informed account designed to illuminate underlying and generally overlooked developments in ethnicities and identities amongst young people of South Asian descent in Britain. In the following account what is important is not that any given speech characteristic in the speech of the Blackhill youth can also be found in use in other locations around the country. My emphasis is on the *co-occurrence* of all those elements in their speech which I have chosen to foreground. What is distinctive is that each of these elements forms part of an integrated use of language serving to reveal something significant about how new ethnicities are constructed and operate in the flow of everyday life. The marked presence in their routine speech of an ensemble of certain key heightened components of London ('cockney') speech, fixes them as Londoners regardless of the familiar distractions of their physical appearance; and other echoes of South Asian ethnicities such as their names, nominal religions and ethnic groups, and their parental and grandparental origins. Another strand of language which co-exists with this rooted local constituent, is their South Asian and other extra-British languages and the ways in which these are woven into the pattern. This does not exhaust the mix, since their engagement with these languages does not seal them off from patterns of language use in English typical of those used contemporaneously by young people all over the world. Finally, embedded within their use of English itself are residual traces of patterns of language drawn from the other side of the globe in the Indian subcontinent. At any specific moment when a member of the Blackhill youth is speaking, the London element is always present, but any or all of the other elements may well also be present. Not in the sense of a series of alternating currents, but as a continuous vein running through their cultural lives. No portrayal of the ethnicity of young people like these in Britain is quite adequate without this kind of sociolinguistic perspective. A more fine-grained sociolinguistic analysis is beyond the scope of this book,[4] but the illustrative material which follows paints the canvas with broad but careful brushstrokes.

The local in language: Maybe it's because they are Londoners

Neither of two major ethnographic studies of Southall, Baumann (1996), Gillespie (1995) pays close analytic attention to the local London inflections of the speech of the South Asian-descended youth of the area. Nevertheless, and relevantly, Baumann does make a brief reference to the young people he researched speaking, 'a West London dialect of English interspersed with various Americanisms and Indianisms' (*ibid.*: 2). Baumann amplifies this by describing the English language use of young Southallians thus,

> Phonetically, it is clearly recognizable as a West London accent, and its lexis integrates Americanisms (*'bad'* or *'wicked'* for 'good'), Afro-Caribbean usages (*'cool, man'*) and Indianisms (*'innit'* for 'isn't it', 'aren't you', 'aren't they', etc.).
>
> (*ibid.*: 47)

A sociolinguistic study of a part of the South Asian community of the area, including the youth, and one claiming ethnographic status, (Saxena, 1995), has nothing to say on the matter. Although not researching ethnic minority youth in the same geographical location, both Hewitt (1992, 1989) writing of 'a local multiethnic vernacular'[5] or 'community English', and Rampton (1995) referring to a 'local vernacular' show a strong awareness of the salience of the phenomena which this section of the chapter seeks to address. More specifically, Hewitt (1986) and Sebba (1993) show a marked recognition of its London inflection. What immediately follows is not an exhaustive analysis of all the features of the speech of the Blackhill youth which are redolent of Londonness. Instead, a limited, but suggestive, selection of such features is presented under three main headings; the phonological, the grammatical, and finally, slang and tags.[6]

London phonology: sounding London

Of immediate relevance, are some observations from variationist sociolinguists concerned with accent variation in Britain. Milroy *et al.* (1994), and a wide variety of contributors to the volume *Urban Voices: Accent Studies in the British Isles*, Foulkes and Docherty (1999), have commented on 'T–glottalling' – the replacement of a /t/ sound by a glottal stop /ʔ/[7] in words of the type /butter/, /letter/, /not/, /what/. They observe that it has for a long time been on the increase in Britain, not just in urban areas such as London where it has been heavily stigmatised as a working class speech characteristic, but in many other regions and amongst the middle and upper classes. Milroy *et al.* (1994: 328) state baldly that 'The spread of the glottal stop is so rapid that it is now widely perceived as a stereotype of urban British speech ...' . Wells (1986: 327) observes that '... the use of / ʔ / for / t / is widespread in all kinds of popular London speech ... '. He adds that,

> the glottal stop is widely regarded as a sound particularly characteristic of Cockney. Matthews (1938: 80) even goes so far as to assert that 'the chief consonantal feature of the dialect is the prevalence of the glottal stop'. It is certainly plausible to suppose that one of the principal factors contributing to the apparently recent geographical spread of T Glottalling is the influence of London English, where it is indeed very common.
>
> (Wells, 1986: 323)

Hughes and Trudgill (1996: 70), assert that 'The glottal stop, [ʔ] is extremely common in cockney speech'.

However, Foulkes and Docherty (1999: 16), note what they call, a 'lack of interest in the phonetics and phonology of ethnic subcommunities, in particular those of immigrant origin ... the lack of published work on the phonetics and phonology of the *English* spoken in ethnic subcommunities remains conspicuous'. The first of the linguistic features in the speech of the Blackhill youth to which I want to draw attention is, then, their pervasive T–glottalling. During the 30 individual conversational interviews conducted with them it was noticeable that their speech was universally marked by its 'Londonness'. Subsequently, careful listening to the recordings of these interviews, showed that all of the young people T–glottalled extensively, as the following examples show,[8] yeah when parents are watching i[ʔ] and we're ea[ʔ]ing downstairs

(Narjot (m) Panjabi Sikh)[9]

I can wri[ʔ]e like simple le[ʔ]ers bu[ʔ] not technical ones like my sister she carried on yeah and she's just done her G.C.S.E. Gujara[ʔ]i she could wri[ʔ]e a proper le[ʔ]er

(Vishnu (m) Gujarati Hindu)

she was very good a[ʔ] i[ʔ] she can wri[ʔ]e i[ʔ] read it it's just um my brother he doesn't know any of it he's never actually sat down and wri[ʔ]en it or read it

(Shariqah (f) Urdu Muslim)

Although T–glottalling was by far the most noticeable token of London phonology in the speech of the Blackhill youth, it was not the only one that was prevalent. Two phonological features, in particular, are worthy of attention. Wells states that,

Another of the very well known characteristics of Cockney is TH Fronting. It involves the replacement of the dental fricatives, [θ], [ð][10] by labiodentals, [f] and [v] respectively. This makes *thin* a homophone of fin ..., and *brother* rhyme with lover.

(Wells, 1986: 328).

Again these symbolic tokens of Londonness were highly prevalent in the speech of the Blackhill youth. For instance,

I just rhyme I jus word think of a word what rhymes wi[v] it put it toge[v]er

(Karwan (m) Kurdish Muslim)

... they are so pa[f]e[ʔ]ic

(Gurshanti (f) Panjabi Sikh)

and then he speaks English himself so he speaks all the English at work and every[f]ing

(Dhrishaj (m) Panjabi Sikh)

Wells (*ibid.*) mentions in passing that another marked feature of London phonology is the pronunciation of a word like *something* as /somethink/. This is an observation confirmed by Hughes and Trudgill

(1996), while McArthur (1992: 226), extends the example,

> *Everything, nothing, something* are pronounced 'everyfink', 'nuffink', 'sumfink'.
>
> (*ibid.*).

According to McArthur these are features contributing to 'core cockney speech' (*ibid.*). Matthews (1938) concurs, claiming that this phenomenon has been noticeable in London speech since the eighteenth century or perhaps even earlier. This kind of pronunciation pattern occurred quite often in Blackhill youth speech, and can be illustrated in the following examples,

> you know and like my mum doesn't wear any religious um rings or anythin[k]
>
> (Punamdeep (f) Panjabi Sikh)

> it's hard to say someone's somethin[k] when they're not
>
> (Premila (f) Gujarati Hindu)

> no they're they're always saying tha[ʔ] oh 'whenever you speak Urdu it sounds like in a Southall accent' or somethin[k]
>
> (Shariqah (f) Urdu Muslim)

It can, then, be seen that distinctively London phonology, which is a prominent part of the speech of the Blackhill youth, also acts to anchor their ethnicities as ineradicably local. This perspective is strengthened by the presence of grammatical aspects of their speech which are also marked as distinctive elements of a specifically London form of English, and it is worth now turning to these in a little more detail.

London grammar: London through and through

Citing a number of sources Cheshire *et al.* (1993), argue that the grammatical elements just mentioned, are often shared by the populations of other urban centres in Britain and as such are characteristic of the speech of people in the lower socio-economic groups in these areas. I want here to concentrate on a small number of such features as ones which were particularly noticeable in the Blackhill youth speech. The first one is the difference between Standard English and what Hughes and Trudgill (1996: 25) call non-standard dialects with respect to the past tense of irregular verbs, so that where Standard English grammar would produce /*I did it* /, London English and some other urban British grammars would have /*I done it* /. As before, this is a London speech characteristic which is readily present in Blackhill youth speech,

> and um er we never [done] that my mum used to do it when she was
> young
>
> > (Sahima (f) Gujarati Hindu)
>
> bu[ʔ] we only [done] that with the teachers ... I talked in Panjabi with
> my friends
>
> > (Sumandev (m) Panjabi Sikh)
>
> it's been quite a while now since I [done] Gujarati
>
> > (Amod (m) Gujarati Hindu)

In addition, Cheshire *et al.* (1993:63) report that the use of /ain't/, producing, for instance /that ain't working/ where standard English would have /that isn't working/ is a common feature of 'non-standard urban varieties of British English', particularly in southern Britain. It is also a feature which is easy to detect in the speech of the Blackhill youth,

> I have tried it bu[ʔ] I [ain't] re- really goo[ʔ] a[ʔ] it
>
> > (Karwan (m) Kurdish Muslim)
>
> it looks like she is doing it when she [ain[ʔ]]
>
> > (Premila (f) Gujarati Hindu)
>
> I think they met here I [ain't] sure
>
> > (Vishnu (m) Gujarati Hindu)

Furthermore, Hughes and Trudgill (1996) describe multiple negation as a non-standard grammatical form which is typical of working-class British speech but which is not found in Standard English. The Blackhill youth reflect this in their specifically London speech in the following manner,

> I don't speak Hindi to no one
>
> > (Diya (f) Gujarati Hindu)
>
> I don't know nothin[k] about my religion
>
> > (Gurshanti (f) Panjabi Sikh)
>
> this man tried to con my mum and she couldn't take no more
>
> > (Shanice (f) Jamaican Creole Christian)

Additionally, Cheshire *et al.* (1993: 71–2) point out that the use of what they call 'non-standard *was*' is common 'throughout the urban centres of the country'. They suggest this means, for example, that in urban British Englishes a phrase such as /we was singing/ occurs where Standard English offers /we were singing/. This is a marked feature of the grammar of London English speech and, unsurprisngly, it also appears readily in Blackhill youth speech,

> they [was] like classes tha[?] wen[?] on during the actual lessons they [was] like compulsory in a way
> > (Bahiyaa (f) Panjabi Hindu)

> I just spoke to him and we [was] making friends
> > (Patwant (m) Panjabi Sikh)

> they [was] in my book
> > (Nashita (f) Gujarati Hindu)

The final grammatical speech token of Londonness to be examined at this juncture is one that Cheshire *et al.* (*ibid.*) report as being the most widely reported grammatical feature of urban British Englishes and one not found in Standard English. This is the grammatical feature which produces /look at them spiders/ (*ibid.*: 64), by contrast with the Standard English /look at those spiders/. In the speech of the Blackhill youth this characteristic was realised in phrases such as,

> my mum and dad and [them] lot can speak it properly
> > (Manika (f) Gujarati Hindu)

> my mum she worked in one of [them] jewellery shops
> > (Julie (f) Swahili Christian Catholic)

> one of [them] telephone engineers
> > (Bahiyaa (f) Panjabi Hindu)

Although, the foregoing highlighted grammatical features are prominent in a wide variety of urban British vernaculars, their status as distinctive markers of working class London identity is confirmed by the research of Stenström *et al.* (2002) into the nature of London teenage speech. According to them, all the grammatical features just exemplified co-occur in London teenage speech, 'almost exclusively in conversations involving teenagers from the lower social classes, many of whom have an ethnic minority background' (Stenström *et al.*, 2002: 133). The empirical work of Stenström *et al.*, based as it is on a language corpus, is particularly useful to the present study for a number of reasons. Firstly, as they point out, in linguistic circles there is a dearth of investigation into teenage language. Secondly, their investigations attempt to give, 'a comprehensive insight into the London teenage vernacular towards the end of the twentieth century' (*ibid*.: p. x). Thirdly, the nature of its computerised, tagged and transcribed corpus is impressive in its scope and quantity by comparison with other available evidence.[11] It is based on recordings made in 1993 and consists of 'approximately half a million words of spontaneous conversations between 13 to 17 year-old boys and girls from different parts of London and with varying socioeconomic backgrounds' (*ibid*.: 4). As well as confirming the grammatical evidence on London specific speech markers provided by other sociolinguistic sources, the work of Stenström and colleagues identifies other London speech characteristics which the other sociolinguistic literature tends not to have pinpointed so precisely. This is noticeable, for instance, with respect to London teenagers' use of tags as will later be demonstrated. This section has provided evidence indicating that in addition to the routine utterances of the Blackhill youth being saturated with a specific and consistent London phonology, they are also enclosed within a London specific grammatical framework. It must be emphasised once again that the examples provided are by no means intended to be exhaustive. Nevertheless, they are sufficient to justify the claim that such everyday foundational aspects of ethnicity and culture mark the Blackhill youth ethnicities as specifically London British ethnicities. Further, these are bodily inscribed in ways which any would-be analysis of ethnicities and cultures must take into account. However, the grammatical and phonological dimensions of their speech which identify the Blackhill youth as British, and more specifically as Londoners, are not the only linguistic phenomena which do so. There are also their lexical behaviours some of which they consciously label as 'slang' and which linguists would label as 'tags'.

Slang, 'innit' and tags

One consistent representation offered by the Blackhill youth was their contention that a dominant feature of their speech in English with their peers was the use of what they universally termed 'slang'. It was curious, though, that when pressed to give examples of what they meant by this they tended to flounder saying that they couldn't think of any. There was, however, one overwhelming exception. Very many of the individuals stated that they used the term /*innit*/, and that they identified its usage as synonymous with slang. The adding to a phrase of the question tag /*isn't it?*/ in a phrase like /*it's cold isn't it?*/ is generally regarded as an unexceptional part of Standard English speech, although it is somewhat stigmatised when appearing in working class London speech as /*it's cold innit?*/. The Blackhill youth are definite and regular users of this linguistic form in its London inflection as can be seen in the following examples,

> its like its like my home language [innit]
>
> > (Vishnu (m) Gujarati Hindu)
>
> yeah bu[?] that's all life's abou[?] [innit]
>
> > (Premila (f) Gujarati Hindu)

However, this is not the only way in which the Blackhill youth use the /*innit*/ tag. They also use it in a way that transcends the traditionally London ('Cockney') usage just illustrated above. Stenström *et al.* (2002: 167–8), describe the use of /*innit*/ as an invariant tag, named as such because it, 'is used in London adolescent speech as a tag that can be appended to any statement, regardless of the grammatical features of the statement'. They add that this invariant tag occurs both, 'typically in multilingual settings' and, 'occurs typically in the speech of ethnic minority youth' (*ibid.*: 168). Nevertheless, rather more precisely, Baumann (1996), McArthur (1992) and Nihalani *et al.* (1979) link this usage with specifically Indian forms of English perhaps derived from diasporic roots in India; and Hewitt (1986) with specifically London forms of Jamaican language.

According to Nihalani *et al.* (1979), in a book on Indian English in India,

> In [British Standard English] the question-tag 'isn't it?' only occurs when the sentence preceding the tag has a neuter subject and includes the verb 'to be': 'It's raining again, isn't it? ... Indian [Variants of English] speakers use this tag much more frequently and in contexts where [British Standard English] would demand a different tag, for example 'haven't you?' in the sentence quoted [i.e.] 'You've heard him make that claim isn't it?'.
>
> > (Nihalani *et al.*, 1979: 104)

In the London context this tendency is seen as representative of 'Indianisms -/*innit*/ for /*isn't it*/, /*aren't you*/, /*aren't they*/, etc.)' (Baumann, 1996: 47). It is, though, on the other hand, possible that the processes by which this has occurred, parallel those described by Hewitt in his description of what he calls the 'London English of black [meaning Caribbean-descended] adolescents',

> 'innit' has become particularly well established over the past few years. Its distinctiveness from the common English usage, which is

found in such phrases as 'it's a nice day, innit' resides in the fact that the 'it' morpheme does not refer back to a previous 'it' but to any general state, as in 'we had a lovely time, innit', and 'she's really nice that girl, innit'. Of all the items to penetrate white speech from the Caribbean, this is the most stable and most widely used among adolescents and amongst older people.

(Hewitt, 1986: 132).

In addition to naming their own use of /*innit*/ as being representational of their use of slang, the Blackhill youth regularly and unselfconsciously used it in their naturally occurring speech, as an invariant tag, in the way just described, as can be seen from the following examples drawn from their individual conversational interviews,

she speaks Gujara[ʔ]i inni[ʔ]

(Diya (f) Gujarati Hindu)

they're my mum's youngest sisters inni[ʔ]

(Shariqah (f) Urdu Muslim)

you're always speaking Gujara[ʔ]i at home as well enni[ʔ][12]

(Vishnu (m) Gujarati Hindu)

This usage is an apt reminder of the overall argument that the Blackhill youth ethnicities are multiply constituted at the same instant, of both traditional London elements and Indian ones, amongst a number of syncretic features.

So far, though, the present chapter has shown that the Blackhill youth have as a fundamental and dominant element of their ethnicities and cultures an unerasable local 'Londonness' which is all the more powerful for being inscribed into their bodies through the low-key, unremarkable human actions of everyday speech utterances. However, as previously suggested, this 'Londonness', is interwoven synchronically in complex ways with the powerfully residual cultural markings inherited from their parents and grandparents. One of these cultural markings is, again founded on language in its everyday use as the next section shows.

The global in the local (i) : 'My Language'

One of the occurrences in the research which at first seemed puzzling was the way in which Blackhill individuals made what appeared to be paradoxical statements concerning their relationships with their home/community languages other than English. On the one hand they tended to refer to these languages, using proprietary pronouns, as 'my language'. On the other hand they were on the whole emphatic about their lack of expertise in the use of these same languages. Eventually, it became clear that these young people, whatever their linguistic mastery, inhabited a multilingual universe both inside and outside the home. Rampton (1990) has pointed out the limitations of linguistic concepts like 'native speaker' and 'mother tongue' and has suggested, instead, the heuristic utility of assessing the linguistic positioning of individuals in terms of 'expertise', 'affiliation' and 'inheritance'. Rampton considers that 'affiliation' and inheritance are constituent elements of 'language allegiance' or 'language loyalty'. The Blackhill youth depict themselves as having limited expertise in community languages in comparison with their strong expertise in English. Simultaneously, though, they declare a firm language loyalty or language allegiance to the community languages which, firstly, they have inherited, and for which, secondly, they have developed a strong emotional affiliation. The challenge is to understand more clearly how the community languages, with their synchronic and diachronic global reach, interact with the locally inscribed Englishes in Britain as the routine business of everyday life proceeds. This greater understanding contributes to our knowledge of how 'new ethnicities' and 'new cultures of hybridity' are constructed and maintained. The Blackhill youth offer ample intricate representations as to how these linguistic relations are played out in their homes.

The home

As has already become evident in Chapter 3, the question of patterns of language use at home is a complex one for the Blackhill youth, and cannot be answered simply and definitively in the way that the language survey questionnaire invited. In answer to the question concerning which languages they speak at home, the Blackhill youth were forced to respond along the lines of, 'it all depends to whom I'm talking for what purposes at what moments'. For these young people, language use at home can involve, at the very least, different patterns of language use with parents, grandparents, uncles and aunts, siblings, cousins, and wider family friends. As the language survey data indicated, the early lives of most of the Blackhill youth were experienced through languages such as Panjabi, Gujarati, or an alternation between either of these and English. For them a decisive shift to English language dominance occurred only during their years at infant school.

The first pattern of interaction with parents presented by Blackhill youth was that of spoken exchanges characterised by considerable linguistic codeswitching which occurred for a variety of reasons.

Sometimes this occurred because of what the Blackhill youth perceived as their own limited expertise in the community languages and consequent inability to sustain prolonged conversation with their parents without the assistance of English,

> 'If I am talking to my father, I speak in both Gujarati and English which is usually mixed together. My Gujarati is muddled and so when I am speaking it, I always add in words in English if I do not know how to say them in Gujarati'.
>
> (Sahima (f) Gujarati Hindu)

> sometimes I have difficul[?]y like speaking Panjabi there's some words I can't say in Panjabi and so it'll be like English and Panjabi and when I speak to my dad it'll be like I'll be speaking English like and he won't answer me (laughs).
>
> (Punamdeep (f) Panjabi Sikh)

A number of the youth, however, did claim a sufficient level of expertise to communicate comfortably with their parents in a language other than English. This seems to have been nearly always prompted by the limitations of one or both parents in the speaking of English,

> 'Although I am in England now and I speak in English at school and outside my house all the time, I still speak in Punjabi with my mum and dad. I have to speak Punjabi with my mum because she doesn't understand English. My dad can understand English but he prefers if I speak in Punjabi to him'.
>
> (Sumandev (m) Panjabi Sikh)

> if I speak to my mum she she only speaks to me in Gujarati she doesn't speak English … she knows how to speak i[?] but she's no[?] fluent … she doesn't feel as though she can speak it properly
>
> (Sahima (f) Gujarati Hindu)

The statement above by Sumandev hints that his father has a greater degree of English language expertise than his mother. This differential pattern was often repeated in the accounts offered by the Blackhill youth. Where this occurred it appears to be for two reasons.

First, their mothers tended to have come to live in Britain at a later stage in their lives than their fathers. Second, their mothers were less likely than their fathers to have spent time working in English-speaking environments outside the home. This points to the heterogeneity of their parents' ethnicities and is something that will be examined more closely in Chapter 6. Sometimes the Blackhill youth made it clear that their parents, while competent at speaking English, preferred to speak to their children in community languages at home as part of their efforts to secure the reproduction of diasporic languages and traditions,

> 'In my house and family the main language spoken is Kurdish, both my parents, both brothers and all cousins and family originate from Kurdistan, and all believe that by speaking our language we remember our roots ...'
>
> (Karwan (m) Kurdish Muslim)

> she [mum] doesn't like it when we speak English to her she's like, 'you speak your own language', she has a go at my dad you know for speaking English with us.
>
> (Shariqah (f) Urdu Muslim)

The strongest and most consistent reason given by the young people for speaking community languages at home was in order to communicate with their grandparents. Here there were two principal motivations. Firstly, there were occasions where they wanted to assist one or more of their grandparents who did not understand English. The second reason was in order to show their grandparents respect. The presence in the family home of a grandparent who understood little or no English was common amongst the Blackhill group as indicated here,

> 'my grandma does not speak English. My whole family can speak Gujarati, but my Grandma uses it the most because this is the only language she can speak which the whole family can understand'.
>
> (Amod (m) Gujarati Hindu)

> 'Punjabi had to be spoken at home because that was the only language my grandmother and grandfather could understand (fathers side) ... I will only speak Punjabi when I have to. For example if my grandmothers speak to me in Punjabi I would have to reply in Punjabi because that is the only language that they understand'.
>
> (Gurshanti (f) Panjabi Sikh)

> I don't really speak i[?] [Panjabi] apart from when my gran stays at my house cos she doesn't understand English so er when I um speak to her I try to communicate with her in er by using my language Panjabi.
>
> (Sachdev (m) Panjabi Sikh)

Using community languages with grandparents as a mark of respect appeared to be one of the everyday practices which was almost universally shared by the Blackhill youth, and almost all of them, individually and spontaneously, volunteered this information,

'The only time I don't speak english is when I am talking to my dad or grandmother ... Punjabi has to be spoken to my relatives because that shows that I have respect for them'.

(Amar (m) Panjabi Hindu)

'I think when you're in a situation it naturally comes to you as to what language you use for example if you were in a situation talking to your elder relatives you would talk in your mother tongue language as it would mean respect to your elders'.

(Neetaa (f) Panjabi Sikh)

'I speak to them [grandparents] in Punjabi because it is felt as being rude when or if someone were to talk to them in a language that they do not understand too well, bearing in mind that the person was younger, and related to them. Speaking to my elders in Punjabi also underlines my respect for them'.

(Patwant (m) Panajbi Sikh)

'If I am talking to someone older whom which may be an aunt also my grandparents. I usually speak Urdu. The reason for this is because they sometimes do not understand what I am saying if it is spoken in English and it also shows a sign of respect'.

(Shariqah (f) Urdu Muslim)

Sometimes the young people said that they used community languages with their grandparents as the result of a certain degree of pressure, from the grandparents themselves, for ethnic-ideological reasons. In these circumstances, grandparents spoke community languages rather than English to their grandchildren on a point of principle based on their perception of their right to speak their own languages at home without constraint; and also by a motivation to encourage community language maintenance linked with wider community ethnic cultural practices (including religious ones) in their grandchildren's generation,

'If I was to speak to them in English they would complain to my parents and say that I do not know how to speak my mother tongue'.

(Shariqah (f) Urdu Muslim)

'They believe that even if you know how to speak English and you speak it on a daily basis, you are supposed to speak in Gujarati to them'.

(Sahima (f) Gujarati Hindu)

I think it's because they [grandparents and other elders] origina[?]ed from India and they want you to speak Indian to them and I don't know I just think that it's like par[?] of our religion as well you have to respect everybody everybody older than your parents in the family and so you have to speak in Panjabi.

(Amrita (f) Panjabi Sikh)

Despite these pressures it was something that none of the Blackhill youth complained about. Indeed many of them drew attention to the fact that using community languages as a show of respect and good manners was something that they willingly did as a matter of course with all family elders and with most older visitors to the family home,

RH: why do you still speak Gujarati to your grandparents?
Keshav: ... it's like a show of respect to them that's why we just like and even to our uncles like olders we have to talk in Gujarati unless they're talking in English then you just talk back in English

(Keshav (m) Gujarati Hindu)

The readiness with which the Blackhill youth used the term 'respect' and offered tokens of respect through their speech behaviour seemed to be a distinctive aspect of their ethnicities. It is difficult to think of a similar symbolic routine practice among white British youth or black British youth of Caribbean descent.[13] It is more common for the youth of these groups to demand respect from others, including elders, than to willingly and unashamedly offer respect to them. The aspects of the interrelationship between the Blackhill youth and their grandparents already described offer an example of how symbolic emblems of residual aspects of South Asian cultures, represented in the continued use of languages like Gujarati and Panjabi, can be retained in the present, and retained without resistance or resentment, while intermingled with newer emergent elements of culture.[14]

However, in stressing the role of community languages in the lives of the Blackhill youth in their homes, it would be a mistake to underplay the everyday importance of English there. Chapter 3 has shown that 8 of the 31 Blackhill youth who completed the language survey questionnaire indicated that the language they first used at home before going to school was English. In fact an important facet of their language use at home is the extent to which English is used, by whom, when, and for what purposes. The Blackhill youth were emphatic in representing their homes as spaces where English language use is certainly not marginal and is often central,

> 'The language spoken mostly in my family is English'.
>
> (Amar (m) Panjabi Hindu)

> 'In my life there are three languages that I use, English I feel is my mother tongue because I speak it at school and a lot at home'.
>
> (Dhrishaj (m) Panjabi Sikh)

> 'My mother-tongue language is Punjabi, but at home I normally speak in English'.
>
> (Bahiyaa (f) Panjabi Hindu)

> they (parents) still speak to me in English so I never really caugh[?] on to language in Panjabi.
>
> (Narjot (m) Panjabi Sikh)

One strong feature of the presence of English language use in the homes of the Blackhill youth was its ubiquity in their habitual communications with their siblings. Most of the young people made it clear that in their interactions with their brothers and sisters they nearly always spoke English,

> 'I rarely speak Gujarati with my brother because we both feel more comfortable by speaking to each other in English. We also understand each other better speaking English rather than Gujarati as my brother gets a few words mixed up speaking Gujarati'.
>
> (Amod (m) Panjabi Hindu)

> 'When I talk to my sisters or cousins of my age I will speak english because they all have been to school and speak English as their first language and if I started to speaking punjabi then they would start laughing at me as it would be inappropriate'.
>
> (Dhrishaj (m) Panjabi Sikh)

> 'At home I only speak in English to my sister and my cousins'.
>
> (Sumandev (m))Panjabi Sikh)

This is not to say that there are no occasions on which languages other than English are used with siblings. However, these usages appeared to be spasmodic and linked with the achievement of certain effects, for example for ludic purposes, rather than being utilised as part of lengthy passages of continuous conversation or the discussion of serious topics,

> 'I sometimes talk in Gujrati (sic) to get my sisters frustrated. I do this by going on and on and saying silly things in Gujrati'.
>
> (Nashita (f) Gujarati Hindu)

One other characteristic of their linguistic exchanges at home will be noted briefly here before being explored slightly more fully in the next chapter; namely, their patterns of language use with members of their wider family, that is to say uncles, aunts and cousins. As was suggested by the language survey questionnaire data the presence of aunts and uncles was depicted by the Blackhill youth as occasioning the broadening of the range of languages used in the home, whether or not they themselves were able to be active participants in their use. Aunts and uncles appeared to open a window to the wider family and ethnic diaspora through their lives in other countries. They also sometimes opened access to distinctive patterns of ethnic hybridisation, where they had entered out-group marriages,

> 'Swahili is a language that my parents and relatives know how to speak as it is the language that they used to speak when they lived in Tanzania. I do not know how to speak in Swahili at all but I always come across it when my relatives come to visit'.
>
> (Sahima (f) Gujarati Hindu)

It could be argued that the relationships with their diasporic relatives and with their grandparents represent two perspectives on the global in the local in so far as the everyday, locally situated, patterns of language use are indicative of the practice, consolidation and development of 'new ethnicities' and 'new cultures of hybridity'. There is evidence that the grandparental influence acts as a kind of active residual presence of global-traditional cultures, while many aunts and uncles represent an actively emergent presence of global-contemporary cultures. It is, therefore, useful to look next at some examples of how the emergent in global contemporary culture has come to be bodily inscribed in the Blackhill youth through the medium of their commonplace speech.

The global in the local (ii): Global teenage language

The term *Global teenage language* is being used here to suggest patterns of language use which, while they are common in everyday local speech in London, appear to have originated outside Britain, to be relatively new, and to have currency in the verbal expressions of young people all over the world. As such the use of this kind of language by the Blackhill youth adds another strand to the weft of the developing tapestry of their ethnicities. Two such features, in particular, will be the focus of the current section. The first is what, in sociolinguistic circles, has been identified as the discourse marker /*like*/ used as a focus marker or as a 'quotative'. The other linguistic feature is known as 'upspeak' or 'Australian questioning intonation'.

'Like'

The primary attention here will be focused on the linguistic phenomenon labelled 'quotative be + like' (Ferrara and Bell, 1995). This refers to one of the variety of ways, in the English language verbal system, in which dialogues are conveyed during narrative accounts. The following examples illustrate the point,

> She's *like*, "Right, you know, we're taking you out."
> I was *like*, "Ah I don't want to go out. Please no."
> And they're *like*, "Come on, go and get dressed."
> (cited in Tagliamonte and Hudson, 1999: 147)

Of course the system for the use of like as a discourse marker as a whole is enormously complex in a way which is beyond the scope of the present book. However, it is treated exhaustively by Blyth *et al.* (1990), Romaine and Lange (1991), Ferrara and Bell (1995), Tagliamonte and Hudson (1999), Dailey-O'Cain (2000), and Macaulay (2001). These researchers are agreed that this discourse feature is relatively new or at least did not receive serious academic attention until the early 1980s. They are also generally agreed that it originated in the United States of America, before spreading to Canada and the United Kingdom and possibly elsewhere in the English-speaking world. There is also a consensus that it is characteristically used by young people and that females are more likely than males to use it. More importantly for the current discussion it is taken as symbolic of global cultural change involving youth,

> be like has diffused into the quotative system in a very short period of time among younger speakers in geographically separated

locations in the English-speaking world according to remarkably similar pathways of development. Thus, the diffusion of be like may be a very good linguistic indicator of the types of developments and changes we might expect from the putative ongoing globalization of English ... further research on be like, in conjunction with other linguistic features rapidly innovating in urban areas throughout the English-speaking world, will be a good place to look for, and 'catch,' the burgeoning global 'mega trends' of language change.

(Tagliamonte and Hudson, 1999: 168)

As the following examples show, the Blackhill youth are part of these global developments, which in turn add just one more of the intricate constitutive elements of their ethnicities,

she goes 'we went through it in class' and I'm like 'bu[ʔ] I wanted to do a different one'.

(Gurshanti (f) Panjabi Sikh)

sometimes I'll be like 'yea::h' and she'll speaking Panjabi with me and ... I'm like erm 'yea::h[15] yeah yeah' you know I'll I'll be like 'ye-es'

(Punamdeep (f) Panjabi Sikh)

and they were just like very 'okay, whatever you say'

(Nashita (f) Gujarati Hindu)

she's like 'you should speak proper Panjabi' ... she's like 'you should speak it this way'

(Amrita (f) Panjabi Sikh)

As this selection of illustrative examples implies, my data confirms the view in the sociolinguistic literature that this feature of globalised teenage English usage is gendered in that it appears to be more common in female than in male speech. There is also a hint in the literature that a similarly gendered pattern of usage is perceptible in the globalised teenage English speech phenomenon of up-speak.

Up-speak or Australian questioning intonation

Another ingredient linking the Blackhill youth, through their everyday speech, with global cultural developments and change, is their evident use of what has been termed variously, 'Up-speak', 'up-talk', 'uptalk' or 'Australian questioning intonation'. The expression refers to a way of speaking in which statements are uttered with a rising intonation as though they are questions. The origins of this speech habit are contested. Some serious linguistic observers locate its genesis in the valleys of California on the US West Coast, while others claim that its source is Australia. Algeo and Algeo (1994: 185) describe it as 'An almost Irish, sort of Canadian, not quite Valley-girl intonation that makes declarative statements sound like questions?'. They add, referring to the work of American linguist Cynthia McLemore,

> While doing research for a Ph.D. dissertation on intonation, she spent six months "hanging out with a tape recorder" in a University of Texas sorority house. ... It wasn't until she started lecturing about her findings that she realized that repeatedly rising intonation – or "uptalk" as it's been called – has spread all over the country.
>
> (*ibid.*: 185)

On the other hand, Guy *et al.* (1986), dubbing the same phenomenon Australian Questioning Intonation (AQI), claim its earliest and certainly most extensive use for Australia,[16]

> We do not wish to claim that 'AQI' is a feature unique to the English of Australia. In fact, we would not be surprised if the verification-seeking meaning we discern in AQI were found to be possible in certain situations for most dialects of English, since it seems a modest and natural extension of the English intonational meaning system. Anecdotal reports from Canada, California, and the southern United States support this view. But we are suggesting that, to our knowledge, it is used with the characteristic meaning we have described more widely and more often in Australasia than in any other part of the English-speaking world.
>
> (Guy *et al.*, 1986: 27)

Nevertheless, there is general agreement that it is a relatively recent linguistic development from the point of view of academic research, since it has become apparent within approximately the last twenty five years. Once again it is possible to trace links between the everyday unselfconscious language use of the Blackhill youth and global cultural and linguistic innovations,

> one thing I do remember is once my mum [forgot me ↑][17]
>
> (Gurleetaa (f) Panjabi Sikh)

> you know just English cos you [live here ↑]
>
> (Shariqah (f) Urdu Muslim)

I didn't like [learning it ↑]

(Sahima (f) Gujarati Hindu)

that means who [sent you ↑]

(Diya (f) Gujarati Hindu)

The foregoing examples give a glimpse of some of the ways in which the use of certain linguistic items by the Blackhill youth links them with practices shared by adolescents of other ethnicities in Britain and elsewhere in the world. In this respect the analysis demonstrates the inadequacy of binary approaches to the analysis of ethnicity and culture which operate somewhat mechanistically through contrasting categories of traditional and modern, old and new. At this point it can be clearly seen that the ethnicities of the Blackhill youth are partly constituted by at least three distinctive strands. The London strand, the Global-traditional and the Global-contemporary. In this tripartite configuration, the London component represents the ever present, the unerasable. The Global-traditional indexes currents of linguistic and cultural practice which echo back to retentions from past ways of life in South Asian contexts where they are still strong and deeply rooted. The Global-contemporary, in turn, reflects synchronic practices which co-occur amongst young people all over the world, and as such are an integral part of a speeded-up and restless media-induced globalised culture. The next and concluding section of the chapter will draw attention to a number of examples of ways in which for the Blackhill youth, what could be described as residual elements of the Global-traditional are embedded in expressions of both the London *and* the Global-contemporary in their cultural and ethnic articulations.

The global in the local (iii): Other 'Indianisms'

Earlier in the chapter, the discussion of the use by the Blackhill youth of the term /*innit*/, characterised one of its usages as representative of what Baumann (1996), termed 'Indianisms' retained in English language use. To this, two other examples found in the speech of the Blackhill youth can be added. The first, for which independent verification is available, is the use of the terms 'cousin-brother' and 'cousin-sister'. The second, whose status as an 'Indianism' I can only speculatively assert, is a particular usage of the phrase 'gives it'.

'Cousin-brother' and 'Cousin-sister'

Nihalani, Tongue and Hosali (1979: 59), with reference to the terms 'cousin-brother' and 'cousin-sister', connect them directly with a specifically

Indian usage of English linked directly with literal usages in languages of the Indian sub-continent,

> Since the word 'cousin' does not contain a sex-denoting marker, where sex is important it has to be indicated (rather awkwardly) in British Standard English by a phrase like 'female cousin'. Most languages in India indicate sex in the word itself and 'cousin-brother' is an attempt to do this in English.

McArthur concurs with this interpretation describing /*cousin brother*/ and /*cousin sister*/ as 'calques[18] from local languages' (McArthur, 1992: 506). The expressions /*cousin brother*/ and /*cousin sister*/ were extremely common in the conversations of the Blackhill youth as can be seen in these selected examples,

> my cousin sisters and cousin brother ... actually they speak fluent English.
>
> > (Amar (m) Panjabi Hindu)
>
> my cousin sisters and um aunties and that they really sit down and watch they've got Sky
>
> > (Narjot (m) Panjabi Sikh)
>
> to my cousin sister I just speak English I don't speak Panjabi a[?] all
> > (Punamdeep (f) Panjabi Sikh)
>
> I think it's unfair cos my cousin brother he got married to a Muslim and then they did nothing to him
> > (Premila (f) Gujarati Hindu)

What was particularly fascinating, and instructive, was that whenever I drew the attention of any of the Blackhill users of the terms /*cousin brother*/ and /*cousin sister*/ to these utterances, they were nonplussed and found it extremely difficult to apprehend that the usage was unknown to British English. In other words their usage of the terms formed an integral part of their ordinary, everyday, unselfconscious local London speech yet at the same time bore residual traces of their 'Indianness'. In this respect it provides a vivid exemplification of ways in which 'new ethnicities' and 'new cultures of hybridity' are constituted simultaneously of the residual and the emergent. However, as indicated above, the provenance of another expression, 'gives it', which was also prominent in the speech of the Blackhill youth is less certain, but I want to suggest that it operates in a similar way to /*cousin brother*/ and /*cousin sister*/.

'Gives it'

Careful listening to the audio recordings of the conversational interviews with the Blackhill youth and reading of the subsequent transcrip-
tions revealed that the young people frequently used the expression
'gives it', when referring during a narrative recount to how a protagonist
said something. This was something akin to the colloquial English conversational narrative device, 'so she goes ...'.[19] Here are some examples,

and mum [gives it] 'oh it's a letter' and I get 'let me read it' and she
[gives it] 'you can'.

(Rishab (m) Panjabi Hindu)

I was actually speaking to a girl in our class and [give it] 'you know
what man' and she [gives it] 'I'm not a man'.

(Amar (m) Panjabi Hindu)

I'm gonna phone up and ask him why he talked to me like tha[ʔ] and
she [gives it] 'no you can't'.

(Gurleetaa (f) Panjabi Sikh)

So she wants us to be like that and she wants us to be able to write it
as well. So she [gives it] 'because if everybody can do it you can do it
as well'.

(Nashita (f) Gujarati Hindu)

I am by no means certain that this usage represents an 'Indianism',
but I have never previously encountered it in British English usage and
am prepared to speculate that it is an instance of an Indian language
retention. Even with this caveat this concluding section of the present
chapter has added another exemplifying strand to the substantive
argument that the residual, emergent and dominant in culture are co-
occurring rather than separate alternating elements or even that they
represent old versus new elements.

Conclusion

One of the contentions of this book is that an investigation into representations of patterns of language use is an important way of understanding how individuals and groups might construct and perform their
own sense of their ethnicities. It is further argued that within the British
Cultural Studies tradition, and also more broadly within sociology, the
question of the everyday language use of ordinary people has been

virtually entirely neglected as an important element of culture and/or ethnicity. This chapter has shown that the overwhelming majority of the Blackhill youth are continuously engaged in the negotiation of what could be called everyday multilingualism, which amounts to a kind of structured linguistic ecology. By this I mean that they live in multilingual environments both inside and outside the home, and on a low-key, routine basis negotiate their way through this world in complex but unspectacular ways which in themselves constitute constructions of important elements of their ethnic formation. Just one aspect of this, and one which is rarely noticed or commented on, is the local British marking which is apparent in virtually every utterance they make. Attention has been drawn to the circumstance that while most British observers concentrate on visible markers (appearance, dress, religion, cultural practices and even foreign language use) of separateness and difference, a deeply routine vernacular marker of Britishness in visible ethnic minority youth such as the Blackhill youth – their everyday pronunciation pattern, is overlooked. It has been demonstrated how the Blackhill youth mark their essential 'Londonness' every time they speak with their use of specific well known tokens of London speech. These tokens include elements of pronunciation such as t-glottalling, and elements of grammar such as the London-marked use of the verbal token 'done'.[20]

Thus I have contended in this chapter that a vital part of any construction of new ethnicities is the pronunciation patterns in the naturally occurring speech of the ethnic formations under analysis. Some authoritative psycholinguistic research has suggested that in naturally occurring speech the phonological, grammatical/syntactical tends to be relatively weakly susceptible to conscious control (Malmkjær, 1995: 363–6). In other words, whatever declarations of allegiance ethnic minority youth make to the symbols of ethnic affiliation available from their grandparental or parental generations, or in the ethnically marked wider community, an ineluctable fragment of their ethnic identity is their local Britishness, signalled in part in the ways shown in this chapter. If the young people concerned live in other areas of Britain, such as Glasgow, Newcastle, Manchester, Leeds/Bradford, Birmingham and so on, as the cousins of many of my informants do, their Britishness will also be marked in linguistically specific local ways. That is to say, when they routinely speak, even in languages other than English, their pronunciation patterns will mark them as belonging to Glasgow, Newcastle, Manchester, Leeds/Bradford and Birmingham and so on. This is not all. This tendency is augmented by language patterns which are also marked by specific local British identifications centred on grammar, idiomatic phrases and lexical choices. The difficulty of readily perceiving these phenomena in the case of young people of South Asian descent, as was suggested earlier, may be exacerbated by the habit of allowing the visual rather than the aural to dominate in considerations of ethnicity. At the same time these localised inscriptions do not stand in isolation. They are interwoven in dense ways with the unspectacularly negotiated everyday multilingualism which the Blackhill youth articulate with globally extended languages like Panjabi and Gujarati, and with the globally influential speech patterns of their worldwide adolescent generation. The next chapter concentrates on some different ways in which local and global, cultural and ethnic forces are articulated together in the lives of the Blackhill youth, as an effect of membership of, and practices in, communities.

6

'My Culture', 'My Language', 'My Religion': Communities, Practices and Diasporas

Introduction

In Chapter 5 I noted that the Blackhill youth regularly used the proprietary pronoun 'my'[1] when they wanted to refer to Panjabi, Gujarati and other languages besides English, which were strongly associated with their families and communities. There was an apparent paradox between their proprietary claims and their simultaneous disavowal of a high level of expertise in the use of these languages. A similar pattern occurred when they referred to communities, both local and globally diasporic, of which they felt themselves to be a part; and also, more specifically, when they referred to the religious formations to which they were nominally attached. Consequently, with regard to these contexts, phrases like 'my culture', 'my language' and 'my religion', regularly occurred alongside bashful and rueful acknowledgements of their own deficient expertise in the tenets of idealised community emblematic practices,

> my language [Panjabi] I- I don't really know all of it because m- I was just when they were raising me they were just speaking English all the time and I just learned English I never really learned [Panjabi]
> (Narjot (m) Panjabi Sikh)

> I know I should be bothered it's my language [Panjabi] bu[?] English just seems a bit easier for me to understand and speak ... but I – I think I – I would like to learn it more if I had the chance
> (Sachdev (m) Panjabi Sikh)

> When it comes to um being able to understand wha[?] my religion is about I hardly know i[?] I hardly know anythin[k] abou[?] my religion and I- I reckon that's true with a lo[?] of my friends I- I don't think

any of them know about their religion ... but seriously if I had to come down to i[?] I (long pause) don't know nothin[k] about my religion ... I don't pray I don't I don't really believe in a god or I question it and I don't I don't er know if my religion is I think our whole religion is based on a god I'm not sure

(Gurshanti (f) Panjabi Sikh)

RH: how did you feel about the [community language] classes when you were going
Rishab: they were okay I I felt yeah tha[?] I was learning more abou[?] my culture

(Rishab (m) Panjabi Hindu)

On the face of it the question of how to reconcile what appear to be competing cultural forces seems to arise. However, I have already indicated my dissatisfaction with, and rejection of, the notion that such young people are 'caught between two cultures'. How else, then, might these phenomena be better understood and interpreted? In this chapter I suggest that the Blackhill youth inhabit a number of ethnic and cultural subcommunities which they articulate together in ways which draw *both* on residual traditional elements informed by diasporic influences *and* on emergent local elements, with different emphases dominant at contingent moments. Furthermore, that all this is accomplished in low key ways with little or no overt sign of crisis or serious discomfort. Their multifarious manoeuverings and negotiations are experienced through the everyday practices of subcommunities organised on the basis of dimensions such as (a) community language use, (b) interactions with adolescent peers, (c) religious practices and (d) diaspora connections and continuities. In all of these dimensions factors related to language use play an important constitutive part. The constitution of new ethnicities and cultures of hybridity, can then, be imagined within the framework of two broad interlocking perspectives which challenge the ways in which members of visible minorities in Britain are customarily seen. Typically, for instance, people with origins in the Indian subcontinent are portrayed as members of a variety of tightly bounded homogeneous 'South Asian' cultures which allegedly contrast with so-called 'British' culture. People with this experience supposedly have to live with the daily anguish of having to choose between one culture or the other. The evidence from the Blackhill youth destabilises these notions. They experience mostly comfortable everyday membership of a variety of communities, some of which this chapter will describe. The second important consideration is that what counts is not merely nominal membership of any given community, but the nature of the accompanying cultural practices of everyday life in which they participate along with co-members of the various distinctive communities of practice which can be identified.

To put it more specifically, the Blackhill youth shared with each other the experience of inhabiting distinctive ethnic and cultural subcommunities each operating within the same local London physical spaces, each mediated by a specific religious affiliation and linked to a worldwide family and religious diaspora. Chapter 3 indicated that of the 31 young people who completed the language survey questionnaire, 13 claimed a Sikh religious affiliation, 11 said that they were Hindus, four declared themselves as Muslims and three claimed an attachment to Christianity, including one Catholic. The present chapter identifies some of the ways in which most of the Blackhill youth, and most markedly in the case of the overwhelming majority who were not Christians, found that their community, religious and diasporic experiences and practices were heavily influenced by factors relating to perceived linguistic expertise and consequent levels of relative detachment from purported ethnic and cultural ideals. It will also be clear to see how the Blackhill youth principally sense their place within specific communities in terms of (i) how well they feel they know community languages (ii) how much they know about and how much they practise community religions; (iii) how they interact linguistically with their peers, and (iv) how they feel when visiting, or otherwise interacting with, parental and grandparental homelands. In all these dimensions they inhabit a series of intricate and interlocking communities of practice. The notion of communities of practice has been described in the following terms,

> They are so informal and so pervasive that they rarely come into explicit focus, but for the same reasons they are also quite familiar ... Most communities of practice do not have a name and do not issue membership cards. Yet, if we care to consider our own life from that perspective for a moment, we can all construct a fairly good picture of the communities of practice we belong to now, those we belonged to in the past, and those we would like to belong to in the future. We also have a fairly good idea of who belongs to our communities of practice and why, even though membership is rarely made explicit on a roster or a checklist of qualifying criteria. Furthermore, we can probably distinguish a few communities of practice in which we are

core members from a larger number of communities in which we have a more peripheral kind of membership.

(Wenger, 1998: 7)

The central purpose of this chapter is to identify, describe and analyse a number of such communities of practice in the lives of the Blackhill youth so as to create a closer understanding of how new ethnicities are enacted.

Community languages as symbols of worthiness

A fascinating aspect of their discourse on community language use was the way in which the Blackhill youth were so frequently apologetic about, or lamented, what they perceived as their lack of expertise in these languages, while taking no concrete actions to remedy these deficiencies. This was all the more striking since most of them had been sent by their parents, at one time or another, to community classes for the maintenance of community languages, religions and cultural traditions. All had discontinued their attendance by the time of my research. But what is most interesting is that when asked why they had stopped attending these classes they appeared to be struggling to supply answers. Not one was coherent on this matter.[2] The following exchanges were typical,

Gurshanti: it's just I don't know what to do because I can't speak i[?]
RH: does it worry you or
Gurshanti: yeah sometimes like erm one of my friends she takes lessons but I'm not I can't be bothered to do that I wouldn't want to do i[?]
RH: what why don't// you want to do it[3]
Gurshanti: //I mean I have I have taken lessons like um (.) my mum sent me to them sometimes bu[?] I didn't learn anything u- th- I'd practise the same thing over and over again and still not learn it
RH: so how long did you do it for
Gurshanti: I did it for a little while//
RH: //inaudible)
Gurshanti: when I was young
RH: when you were young I think I ha- s- made a note of it you so I mean when you say do you remember how long you actually went for

Gurshanti:	not that long I mean the first time I went for a li[ʔ]le while my mum sent me for a li[ʔ]le while and then the second time I went for about two weeks
RH:	mm
Gurshanti:	and I just got bored and my mum jus- couldn't be bothered to take me either
RH:	mm so I mean you- from your point of view you just didn't want to do it
Gurshanti:	mm I jus- didn- (.) didn't want to

(Gurshanti (f) Panjabi Sikh)

or again,

RH:	mm bff bu[ʔ] you also said that you did have a little bit of time going to classes to learn Panjabi
Sachdev:	yeah I c- I went for a couple of months I think a couple of weeks a couple of months I'm not sure erm=
RH:	=you were about seven
Sachdev:	yeah seven or eight and I didn't enjoy it much I don't think I learnt much as well I learnt h- erm (.) I think basically I learnt the five letters of the alphabet which wasn't much so I just decided to leave it
RH:	can you remember why you didn't like it so much
Sachdev:	er (.) I th- I think it was just the way the teacher taught the the erm the class it wasn't really good enough for us lo[ʔ] er to understand because I remember when er me and my sister went with our next-door neighbours and they understood i[ʔ] um er Panjabi pretty well so I think the whole class really did understand it more than we did so it was just difficult for me and my sister to understand it I think that's why we left
RH:	and and so what happened to you if you didn't understand it (inaudible)
Sachdev:	erm no not really erm I just left it I I decided I didn't w- er wanna to learn i[ʔ] so I just left i[ʔ] I just ca- erm from then I just carry on speaking with my grandma
RH:	yeah right and I mean you said earlier on that well you should know it bu[ʔ] 'I think it's too late' what makes you think it's too late
Sachdev:	er:m well I'm not sure it's just that I'm no[ʔ] I don't think I can be bothered

RH:	yeah huh (chuckles)
Sachdev:	I know I should be bothered it's my language bu[?] English just seems a bit easier for me to understand and speak from but I I think I I would like to learn it more if I had the chance
RH:	so I mean bu[?] um there are classes in it aren't there
Sachdev:	yeah it's um the time and w- er I I I'm normally busy and it just doesn't fi[?] in
RH:	right and also in this school they don't have classes for Panjabi
Sachdev:	um I'm not sure I didn't really ask anyone

(Sachdev (m) Panjabi Sikh)

Neither Gurshanti nor Sachdev is unduly concerned about passing up available opportunities to consolidate their knowledge of, or expertise in, Panjabi language. So to re-iterate, the question that arises is why these young people and their peers should, in relation to languages like Panjabi and Gujarati, claim ownership, go on to bemoan their inexpertise, but spurn opportunities for improvement of their capabilities. One explanation may lie in the phenomenon of language shift which is well known within Sociolinguistics and the Sociology of Language, and is characterised by Fishman in this way,

> The basic datum of the study of language maintenance and language shift is that two linguistically distinguishable populations are in contact and that there are demonstrable consequences of this contact with respect to habitual language use.
>
> (Fishman, 1964: 33)

According to Fishman, these forces mean that with regard to minority populations and minority languages '... intergenerational mother tongue continuity is very frequently not only endangered but actually not attained' (Fishman, 1989: 225). Fishman argues that these developments are often seen as undesirable, but suggests that they are in fact inevitable,

> Language is both part of, indexical of, and symbolic of ethnocultural behaviour. As ethnicities meld, change or absorb and replace one another, it is inevitable that the languages of these ethnicities will be modified as well. Language change, *per se*, in the usual linguistic sense of alteration in lexicon, semantics, syntax and phonology, is, of course, always ongoing, particularly between languages in contact ...
>
> (Fishman, 1989: 673).

Looked at in this way the condition of the Blackhill youth, with respect to community language expertise, looks predictable and does not require undue melancholia on the part of grandparents, parents or sympathetic observers. The young people are, here, clearly subject to larger social structural forces, which defy voluntarism. In other words there is something in their British ethnicity which constrains the utility of the community languages and reduces them gradually to the kind of symbolic status which accommodates the continued use of phrases like 'my language' and 'my culture'.[4] It should be emphasised that the Blackhill youth did not show any particular discomfort about these circumstances. Their attitudes towards taking steps to enhance their community language use remind me of a British person resolving on New Year's Eve, that in the approaching year he/she really must join a gym, lose weight, learn a foreign language, give up smoking etc. In other words it is a general aspiration to take action, but not just yet, and certainly not if it involves specific effort. Often the young people said that the reason why they did not attend community language classes was that they couldn't fit them into their busy timetables and they frequently cited homework and exams as the impediment. When I asked whether or not Blackhill school itself had offered the option of studying languages like Panjabi as a school subject, they appeared initially confused before admitting that they had been given this option in earlier years but had declined to take this up as Sachdev has already indicated above.

It could be argued that the protestations by the Blackhill youth that they were seriously deficient in community languages might have been simply a reflection of the substantial amount of perceived expertise possessed by many others in their families and communities. However, the volume and persistence of their claims that they felt inadequate in their community language performance convinced me that this perspective had to be taken seriously. To do, otherwise I concluded, would amount to the practice of 'Romantic Bilingualism' (Harris, 1997).

At the same time, perhaps because they were trying to be helpful to me as an enquiring 'outsider' researcher, there were a considerable number of occasions in which they adopted the role of at least relative experts in supplying elements of linguistic infomation in didactic or instructional mode,

my mum she tells my li[ʔ]le sister off cos like she says [tu] which means like 'you' but it is meant to be [tuseen] it's like more respectful[5]
(Dhrishaj (m) Panjabi Sikh)

Rishab: [namaste] means um sort of saying that 'hello how are you welcome come in

RH: yeah yeah

Rishab: yeah and [sat sri akal] is just 'hello'... [namaste] yeah that's Hindi and [sat sri akal] is in Panjabi ... me and my friends we were walking across the pavement saw an old woman she was walking slowly and she looked up and actually smiled in a sort of friendly manner so me and my friend just sat sri akal and namaste and just to you know be friendly back

... mum and dad give it 'yeah we're going to Wembley do you want to come' and I said [nahī ma paRhnā][6] yeah that means 'no I wanna read'

(Rishab (m) Panjabi Hindu)

Whatever conclusion is reached on these matters, it is clear that the primary significance lies in the collective perception of the Blackhill youth that in a number of different ways they share certain related communities of practice and experience. One of these is shaped by orientations to community languages and to attendance at community language classes. Another, which will now be sketched, and which is also distinctively shaped by language practices, emerges in adolescent peer to peer interactions.

A linguistic community of adolescent peers

Frequently in their discourse the Blackhill youth positioned themselves as part of a local community of adolescent friends in and out of school. This peer and friendship group appeared to be dominated by young people with a broadly similar ethnic profile; that is, of South Asian descent.[7] One of the factors binding them together was their identification of their group as a group of English-speaking peers. Just as was the case with their own siblings, the Blackhill youth claimed to almost always speak English with their friends. They were also insistent that the kind of English they spoke with their peers was heavily marked by the use of slang, although they were hard pressed, as indicated in Chapter 5, to be precise about what form this exactly took.

Swearing and cussing

Alongside the use of slang they made remarkably frequent mention of the fact that they shared with their friends a propensity for swearing and cussing. These aspects of speech are what one might expect from any English-speaking adolescent in contemporary Britain (Stenström *et al.*, 2002). In my research data both girls and boys referred to themselves and their peers as active and regular participants in swearing,

> 'When I talk to my friends I do not really care about the sort of language I use because when you are with your friends you are not really bothered and I have noticed that you do tend to swear a lot when you are with your friends'.
>
> (Manika (f) Gujarati Hindu).

'Standard English:	"Satpal, can you pass the football!"
How I'd say it casualy (sic):	"Oi Satz, pass the fucking ball!"
Standard English:	"Do you know where the football is?"
How I'd say it casualy (sic):	"Where's the fucking ball?"
Standard English:	"Why is he doing those football skills for?"
How I'd say it casually:	"What the fuck's he doing those shit skills for?" '

(Japdev (m) Panjabi Sikh).

The Blackhill youth were also emphatic that in their patterns of casual swearing they were influenced by their consumption of American popular culture; especially music and films,

> 'Man I'm fucking going ... They've got the same shit over there that they've got here ... They wouldn't know what the fuck a quarter pounder is ... Any of you fucking pricks move and I'll execute every motherfucking last one of you'
>
> [extracts from the film Pulp Fiction,
> (Gurleetaa (f) Panjabi Sikh)
> self-made audio recording].

Sachdev: ... there's a main rapper Tupac[8]
RH: yeah
Sachdev: ... I pick up things he says like 'f' words swear words and same thing happens with my friend Amar me and him normally when we want each other to shu[ʔ] up we ju- just say 'shu[ʔ] up bitch'

(Sachdev (m) Panjabi Sikh)

The issue of popular cultural influences on the identities and tastes of the Blackhill youth will be explored more fully in Chapter 7. However, the specific issue of the part played by cussing in the formation of Blackhill youth masculinities, as foreshadowed by Sachdev's comments will be discussed below in the references to the form of swearing known as cussing. Before turning to that topic it is worth mentioning that the Blackhill boys were much more likely than the girls to refer to swearing in community languages as well as in English. On one occasion when it was Amaljeet's birthday and I was walking with him across the school playground he was approached by a boy who handed him a card in a blue envelope and uttered what appeared to be friendly but disparaging remarks. Amaljeet confirmed to me that the utterances constituted swearing in Panjabi, adding that the boy was his cousin. Sumandev confirmed and extended the salience of this phenomenon,

'Occasionally, I speak in Punjabi at school with my friends who know it. Most of the time it's swearing in Punjabi. The Punjabi swearing is so common that even people from completely different ethnic groups know how to swear in Punjabi. At school, I have come across swearing words in Swahili, Gujarati, Punjabi, English, Arabic, Somali and even German'.

(Sumandev(m)Panjabi Sikh).

In London and other British urban schools from at least the 1980s onwards, 'cussing' routines, as distinct from routine swearing were a commonplace in the day to day interactions of young males, where they sometimes provoked jocularity and sometimes serious conflict. Rampton (1995: 171–83) provides an extended discussion of multiethnic and multilingual contexts of this kind where Panjabi language use amongst young people plays a symbolic and mediating role. However, the more frequently occurring instances appear to be related to 'cussing' rituals led and dominated by black males of Caribbean descent (Sutcliffe, 1982: 56–57; Hewitt, 1986: 136–38, 179–82, 236–8). In these cases the key point of reference seems to be highly developed 'cussing' and abuse rituals practised by African American, predominantly male youth.[9] As suggested these exchanges can be jocular or explicitly hostile, with the hostile dimension perhaps being provoked because the subject of the cussing, replicated from the African American tradition, frequently involved derogatory commentary about the mothers, sisters or girlfriends of male youths. Amaljeet, in a written representation of a typical interaction between him and his brother in Panjabi, portrayed the following,

'*Brother:* Kidha Prawa.
English: Alright brother
Me: Tikhaye.
English: I'm alright.
Brother: Teri tati wale mu wargi kuri kidha.
English: Hows your shit faced girlfriend.
Me: Teri kangeri nalu changi ha
English: Better than your prostitute'

Amaleet's accompanying written commentary added, 'I put in a bit more action to show my brother I am better than him in cussing'.

The foregoing discussion of swearing and cussing amongst the Blackhill youth shows one aspect of the kinds of practice which help to construct them as members of highly specific local adolescent communities of linguistic, ethnic and cultural peers. As Back has suggested cussing exchanges amongst youth,

> have greater sigificance than just play for play's sake. They not only mark the boundaries of tolerance within dyadic friendships but they also mark those who are included in the peer group.
>
> (Back, 1996: 74–75)

However, this amounts to just one dimension in the intricate constitution of such communities. As the Blackhill youth made clear most of their communication with each other was in English of one kind or another, with their mutual usages of additional community languages confined to particular, carefully defined, circumstances.

Community language use with peers

Sometimes the young people alluded to the suggestion that there might be social moments when someone, for instance, from a Panjabi speaking family was with peers from Gujarati-speaking families, and that these circumstances might induce them to communicate with each other in Gujarati. Generally speaking one of the reasons they gave for nearly always speaking English with their friends was to ensure that, in a potentially highly multilingual environment, no one was frozen out. There were, though, occasions when they saw their community languages as providing a useful exclusionary device. However, when this tactic was deployed among friends it generally seemed to have benign characteristics,

> RH: you said that sometimes you might um Panjabi might be used to talk about something behind their back
>
> Dhrishaj: yeah i[?]'s like if there's someone who is Hindu and they speak Gujarati then we might speak behind their back but the thing is they understand like Keshav he he like speaks Gujarati say if I want to s- um swear at him yeah he'll understand wha[?] it means because he's heard it before
>
> RH: yeah yeah
>
> Dhrishaj: like from his other Panjabi friend
>
> > (Dhrishaj (m) Panjabi Sikh)

On the other hand there were hints at more determinedly exclusionary practices reserved for ethnic (white British?) outsiders,

> I think all of us do know how to swear in Panjabi some differ some words so we either use it to cuss each other or say there's um a different race around us and we don't want them to hear i[?]
>
> > (Sachdev (m) Panjabi Sikh)

As well as this kind of highly circumscribed pattern of 'in-group' community language use, many of the Blackhill youth also recognised themselves as affiliative members of a community of 'out-group' language users of the language of black youth, particularly black youth of Caribbean descent.

Black talk: Caribbean, Black London and African American

The Blackhill youth were conscious of the influence, on their collective speech, of language associated with black people, both those in Britain of Caribbean descent, and those in the USA. For the purposes of analysis it is useful to sketch out the dimensions of these usages in relation to phonology, lexis, and idiomatic style, as they emerged from the research data, and using Jamaican as the paradigm case of Caribbean language use. The most noticeable orientation to Caribbean language use by the Blackhill youth took the form of conscious declarations of affiliation as Chapter 4 demonstrated with respect to Amaljeet and Karwan, who linked their interest to matters of music and style, and to the use of a few symbolic phrases such as the Jamaican language greeting, 'wha a gwaan'. There was some evidence that other young people in the peer group were significantly influenced in this respect by the example of Amaljeet, even when the connection was more weakly and hesitantly expressed,

> yeah I hear him [Amaljeet] say like these days the main greeting is saying I'm not sure how to say it properly bu[?] it goes … 'wha a gwan' something like that … and that's how they greet each other
> (Sumandev (m) Panjabi Sikh)

Much more common, though, amongst the Blackhill youth, was their unconscious use of Jamaican language forms which had to some extent become absorbed into their routine speech. These were filed in their minds, when they were aware of it at all, under the heading of slang. This practice was observed by Hewitt (1986), and is exemplified in these exchanges with Rishab,

> *Rishab:* … when I'm with my friends I talk a lot of slang like 'innit' 'cos' 'chip'…'you seen' in things like that yeah 'seen' so if someone said says 'oh she's lookin old ennit' and I say 'seen', that means 'I understand what you're saying'
> *RH:* yeah
> *Rishab:* like slang words like tha[?] tha[?] have come in like//
> *RH:* tha- tha- that's Jamaican[10]
> *Rishab:* is it?
> (Rishab (m) Panjabi Hindu)

Interestingly, and again unlike Amaljeet and Karwan, Rishab sources his own usage and that of others he knows, not to local contacts of Caribbean descent but to popular cultural influences, and mentions specifically the film 'Cool Runnings'.[11] It will be observed that Rishab also mentioned his own usage of the word 'chip' which Hewitt (1986: 129) cited as an example of a Jamaican language usage among young white people in South London, whether or not they were conscious of its origins. As I have reiterated many times, the Blackhill youth seemed to have a sense that usages like this were slang in general rather than specifically Jamaican,

> *Suhir:* the way the kids er speak in the playgound is slang I've just always thought that
> *RH:* yes
> *Suhir:* because it's it's just different and like you use different things like er there's chip and everything
> *RH:* yes
> *Suhir:* talking about leaving
> (Suhir (f) French Creole Muslim)

This question of the unconscious usage of Caribbean speech tokens sometimes appeared too, unmarked, in passages of speech rather than in a referential way,

> I don't like it a[?] all I just wish they'd stop it it's just stupid because there's no reason innocent people get killed and buildings get [mashed up] people lose their lives businesses everything
>
> (Sachdev (m) Panjabi Sikh)

Again in Hewitt's work (*ibid.*) the term 'mash up' was identified, but as an example of the leakage of Caribbean usages into white youth speech. In my research data the most prominent examples of unselfconscious usage occurred in the pronunciation of the voiced th (ð) as /d/ which, as has been well noted by many sociolinguists (Roberts 1988 for example), is characteristic of Caribbean speech. As Roberts observes (*ibid.*: 54), the reason why this is especially noticeable is because they are continually highlighted in some of the most high frequency words in English so that words such as /the/, /this/, /them/, /then/ and so on, are rendered as /de/, /dis/, /dem/, /den/. This example is brief but typical,

> [dat] was up to [dem] [den] really
>
> Narjot (m) Panjabi Sikh)

One other area of influence of the language of black youth on the speech of the Blackhill youth, lies in emergent black-led English usages in London. Two examples serve as illustrations. The first instance is the use of the phrase, 'what are you saying?' as an opening greeting in a face to face meeting or in a phone conversation, instead of an expression like 'hello'.

> *Sumandev:*   there's, 'what are you saying?'
> *RH:*   'what are you saying?'
> *Sumandev:*   oh er yeah it goes, 'wha[?] are you saying?', bu[?] u- it's short for what are you saying
> *RH:*   yeah
> *Sumandev:*   and that's supposed to be another way of greeting
>
> (Sumandev (m) Panjabi Sikh)

I first noticed this phrase in the 1990s in black youth speech in London but have not been able to find it attested elsewhere in the sociolinguistic literature. The other example is much more pervasive in the speech of the Blackhill youth. This is the chronic use of the tag /*yeah*/. According to Stenström *et al.* (2002: 172) this tag is common in London teenage speech but, 'has not previously been described in the literature'. In their findings it was more frequent in working class than in middle class speech and was used equally by boys and girls. They depict it as serving the interactional function of checking, 'the mutualness of the concepts referred to' (*ibid.*: 173), and they add that, spoken with a rising intonation, it invites 'the hearer's evaluation of some aspect of the utterance' (*ibid.*: 173). Here are some examples of its use in the speech of the Blackhill youth,

> my grandfather sometimes gets let- gets letters from his relatives or brother or something yeah↑ he usually has to ask my dad to read it when sometimes yeah↑ because he can't see properly inni[ʔ] yeah↑ but they're usually in Panjabi though yeah↑[12]
>
> (Neetaa (f) Panjabi Sikh)
>
> my brother sister dad and mum they don't exactly really religious yeah↑ bu[ʔ] we do yeah↑ keep our long hair
>
> (Narjot (m) Panjabi Sikh)

I agree with Stenström *et al.* (2002) in stating that I have not found this speech characteristic described in the sociolinguistic literature, however I first noticed it in the speech of black London youth of Caribbean descent in the early 1980s and am prepared to speculate that these youth were the originators of this speech form. Like Hewitt (1986), when referring to the use of Caribbean speech forms by white London youth, I do not want to exaggerate the extent of these usages in the speech of the Blackhill youth. Rather, I want to register that they are deeply embedded as emergent cultural elements in their routine everyday language use both as young people of mainly South Asian descent, and as unexceptional London teenagers of their social class positioning (see Appendix B). On the whole the Blackhill boys were more likely than the girls to claim a greater usage of Jamaican influenced speech beyond the expression of individual words, and a greater affiliation to them. This type of affiliation formed, for the most part, a vicarious attachment to forms of masculinity, associated with working class black young men of Caribbean and African American heritage, which are much admired on the London street and which constitute for boys in London as early as age 11 part of a 'hegemonic' masculinity (Frosh *et al.*, 2002). In this conceptualisation, South Asian masculinities have not often been sources of admiration or objects of desire. As DJ Ritu, a female DJ of South Asian descent put it,

> we could see that it was cool for Asians, Cypriots and white kids to be down with the black, be down with Afro-Caribbean culture in terms of music, language, dress, style, everything, and one of the things I said ... was 'wouldn't it be nice to see a day where it'd be cool to be down with the Asian?'
>
> (Huq, 1996: 76)

It is probably most satisfactory to interpret the Caribbean/Jamaican language orientations of the Blackhill youth, especially the boys, within this frame. Their speech habits in this respect are for the most part playful. As such they may well be expressing speech allegiances representing merely a transient phase of adolescence, and therefore unlikely to last into adulthood. Nevertheless, for the time being they appear to be an important marker of identity which a significant number of Blackhill males seemed eager to assume. However, it is important to note that none of them claimed that they had current close friends who were of Caribbean descent, although they were influenced by the speech and other style behaviours of such youth in the locality.[13] At the head of this section of the present chapter I mentioned African American language as an influence on the language of the Blackhill youth. However, unlike the Caribbean language influence which was at least partly influenced by direct interpersonal contact on an everyday basis, whenever the young people referred to their attraction to African American language, this was always an attraction mediated and developed through popular cultural sources. The nature of these influences will be explored a little more fully in Chapter 7.

Most of the Blackhill youth described their linguistic interactions with their friends and peers in ways which could be described as representing a kind of fragmentary multilingualism. In this formulation, a bedrock of English language use founded on a London English, underpins the interplay of interjections from South Asian languages like Panjabi, Gujarati, Hindi or Urdu, sprinkled with dashes of London Jamaican and African American Vernacular English.[14] It should also not be forgotten that the Blackhill youth also shared the everyday school experience of listening to, speaking, reading and writing German, which they were all studying as a school subject to GCSE level. A significant number said that they used it outside the classroom, usually for a combination of playful and social exclusionary purposes.[15]

Yet amongst this potentially dazzling array, it is important not to lose sight of the fundamentally British and specifically London community identities which are dominant. It is, therefore, worth considering whether a similar trajectory can be traced with respect to another of the communities which help to frame the ethnicities and cultures of each of the Blackhill youth. I refer to the everyday transactions and discourses of the religious communities to which they claim nominal allegiance.

A community of religion

For each of the Blackhill youth another significant marker of community belonging was their religious affiliation. To repeat, 13 of the young people claimed a Sikh affiliation, 11 a Hindu one, four Muslim and three Christian. In this section of the present chapter there will be a glimpse of some of the ways in which religion was, for them, another community, cultural, and ethnic identifier which again prompted the articulation of the proprietary pronoun 'my'. The Blackhill youth often referred to 'my culture' or 'my religion' just as, as has already been established, they referred to 'my language'. As was the case with community language, this claim of ownership by the Blackhill youth in relation to their nominal religion, was accompanied by numerous statements about their limitations in knowledge and understanding of its procedures and practices, 'I don't think ea[ʔ]ing meat's against my religion I dunno' *(Bahiyaa (f) Panjabi Hindu)*. This went together with extremely modest levels of participation in its regular, locally available, rituals in the gurdwaras, temples and mosques.

One of the reasons why the Blackhill youth appeared to have limited knowledge and understanding with respect to their family religions, was related to the fact that some of the key religious texts were written in languages like Panjabi or Hindi which they could not read.[16] As Shariqah, a Muslim, put it,

> the prayers I do know how to read but no[ʔ] (.) no[ʔ] properly I usually need my mum reading out aloud so then I can just follow what she is saying[17]
>
> (Shariqah (f) Urdu Muslim)

Shariqah's comments were echoed by Amaljeet, speaking of his encounters with Sikh religious observances,

you get tapes yeah↑ translate the book cos you can't read it it's more
or less like that's really standard sort of Panjabi it's hard to take in but
um it's just hard to read the Book it's really hard to read it.

(Amaljeet (m) Panjabi Sikh)

There was also the suggestion that the sung and spoken utterances of
their religious leaders in the places of worship were delivered in versions
of the languages which were perhaps heightened, poetic and somewhat
antiquated; in other words the antithesis of everyday contemporary
speech in these languages. A possible point of comparison might be
between the ordinary spoken vernacular Englishes used in Britain today
and the language of the Old and New Testaments in the King James version of the Christian Bible, or the language of the Psalms. Consequently
the Blackhill youth often said that they could not understand the pro-
ceedings in the places of worship and therefore felt detached from them,

when you're praying yeah↑ I can understand parts of i[?] bu[?] erm
the way they speak is they speak like in Hindi which originated from
many many years back like hundreds of years back cos that that's
been wri[?]en a hundred years ago

(Rishab (m) Panjabi Hindu)

with Panjabi they use in the Gurdwara I think it's slightly more complicated cos I don't really understand it you know sit there and and
then they tell you stories and then they sing and then you go into the
langar which is um a place where you eat

(Jasjoti (f) Panajbi Sikh)

These observations with respect to the experiences of the Blackhill
youth have been endorsed from outside their ranks by Jeevan Singh
Deol, a Cambridge University Research Fellow who has stated,

Most people in Britain conduct their religious life and moral thinking
entirely in English. I suspect that they would find the real issue here
somewhat unfamiliar: it can be tough for those born in Britain to
engage with their beliefs in a language they don't fully understand.
Those of us in the Sikh community who have been born in Western
countries can sympathise more readily. The language of worship, teaching and discussion in our Gurdwaras the world over is usually Panjabi.
Many of us have a rather basic command of the language which does-
n't extend very far beyond the world of home and family. It's difficult

for many of us to really understand and discuss complex issues and ideas in any depth in Panjabi, especially matters of religion and morality. The same often holds for British-born Hindus and Muslims, whose command of their parents' languages may be equally shaky.

(Deol, 2003)

Another factor contributing to the relative religious detachment of most of the Blackhill youth, was their perception that it was possible to feel attachment to a religion while being relaxed about following its practices rigorously. This was an outlook which they sometimes attributed to the attitude of one or both of their parents. In most cases the parent concerned was the father,

> my grandmother says how I shouldn't ea[ʔ] mea[ʔ] and all tha[ʔ] but I do anyway cos my dad thinks it's dippy my dad makes me ea[ʔ] i[ʔ]
> (Bahiyaa (f) Panjabi Hindu)

> it was an early age that ... I had my hair cut and my dad used to cut my hair an er now he's saying 'if you want to grow a turban grow it I don't mind you do what you want to do'... my dad he used to have a turban but he cut ... his hair
> (Patwant (m) Panjabi Sikh)

Conversely, usually when a parent was depicted as being a strong adherent to the following of religious observances, it was represented as being more likely to be the mother or often older female family members in general. For instance, Vishnu, a Hindu, says, 'my mum prays every day'; and Dhrishaj, a Sikh, observes, 'most of the time now my mum goes [to the temple] in the morning about five o'clock I'm asleep then'; and Julie, a Catholic, comments, 'my aunty asks me like oh about something in the Bible and I don't get it she says you should read it she gets angry with me'.

Even where the Blackhill youth professed a comparatively strong attachment to their family religion they still seemed to regard themselves as seriously deficient in their knowledge and understanding of it. As Gurshanti confessed earlier,

> with a lo[ʔ] of my friends I I don't think any of them know about their religion and I know like the things that have happened in the past and stuff I've bough[ʔ] books abou[ʔ] i[ʔ] but seriously if I had to come down to i[ʔ] I don't know nothin[k] about my religion
> (Gurshanti (f) Panjabi Sikh)

A number of the youth said that their families had small prayer rooms or shrines at home, but the most convincingly described types of religious participation which they reported were their own slightly naive personal prayers for good fortune at challenging moments or for the fulfilment of pressing wishes and dreams. However, perhaps the most heartfelt expressions made in relation to religious identities and self-positionings came from a number of individuals who described themselves as universalist rather than sectarian on religious questions. For example, Punamdeep, a Sikh, explains,

> my dad always taugh[?] us you know everyone's equal there's no difference and um he goes 'treat others how you wanna be treated in return' and that's how you know I am.
>
> **(Punamdeep (f) Panjabi Sikh)**

Although there were known to be open religious conflicts in their local area, none of the Blackhill youth expressed partisan positions on these matters.[18] On the contrary, some girls expressed disapproval of the provocative coat-trailing activities of their own young male relatives in courting confrontation with young men from other faiths by trying to disrupt their key community religious celebrations; hooting and jeering in hooligan fashion from cars. One Blackhill boy, Sachdev, says that he went to elaborate lengths to avoid religiously inspired conflict by wearing one of his favourite t-shirts, which bore Sikh religious symbols, under his shirt to avoid causing offence to, or attracting aggression from, other groups. Referring to gang fights between local Muslims and Sikhs, he says, 'I don't like it ... so I wouldn't try and do any[f]ing which would cause any trouble between Sikhs and Muslims' (*Sachdev (m) Panjabi Sikh*). In addition to the foregoing descriptions of the relative detachment of the Blackhill youth from idealised versions of community religious practices, a significant number of them made passing mention of open and outright transgressive acts by older male relatives.

Acts of transgression

Much is made, in essentialised British discourses about South Asian people, of their supposed fervent observance of religious principles across a variety of faiths other than Christianity. This sentiment has flared with a particular emphasis on Muslims ever since the fatwah against Salman Rushdie over his book *The Satanic Verses* in the late 1980s (Khan, 2000, Runnymede Trust, 1997); and again after the events of 9/11 in the

United States of America as well as after the London transport bombings of July 2005. However, many of the Blackhill boys identified their fathers or grandfathers as significant transgressors of some key religious community mores, and admired them for it. Examples of this were seen in what Amaljeet, a Sikh, and Karwan, a Muslim, had to say in Chapter 4. These transgressions included the flouting of dietary rituals, heavy drinking and profuse swearing.

The idea of strict and unbending religious community rules affecting young people of South Asian descent encompasses the notion that there is a severe taboo on out-group marriages. Certainly, it is a favourite trope of media stories in Britain as well as of broadcast drama, and political discourses. The phrase which acts in these contexts as a triggering signifier is 'arranged marriages' or 'forced marriages' as they are sometimes indiscriminately referred to, and are often said to trigger so-called, 'honour killings' (Dalrymple, 1998). It might therefore be reasonably assumed that anyone marrying outside their religious group is committing a serious act of transgression with harsh consequences. Such marriages would be described in familiar British parlance as 'mixed marriages', a type of social arrangement which has been heavily stigmatised and portentously characterised in the post-1945 era as being inevitably doomed.[19] Yet a number of the Blackhill youth mentioned in passing that their parents came from different religious communities. Rishab, for example, explains that his mother is from a Hindu family while his father is from a Sikh one,

> my grandma and grandad they're strong believers of the Sikh religion they follow Sikh but my mum's dad and mum they're strong believers of the Hindu ... they [his parents] go to each other's things they respect each other and both they also like both each others.
>
> (Rishab (m) Panjabi Hindu)

Consequently, despite his claimed Hindu affiliation Rishab cheerfully points out that he has attended both Hindu temples and Sikh gurdwaras with his parents.

Additionally, one or two of the youth recounted vignettes of individual family members like aunts or uncles who had transgressed religious and ethnic community conventions in their choice of marriage partner, but had suffered no onerous penalty. Premila, who claims a Hindu affiliation, points out, 'my cousin brother he got married to a Muslim and then they did nothing to him' (*Premila (f) Gujarati Hindu*). It must be emphasised that such comments by the young people were made in a matter of fact, low key way. This apparent complexifying of their ethnicity and culture caused them no particular concern.

As mentioned earlier, British politicians and social commentators have been fond of holding up what they call 'Asian families' for approbation on the grounds that they are models of family cohesion.[20] This, of course, when they were not contradictorily being said to be stereotypes of dire family friction concerning arranged and 'forced' marriages. The favoured idealising discursive representation of families of South Asian descent is disrupted by a number of the Blackhill youth who mentioned in passing that their parents were divorced or separated.[21]

Again their comments on this subject were unprompted and matter of fact. This was decidedly not crisis talk, nor offered by the youth as representative of remarkable phenomena. However, it would be a mistake to give the impression that, on matters related to the notion of communities of religion, what is being discussed is an arena entirely free of constraints and pressures.

Not all laissez-faire

There were a number of ways in which the Blackhill youth said that they sensed and experienced community pressures to conform with religious and ethnic ideals. Girls, in particular, often had a strong awareness that there were expected religious and ethnic norms which might enter their futures; for instance in terms of what a suitable wife should be like in the eyes of prospective in-laws, as Gurleetaa illustrated in Chapter 4. None of the girls intimated that such pressures were of the potentially dangerous order of the forced marriage scare stories. Nevertheless, the existence of these community-derived constraints were an inescapable part of the ethnic universes of the Blackhill youth as a whole, and the girls in particular. According to some of the Blackhill girls, another requirement for a suitable wife in the view of some influential community elders was a very good proficiency in the relevant community language. This was also something that Gurleetaa mentioned in Chapter 4.

An additional community pressure with quasi-religious overtones was the continuing background existence and influence of conceptions of caste. A few of the Blackhill youth mentioned this, usually naming the caste to which they thought they belonged. Amaljeet and Diya provided illustrative examples in Chapter 4. On the whole though, none of the youth displayed anything more than an extremely vague notion of what caste meant and what its consequences might be, beyond the certainty that some castes were higher than others. As Manika *((f) Gujarati Hindu)* put it, when discussing the topic, 'there's loads of them but I don't even know half of them'. However, the important point for the present discussion is that, in any imagining of 'new ethnicities', the residual and traditional elements form an important integral strand. No matter how peripheral these elements might be in the lives of young people like the Blackhill youth, they are still salient constituent parts of their putative cultures of hybridity, however conventionally British they might otherwise be. Still, in the final analysis, with the Blackhill youth, whatever community forces might attempt to pull them in other more austere and purportedly authentic directions with respect to religion, what was most apparent was their typically contemporary British responses in this domain. By this I mean that while claiming a nominal affiliation to a religion, they rarely attended the relevant places of worship, but did participate in religious rituals connected with births, initiations, marriages and deaths. Their most enthusiastic participation was in the big community festivals like Divali, Vaisakhi and Eid,[22] which involved the whole family and community in enjoyable celebrations often accompanied by the exchange of gifts.

In these respects it is difficult to see any vital difference between the behaviour of the Blackhill youth and the behaviour of a white British person, who claims allegiance to the Church of England, rarely attends church except for christenings, weddings and funerals, but who enthusiastically celebrates the Christian festivals like Christmas and Easter which involve public and private family and community celebration and gift giving.[23]

Once again it is possible to discern clearly among the plethora of influences, the strongly British inflections to the ethnicities of the Blackhill youth. Yet this is not the only dimension in their lives where the obligations, practices and experiences linked with a strong residual sense of traditional community are negotiated in articulation with a strongly dominant foundation of Britishness. Britishness here refers to widely recognised contemporary behaviours and practices sitting with comfort and ease within any given local British landscape. The wider transactions surrounding the reconciling of diasporic and British ethnicities and cultures constitute another such dimension.

Diasporas and Britishness

A potential disruption to the Britishness of the Blackhill youth is their continuing membership of, and involvement with, global diasporic communities through their families. At first sight these connections would seem likely to emphasise the 'otherness' of the Blackhill youth when set next to what might be considered to be quintessentially British. It could be argued that diaspora is a useful conceptual mechanism for understanding how the residual and emergent in culture are inextricably linked in the various communities of practice in which the Blackhill youth are involved in their everyday lives. Diaspora might, for the most part, be seen as constituting a pull towards, or at least a reminder of, the residual and traditional. Clifford draws attention to a formulation that characterises the main features of diaspora in this way,

> a history of dispersal, myths/memories of the homeland, alienation in the host (bad host?) country, desire for eventual return, ongoing support of the homeland, and a collective identity importantly defined this relationship.
>
> (Clifford, 1994: 305)

All but the desire for eventual return might be seen as figuring in the active experiences and cultural and ethnic imaginaries of the Blackhill youth. Writers in the British Cultural Studies tradition have played their part in the recasting of the concept of diaspora for purposes of analysis in relation to Britain's black and brown minorities (for instance, Hall, 1990; Gilroy, 1993a; Mercer, 1994). However, these authors have concentrated on the African diaspora of Africa, the Caribbean, North America and Europe, and tend to mention, only rarely and in passing, the global South Asian diaspora. There has, however, been a steady development in the utilisation of diaspora as a theoretical tool by scholars who are themselves members of the South Asian diaspora (Brah, 1996; Sharma *et al.*, 1996; Raj, 1997; Banerjea, 1998, 2000; Qureshi and Moores, 1999; Dudrah, 2002a, b; Puwar and Raghuram, 2003). Brah in an extended discussion of how a South Asian Britishness might be theorised, states that,

> the identity of the diasporic imagined community is far from fixed or pre-given. It is constituted within the crucible of the materiality of everyday life, in the everyday stories we tell ourselves individually and collectively. All diasporic journeys are composite in another sense too. They are embarked upon, lived and re-lived through multiple modalities: modalities, for example, of gender, 'race', class, religion, language and generation. As such, all diasporas are differentiated, heterogeneous, contested spaces, even as they are implicated in the construction of a common 'we'.
>
> (Brah, 1996: 183–4)

Cohen (1997), has added to this a positioning of diaspora within wider theorisations of contemporary globalisation. It is with all this in mind that I will examine next some of the more explicit ways in which diaspora was visible in the lives of the Blackhill youth. One dimension concerned the origins of their parents and grandparents. The other involved their own journeys to the homelands of these close relatives.

Parental and grandparental origins

Having stated that a key source linking Blackhill youth with diaspora communities was the birthplaces of their parents and grandparents, it is worth reiterating that the overwhelming majority of the Blackhill youth's diaspora roots were located in the broadly Indian ethnicities of East Africa and India. Here, two factors stand out. Firstly, their parents rarely had precisely homogeneous ethnic backgrounds. Often, one parent was born in East Africa and the other in India. Frequently one parent arrived in Britain for the first time in childhood while the other arrived in adulthood. These differences suggest potentially substantial variations in ethnic formation between such parents. Nevertheless, virtually all the parents of the Blackhill youth appear to have been born in either East Africa or South Asia,[24] as had their grandparents and most of their aunts and uncles. Members of their wider families, with whom they were in active contact, continued to live in these locations as well as in Canada and the United States of America amongst other places. The second thing to stand out was the extent to which the Blackhill youth struggled to piece together precisely where their parents were born, and how, why and when they came to Britain. This might well be important to the extent that it serves to distance the youth to some degree from engaging in a fuller attachment to the cultural meanings and practices of their diasporas. I was surprised by the apparent gaps in their knowledge of their closest family histories, since, in many other respects their parents took steps to try to ensure that cultural continuities were understood and secured in their children's generation. In some cases the ethnic differentiation between parents meant that the Blackhill youth's diasporic global communities were even more widely spread. Narjot, for instance, says, 'my dad was born in India and my mum was born in England'. He adds the further information that his father did not come to England until at least the age of 24. Punamdeep describes how her father spent his childhood and adolescence on an unfolding migratory journey from Kenya to India to the United Kingdom to Canada before arriving in the United Kingdom to settle in Coventry, whereas her mother having been born in Uganda moved to Leeds, Yorkshire as a child. She states that after her parents met and married in the United Kingdom they moved to Canada, where she was born, before finally returning to the United Kingdom when she was about one year old. She makes it clear that her global diasporic family, in the form of aunts, uncles and cousins, remains distributed between these locations.

   Diaspora family members also brought to the young people's families, on visits to Britain, a range of other languages besides English, for instance Swahili, which the Blackhill youth involved said that they could not understand.[25] Another phenomenon to note was that the diaspora communities were not always located outside Britain. A number of the Blackhill youth mentioned relatives whom they considered as subtly different in their ethnicity because they were living out their lives in other parts of Britain. A prime marker of this difference was perceived differences in patterns of language use. Dhrishaj, for example, speaking of his aunt, uncle and cousins who had moved first to North Shields and then South Shields in the Newcastle region of northern England, commented,

Dhrishaj:	they used to live in Southall and I used to see them about every day now I see them what about once a year probably and so when I see them they look a bit different the oldest one's like she was about 11 when they went to Newcastle and now she is about 19 and the boy he was just born and now he's old and he speaks proper like Geordie[26] and the others speak Geordie as well and when I went there they've got a shop there I was standing in the shop listening to the people and it sounds funny they'll come down here we'll laugh at them and when I go up there they laugh at me
RH:	so what do they say about your language
Dhrishaj:	they say I am posh and everything
RH:	posh!
Dhrishaj:	it's like they think I speak weird and they don't really say much though because I just start taking the mickey out of them
RH:	so but they actually say you're posh do they they don't say you're London they say you're posh
Dhrishaj:	em they say I'm speaking cockney and I say 'how am I speaking cockney?' and so it's just like I'd not fit in there the way I speak and they wouldn't fit in here
RH:	um for them what happened to their Panjabi?
Dhrishaj:	I don't know if they speak Panjabi they speak Panjabi with their parents and they're pretty strict but that comes out

with their accent as well It's like I don't know what it is
with the accents

RH: do you mean they speak Panjabi with a Newcastle accent?
Dhrishaj: yes if that's possible

(Dhrishaj (m) Panjabi Sikh)

The existence of these intra-Britain diasporic communities is an indication of the need for an even more fine-grained level of investigation in
the analysis of ethnicities. However, the principal focus in the present
discussion is the diasporic influence generated outside Britain, and for
the Blackhill youth this became most visible when they travelled to East
Africa, but more especially to India, to visit relatives there.

Trips to parental and grandparental homelands

The most vivid way in which they encountered their global diaspora
communities was through visits to the countries where their parents
were born or brought up. Typically this entailed visits to countries like
Kenya, Uganda and Tanzania in East Africa or visits to specific parts of
India such as the Punjab or Gujarat. The visits tended to be for periods
of a month or two at a time. Although in some ways these visits served
to bind the Blackhill youth into their respective global diaspora communities, they also acted powerfully, particularly the visits to India, as
instruments for accentuating not the Indianness of their ethnicities but
their Britishness. This occurred for a number of reasons. In the first place
most of the youth said that they found that their linguistic skills in
Panjabi, Gujarati and other languages were inadequate for the maintenance of extended conversation with their relatives, even the younger
ones. Sometimes the youth attributed these difficulties to their diaspora
relatives speaking more 'proper' or 'standard' versions of the languages
or speaking very quickly or using unfamiliar lexical items. In short, they
were speaking versions of the languages which were sharply different
from those spoken in Britain.

The second, and most telling, type of experience which the Blackhill
youth had during these visits was their encounters, which they found
extremely distasteful, with the somewhat 'third world' material living
conditions they experienced at first hand. These involved illnesses
picked up from the water, rudimentary toilet facilities and flying, biting
insects. Their alienated endurance of these hardships appeared to be
decisive in confirming for them that Britain unambiguously counted as
home. This was seen previously in the vivid description Amod gave in

Chapter 4 of a trip to India. His view of India was endorsed by Bahiyaa in the following extended exchange,

RH:	yeah have you have you ever been to India
Bahiyaa:	yeah
RH:	how many times
Bahiyaa:	three four times
RH:	when was the last time you went
Bahiyaa:	about two (.) three years ago I think
RH:	what do you think of it
Bahiyaa:	don't like i[?]
RH:	why not
Bahiyaa:	it's really differen[?] and er I didn't just didn't fi[?] in I don't think anyone could at my age if they're really young then I suppose they don't really know much
RH:	mm
Bahiyaa:	well I'd never be able to go there again
RH:	so wh- what are the things that made you not fit in
Bahiyaa:	it's just they're all different their way of living and they really know what I did there and all this – jus- I just didn't fi[?] in and it was horrible I didn't like it some places were alright but some places I didn't like um (.) like we went t- sick to the
RH:	huh huh (chuckles)
Bahiyaa:	water there so we really fel[?] ill
RH:	oh
Bahiyaa:	it was a horrible// holiday so I wouldn't go back[27]
RH:	//so which part did your// (family)
Bahiyaa:	//um we went to the p- to the Punjab we went to Bombay and tha[?]
RH:	and there's family there
Bahiyaa:	(.) yeah m- my mum's family some of them and where my dad used to live when he was young the village we've got um farms there
RH:	yeah
Bahiyaa:	lots and lots of farms so we'd stayed there for a li[?]le while
RH:	mm and and um
Bahiyaa:	tha[?]'s it
RH:	the bits that you didn't like you said that apart from being ill
Bahiyaa:	yeah
RH:	what other bits of the way of life

Bahiyaa:	the weather it's too hot for me
RH:	yeah
Bahiyaa:	all those mosqui[?]oes
RH:	oh yeah
Bahiyaa:	(tuts) terrible and it's too (.) I dunno it's too noisy especially where we stayed like we wen[?] ou[?] on the stree[?] too noisy and I dunno it's like they had no medical brig- I thought I was going to die
RH:	huh huh (chuckles)
Bahiyaa:	they've got no proper doctors or nothing and it's not really a secure country I don't think
RH:	(inaudible)
Bahiyaa:	I dunno oh I think the police or anything is dependent enough people die there (..) and I dunno I don't think they're really capable still developing[28]
RH:	mm mm mm and and the the things about the illness what do you know what it was called that you had
Bahiyaa:	no I think it was to do with the water so they we used to buy in the water all but they used to buy all these bo[?]les of mineral water i- it was exactly the same as the tap wa[?]er so I dunno it pu[?] me to the wa[?]er it affected what do I dunno all my sisters fell ill so two of my sisters and myself and it was just horrible

(Bahiyaa (f) Panjabi Hindu)

This lengthy representative example might be viewed as superfluous were it not for conventional dominant British discourses about people of South Asian descent, positioning them as prime symbols of 'otherness'. My argument is that responses like Bahiyaa's are reminiscent of nothing so much as caricatures of the stereotypical ordinary British tourist abroad of recent decades, and provide an aptly pertinent summary of how the proprietary pronoun 'my' which the Blackhill youth deploy to claim 'my culture', 'my language' or 'my religion' is at virtually all times saturated with fundamental kinds of Britishness; but a kind of Britishness which relates to and certainly does not disavow affective diaspora connections and identities redolent of traditional cultures and practices.

Conclusion

This chapter opened by drawing attention to the way in which the Blackhill youth appeared to contradictorily talk of 'my culture', 'my language' or 'my religion', while apparently in the same breath distancing themselves somewhat from these constructs. It is perhaps worth pondering why the youth do not also at other times explicitly refer symbolically to 'my Britishness'. It may be that what is being observed here is a Britishness which is being lived in a relatively new kind of social formation which has not fully matured into a structure which can be lucidly named. Here it is important to repeat Raymond Williams' observational stance,

> Again and again what we have to observe is in effect a pre-emergence, active and pressing but not yet fully articulated, rather than the evident emergence which could be more confidently named.
>
> (Williams, 1977: 126)

This chapter has traced the outline of a series of emergent communities of practice in which the Blackhill youth are active participants. Earlier, Wenger's notion of communities of practice was introduced as a conceptual device which might assist in capturing something of what I have been trying to accomplish here. As Wenger says, in relation to communities of practice,

> Being alive as human means that we are constantly engaged in the pursuit of enterprises of all kinds, from ensuring our physical survival to seeking the most lofty pleasures. As we define these enterprises and engage in their pursuit together, we interact with each other and with the world and we tune our relations with each other and with the world accordingly. In other words we learn.
>
> Over time, this collective learning results in practices that reflect both the pursuit of our enterprises and the attendant social relations. These practices are thus the property of a kind of community created over time by the sustained pursuit of a shared enterprise. It makes sense, therefore, to call these kinds of communities *communities of practice*
>
> (Wenger, 1998: 45).

For the Blackhill youth, their shared enterprises have been shown to constitute communities of practice involving, at the very least, orientations to community language use, language use with peers, communities of practice related to religion and diasporic communities of practice. It is in the operations of these and other communities of practices that 'new ethnicities' and 'cultures of hybridity' can be glimpsed. The Blackhill youth ethnicities develop through their fluid, continuous and nuanced participation in the practices of a series of highly specific and interwoven social, cultural and ethnic communities both local and globally diasporic. In these practices their orientations to language use act as a key marker.

Throughout the foregoing account there is evidence of how diaspora influences act as a link to religious and linguistic practices which seek to consolidate communities, cultures and ethnicities around notions of traditional continuities. At the same time emergent practices can be seen to constitute another organising principle for other identifiable communities of practice with which the Blackhill youth associate themselves. These two cultural forces, the traditional and the emergent, are constantly co-present in their lives, with one or the other perhaps dominant at any given moment. I am suggesting this perspective as more productive than the binary either/or which seeks to configure the old versus the new. On the whole, though, in this intricate mosaic, what is dominant and what is emergent is at most times heavily marked by cultural behaviour typical of contemporary British customs, practices and sensibilities among young people in general. Once again, though, these developments are the product not of spectacular incidents, moments or behaviour, but of countless exchanges, experiences and observations accumulated in the routine ordinary intercourse of everyday life. In this, as more generally, issues of language have been shown to play a significant role. The next chapter examines, albeit relatively briefly, territory which is more familiar in the study of youth cultures, and which often *does* potentially reveal the spectacular. I refer, here, to the orientations of the Blackhill youth towards popular culture.

7
Popular Culture, Ethnicities and Tastes

Introduction

The link between patterns of language use and the construction of ethnicities and popular cultural tastes is not necessarily an obvious one. Yet, when given the opportunity in a variety of ways to describe their own patterns of language use, the Blackhill youth themselves made such a link abundantly clear. This worked in a number of ways. First, as demonstrated in earlier chapters, there were patterns involving affiliation to, and the partial absorption of, linguistic forms drawn from sources like African American Vernacular English or Jamaican Creole. Second, particularly in relation to languages like Hindi and Panjabi, issues of expertise interfered with the consumption and production of popular culture. Films and music were especially affected. At the same time, the wider more general references the Blackhill youth made to popular culture, confounded certain familiar essentialist notions. I had anticipated that when discussing music they would make ample and rich references to Bhangra music and Hindi film music, and would claim strong affiliation to these cultural forms. Such expectations amount to the positioning of the tastes of the Blackhill youth as a kind of 'exotica', an approach trenchantly critiqued by Hutnyk (2000). According to these discourses, when the youth discussed films the expectation would be that they would have much to say about Hindi language films to which they would, of course, be strongly attached. However, the Blackhill youth expressed relative detachment when mentioning what might be characterised as 'Asian' music like Bhangra and Hindi film music, or 'Asian' film in the form of Hindi (or Bollywood) films.[1] Instead their most enthusiastically evaluative comments were reserved for a wide variety of Anglo-American popular music and for *Hollywood* films. This is in no way to argue that there were not individuals who *did* express a relatively stronger attachment to South Asian popular cultural aesthetics, nor to deny that there were gendered variations in these attachments. What this chapter will demonstrate, is that a fixation with essentialist conceptualisations of ethnicity and culture can obscure a clear eyed perception of everyday practices and dispositions. The self-representations of the Blackhill youth indicated popular cultural tastes which were at base typical of those of a large number of other British teenagers from other ethnic formations, including white British ones. In the case of the Blackhill youth, though, the dominance of these emergent British inflected tastes was at all times tempered and interrelated with the constantly present contemporary versions of traditional South Asian cultural expression. This chapter traces briefly these different strands of influence in the domains of music, films, and, in a minor way, television and radio. In the process, a constant eye is kept on the role questions of language are playing. One way of grasping the workings of these various elements is to note the intricate interplay between traditional inheritances and contemporary enthusiasms, and between considerations of expertise and affiliation.

Music

Inheritances

Although, as will emerge later, a number of the Blackhill boys expressed relative disdain for Hindi films and their generic music, these same boys showed considerable interest in what they called Hindi remixes. These were musical tracks drawn from Hindi films and remixed with sampled styles and/or beats drawn from Anglo-American popular music.[2] My impression was that the boys found the remixes congenial because they represented some kind of symbol of the emergent and modern in culture as opposed to the residual and traditional culture suggested by the music in its original form. In these circumstances they felt pulled to partly distance themselves from cultural forms perceived as outdated, being associated with feudal/rural aspects of the diaspora, rather than indicative of the more knowing 'sophisticated' effects of urban/industrial contemporary Britain. I say that they only partly wanted to distance themselves from the traditional, because an engagement with a type of music, in this case Hindi film music, albeit in a modified form, is nonetheless an engagement and not a complete rupture or alienation. In this sense it is typical of how the Blackhill youth ethnicities are formed. As Raymond Williams suggested in some of his propositions about the nature of culture, it is a mistake to look for total ruptures and the discarding of the traditional and the customary. At any given moment the residual, dominant and emergent in culture exist in a complex and fused web of interaction and discourse. It is also important on this point to make it clear that while it is being argued that, for the Blackhill youth, Hindi film music is emblematic of the traditional, this is not intended to imply a tradition which is either static or which claims any kind of homogeneous purity. Here it is worth noting two aspects of the Hindi film tradition. On the one hand as Booth (2000) points out, the Hindi films themselves have established their own musical traditions over more than 70 years and have also always drawn on longstanding narrative traditions emanating from Indian, mainly Hindu, civilisation,

> A huge body of over 40,000 film songs (*filmī gīt*, as they are known in Hindi) has grown along with the thousands of Hindi sound films produced since 1931.
>
> (Booth, 2000: 125)

On the other hand, as Booth also comments, Hindi music has been renowned for its mixing and matching of any and every music style from east or west that it finds useful for its purposes. Indeed this tendency has received severe criticism, not least from western critics. Booth cites the complaints of two such critics Marre and Charlton about certain Hindi film music directors who, 'plagiarise all sorts of music from classics to pop ... what emerges is the hotchpotch that is Indian film music' (Marre and Charlton, 1985, p. 141 cited in Booth, 2000: 126). Banerji confirms the habitual eclecticism of the music of Hindi films, calling the films, 'notorious for their voracious appetite for songs from any and every cultural and stylistic source' (Banerji, 1988: 207). All of this shows, again, the weaknesses inherent in the proposition of dichotomies of 'old' versus 'new' in relation to ethnicities. Clearly, when the Blackhill youth express a liking for Bally Sagoo's remixes of Hindi film music they are indicating an aesthetic preference for one kind of contemporary musical bricolage over another, rather than necessarily for the new and dynamic over the old and static.

I have implied so far that the Blackhill girls were more attached to Hindi film music than the boys. However, this difference should not be exaggerated. The girls were more likely to admit to a certain liking for some Hindi film music whether or not it was remixed with the most fashionable Anglo-American or bhangra beats. Both boys and girls, though, preferred the latter. The boys were more likely to claim a difference in taste between themselves and their sisters and other female relatives. Drishaj, for instance, claims in relation to Hindi film music,

> some of it is good yeah but I don[?] understand i[?] I just like the tune or some[f]ing and the way it sounds it's like my sister likes the old stuff she doesn't like the new songs and every[f]ing because they are too poppy and she likes the older ones because they are like more slower and sadder
>
> (Drishaj (m) Panjabi Sikh)

It will be noticed that language limitations play some part in Dhrishaj's aesthetic choice. Amar concurs, both in relation to his representation of his sister's tastes and with respect to the role that language plays in both of their practices,

> I like the English songs she likes the Hindi songs I'm English and she can listen to Hindi songs and actually understand it but I can only under- well listen to the background music but not the words
>
> (Amar (m) Panjabi Hindu)

Amar also, in a way which is representative of many of the Blackhill youth especially the boys, appreciates the Hindi remixes as symbols of advance and progress in his aesthetic universe,

> if you go down Southall nowadays and you go to one and a couple of shops they do actually i- it's called like remixes Hindi remixes and that and that's like done proper and you won't see tha[?] in the film because it's like too advanced (light laugh) and it's done by people here[3]

This perception is also linked with a view that purely generational factors are also salient,

> normally Indian films have a song every five minutes righ[?] and um throughout the film there'll be about ten songs in which two would be good remixes the rest would be just for old people and that so you go and buy a tape from the marke[?] it'll be here you ge[?] a Hindi song for a pound it'll be a pound because you'll only like two songs for the younger ones and that you know the rest will go on to the adults
>
> (Amar (m) Panjabi Hindu)

So, to sum up, there are Blackhill boys who distance themselves from Hindi film music unless it is in the form of remixes, and girls who quite like it in its original form, and there are both boys and girls who are slightly scornful of its aesthetics. As Punamdeep put it commenting on songs in Hindi movies,

> some are pathe[?]ic it's like they do um an Indian version of an English song and it doesn't always go i- it sounds stupid most of the time and why do that
>
> (Punamdeep (f) Panjabi Sikh)

Whatever the particular positioning of any Blackhill individual on these matters, perhaps the most apt way of characterising their relationship to their inheritance of Hindi film music is that it is *just there*; an ever present routine backdrop integral to their lives; something that cannot be avoided but is neither necessarily wholly rejected nor necessarily warmly and enthusiastically embraced. This kind of interpretation emerges precisely because my research approach pays especially close empirical attention to the unspectacular and the everyday in the expression of the young people's popular cultural tastes. Manika states that she hears Hindi film music, 'when my mum listens to the radio'. Punamdeep describes how she and her mother squabble over which music should be played on cassette when they go out in the car, with her mum wanting to play Hindi films songs, 'she'll say you are not going to listen to English music we'll put an Indian cassette'. Both Sachdev and Jasjoti, for instance, included on their self-made audio recordings, examples of Hindi film songs as one aspect of language use in their everyday lives. In each of these instances, traditional Hindi film music is an inescapable presence at certain moments of ordinary life, but is neither resented nor fervently embraced.

Not concentrating the research gaze on the spectacular in popular music does not indicate that spectacular cases cannot be found. One example was Amaljeet who was portrayed at some length in Chapter 4. It might well have been possible to learn much more about the importance of Bhangra music in the locality and amongst Amaljeet's peers if I had followed the option of investigating the spectacular as embodied in the person of Amaljeet himself and exemplified in his cultural practices. Amaljeet would have provided ideal material for these purposes, with his dhol band and its prolific public performances, together with his relatives who were well known and sought after DJs in the West London area. Yet, for the reasons given throughout the book, primary emphasis has been placed on the ordinary and the everyday and the particular angle of perception this affords. In practice Amaljeet's musical tastes were wide, embracing reggae and other black music styles.[4] Another potential opportunity to develop an analytic frame around an exploration of spectacular youth culture which might have been pursued was represented in the persona of Karwan who was also portrayed in some detail in Chapter 4. Here was a Jamaican-Creole speaking young man from a Kurdish refugee family from Northern Iraq, who was trying to develop himself into a recognised MC in his locality, and who had a number of relatives who were prominent local DJs with their own sound systems.[5]

Although the principal musical focus up to this point has been on Hindi film music, this music and its derivations was not the only kind of music to which the Blackhill youth referred. They also referred to Bhangra music. However, as already indicated, these references were relatively limited. When the Blackhill youth mentioned bhangra, and many did not, it was for the most part without the animated enthusiasm or attention to the specific detail of favourite artists and styles which they employed when referring to their favourite Anglo-American music. In short, notwithstanding the fact that bhangra music has received a significant amount of academic attention, (Baumann, 1990; Dudrah, 2001; 2002(b); Huq, 1999; Kalra, 2000; Sharma *et al.*, 1996; Maira, 1998; Back, 1996; Gillespie, 1995; Hall, 2002; Bennett, 1997) some of it related to the very locality in which the Blackhill youth lived, few of the youth themselves spontaneously mentioned Bhangra as being amongst their favourite music. Of course the academic authors cited treat bhangra with varying degrees of intensity and from radically different positions ranging from the orthodox and seminally influential (Baumann 1990), to the polemically revisionist (Sharma *et al.*, 1996). However, what these writers tend to share is a view that the development of bhangra in Britain occupies a centrally important position in the construction of new and unifying South Asian youth ethnicities and identities. For them bhangra tends to be seen as symbolic of some sort of transition from the old to the new, from the traditional to the modern or even postmodern. According to Baumann (1990: 81) bhangra is traditional urban and rural 'Punjabi folk dance and music' of the Punjab region of India, which has been transformed by South Asian youth in urban British contexts. This transformation is said to have led to the emergence of a distinctively 'British bhangra' which Dudrah describes as the,

> fusion of traditional folk bhangra lyrics and beats with urban black British and pop sounds into a new and distinctive genre of British

bhangra dance and music [which produces] an urban anthem and commentary about the lives of its British South Asian audiences.

(Dudrah, 2002b: 363)

In the light of this then, what remains to be accounted for is the relatively marginal position accorded to bhangra in the popular cultural lives of the Blackhill youth as represented to me in their own narratives. Here two speculative interpretations are offered. Firstly, it may be that my research evidence simply reports the beginnings of yet another generational change in the cultural practice and consumption of music. This judgement is strengthened by discernible evidence of similar forces in the transformation of the musical tastes of black youth of Caribbean descent in London. Research conducted into this group in the 1980s, for example Hewitt (1986), Back (1996), Jones (1988) emphasised the importance of Reggae music in the lives of these particular young people. Yet it is certainly the case that for young people of Caribbean descent born in the late 1970s and early 1980s in London, reggae has become of marginal interest; respectfully acknowledged as a pioneering cultural form which has always been there as a background soundscape to their lives, but no longer a cause for the great excitement which innovation generates. A second speculative interpretation might be that other academic commentators have directed attention and emphasis to spectacular aspects of the engagement of South Asian youth with popular culture, of which British bhangra forms a part. My attention, by contrast, as I have repeatedly emphasised, has focused determinedly on the unspectacular and everyday in the lives of the Blackhill youth as they themselves represented it. In their frame of reference the importance and dominance of bhangra recedes.

Close attention to what might be regarded as musically more prosaic, revealed that when the Blackhill youth described their musical tastes they appeared to fall into three broad groups. The first group, nearly always male, declared themselves to be relatively demanding followers of a variety of musical styles such as Jungle, Hip-Hop, Rap, Swing, House and Garage which were popular amongst black Caribbean descended, urban-based youth in Britain. This group of male Blackhill youth also declared an allegiance to a linguistic style associated with these musics. The second group, nearly always female, seemed to be casual but rather dutiful consumers of traditional Hindi film music, but located their favourite music of choice in the products of a variety of Anglo-American musical performers ranging from pop, to soul, to r&b, to rock, to indie music genres. The third, and highly significant group, and again the least spectacular, was composed of both boys and girls who were reluctant to identify themselves with any one style of music and tended to say that they listened to all kinds of music and were simply drawn to any tunes they heard that they liked whatever the musical genre. They also often described their favourite music as being pop or whatever was current in the national charts of music sales. Importantly, all three groups, located themselves in these positions, not as mere passive objects, constructed within the projected analytic frame of others, but as knowing agents actively describing the nature of their musical enthusiasms.

Enthusiasms

The first of the three groups, those who identified with music associated with the hard edged masculinities of both black youth of Caribbean descent and of urban African American youth, tended to want to distance themselves both from what they saw as the soft, romantic and 'feminine' characteristics of Hindi film music, and the old fashioned and 'uncool' aesthetics of traditional bhangra. They were however, more well disposed and sympathetic to, but relatively detached from, both the Hindi music remixes and the contemporary urban stylings linked with the development of bhangra in Britain in the 1980s and 1990s. It seemed to me that their declared tastes in music were linked with 'hard', prestigious black-led masculinities which they vicariously desired., rather than necessarily participated in as equals.[6] Some empirical evidence of these positionings was glimpsed earlier, for instance in the exchanges between Sachdev and Amar in the 'swearing and cussing' section of Chapter 6. These latter inclinations can also be readily encountered in the realm of music. Two particular favourites of Amar, Sachdev and a number of other Blackhill youth were Tupac Shakur (already referred to in Chapter 6) and Coolio,[7] both of whom projected a view of 'hard', 'street', African American masculinites linked with gang conflict, brushes with the law and often early violent death. Something of the flavour of what is being described can be sampled in the following comments from Amar describing some of the fantasies of one of his classmates linked with his own,

> my next friend he thinks he's Tupac yeah actually like the way he talks bu[?] I just tell them all that I'm Coolio because you know he's kind of cool in his music and tha[?]
>
> (Amar (m) Panjabi Hindu)

By way of illustration, in his audio recordings of language use in his life, Amar presented, amonsgt other things, one of Coolio's album tracks whose contents he described excitedly,

> *Amar:*   he walks into a record thing he wants a seat and the person who manages it and he gives it the manager gives it 'I I heard you's [d]is' and he just says all these swear words and he gives it 'where's my money' the manager gives it 'what money' and he shoots him
>
> *RH:*   mm
>
> *Amar:*   and the other one starts like shou[?]in and that and shoots him again
>
> *RH:*   mm
>
> *Amar:*   and gives it you know swears again and er a woman walks in and she starts shou[?]in and blabberin
>
> *RH:*   mm
>
> *Amar:*   he shoots her and he gives it 'shut up bitch'
>
> *RH:*   yeah who was this
>
> *Amar:*   this one was Coolio
>
> *RH:*   yeah Coolio
>
> *Amar:*   this was Coolio's lyrics and we just actually hooked onto that song
>
> (Amar (m) Panjabi Hindu)

Apart from Amar and Sachdev quite a number of other Blackhill boys – Drishaj and Vishnu, for instance, mentioned Tupac Shakur by name as an admired figure. Apart from the obvious links between musical tastes and configurations of masculinity, what was striking about these boys was the degree of enthusiasm and engagement evident whenever they discussed these particular musical allegiances. Their strength of commitment in this direction, rendered music styles other than those associated with tough black urban male youth as of limited interest or even irrelevant.

The second group who expressed music enthusiasms were, as already indicated, Blackhill girls who, sometimes alongside a moderate degree of interest in Hindi film music, reserved their strongest and most precise musical preferences for a wide and eclectic range of Anglo-American popular music styles.[8] These girls were more likely than any other group of Blackhill youth to name not only their preferred style of music, but also to name specific artists as favourites. Gurshanti states, 'I just like English music you know soul, hip hop stuff like that … my friends like they all like rock and indie.' Punamdeep confirms the range,

I love my English music ... I like a number of things you know I don't like I just don't stick to one music like I love jungle I really like tha[?] whereas some of my friends would be like nah and then I like erm hip hop or soul and then I can like rock on the same time and my friends can't stand i[?] and you know like most of my friends are just like on one thing like hip hop and r&b and stuff

(Punamdeep (f) Panjabi Sikh)

Turning to the question of named favourite artists, an analysis of comments made by nine Blackhill girls Gurshanti, Gurleetaa, Jasjoti, Nashita, Shariqah, Neetaa, Julie, Suhir and Shanice, showed them claiming allegiance to artists as varied as the following: Nirvana, Bush, Everclear, Garbage [grunge]; Bon Jovi [rock]; Kula Shaker [psychedelic rock]; Guns N' Roses [rock/heavy metal]; No Doubt [new wave ska]; Brand New Heavies [acid jazz/r&b]; LL Cool J, The Fugees, Coolio, Warren G [rap/hip hop]; Michael Jackson, Whitney Houston, Peter Andre [pop]; Damage [r&b]. This listing is not exhaustive of the Blackhill youth's specific music interests, but is sufficient to support the argument that the contributors to Sharma *et al.* (1996) make in their book-long assault on essentialist attempts to consign people of South Asian descent to a metaphorical box marked 'asian music' containing only items like bhangra and Hindi film music. Particularly powerful and illuminating, is the account by Banerjea and Banerjea (1996), of the systematic way in which young South Asians in Britain have been excised from depictions of the histories of fanatical followers of soul music in favour of a preferred binary of black and white youth,

Asians were 'understood' through their perceived 'penchant' for spicy food, illegal immigration and small businesses. Similar attachments to Horizon,[9] JFM, Robbie Vincent and Greg Edwards unsurprisingly failed to make it onto this list.

(Banerjea and Banerjea, 1996: 116)

Another example of the nuanced approach needed to develop this sort of analysis can be found in the spectacular music-related event which was mentioned in passing earlier in the book. This was the visit to Blackhill School by the British R&B group called Damage during my research fieldwork.[10] This singing group of young black men were visiting the school because one of the girls in the school had won a competition in the teenage girls' magazine *Smash Hits*, and this was the prize, along with the prize of a personal 'makeover'. What is pertinent to the present discussion on the nature of 'new ethnicities' and 'cultures of hybridity', is the profoundly typical response the visit provoked in terms of historical female teenage behaviour in Britain. Damage did a P.A. performance in the school hall and signed autographs.[11] The Blackhill girls' full and excited participation in the event included the obligatory screaming,

> it was really good and everyone was screaming throughout the whole concert and they [Damage] were just laughing at us and they stopped and they give it time and they said 'if you want to listen to us you want to come on our roadshow' I was really excited everyone was screaming
>
> (Nashita (f) Gujarati Hindu)

Pointedly, the same girls who watched Hindi films, visited India regularly or were strongly aware of community and religious idealised norms concerning what made for a suitable Hindu, Sikh or Muslim wife, were now screaming at a group of working class black London boys of Caribbean descent. Equally typically, in British teenage terms, this behaviour was gendered so that the Blackhill boys said they were not interested in the visit or were not impressed, seeing bands like Damage as being for the girls. As one boy remarked in touchingly honest terms,

> I don't really like Damage though but their songs are okay but them as a whole I don't really like em cos they're a bit too popular ennit to the girls
>
> (Rishab (m) Panjabi Hindu)

The musical enthusiasms of the Blackhill girls, then, project not a confirmation of their South Asian 'exotic otherness', but an affirmation of the ordinary in terms of the range of musical tastes of British teenage girls in general.

Even more typical of ordinary unexceptional British popular music tastes are the third group mentioned above. This was the group of Blackhill youth who were interested in popular music without being committed to any particular style or artist. Vishnu, for instance, is representative of this group in saying,

> I don't really listen to a strict certain style if I like the songs then I listen to it like in the top ten there's some rock 'n' roll songs tha[?] I don't really like so I don't listen to em but if the sounds good I- I- I-listen to em once [it] sounds good then I kinda listen to it or maybe I'll buy it bu[?] if I don't like it I'll always listen to it first before I buy

it for yeah we buy these big albums with all these different songs on it which is be[ʔ]er[12]

(Vishnu (m) Gujarati Hindu)

It is plausible to suggest that any randomly chosen group of young and not so young Britons, asked about what kind of music they liked, would have yielded a core responding in a similar way to the Blackhill youth. It is instructive to note that recent British reality TV pop music talent shows like *Pop Idol* and *Fame Academy* attract millions of viewers who vote in their millions for their chosen contestant, then propel the winner's first few singles and maybe even first album to the top of the charts; then equally suddenly lose interest completely, virtually ending the artist's career. It is also a commonplace for well established and even famous artists to express bemusement about the limited scope of their reliable fan base and their astonishment as to why the public ignores one release then catapults another to massive success. In sum, the Blackhill youth share tastes in music which are just like those of other British teenagers except that their cultural universes also integrate a continuous background soundscape, to which they may or may not pay heightened attention at any given moment or to which they may or may not choose to affiliate; but which is also part of a global, diasporically informed aesthetic experience, forged originally in the Indian subcontinent. A somewhat similar configuration could be perceived in relation to film, which was a constant point of reference for the Blackhill youth, and with respect to TV and radio which appeared far less frequently as reference points in their spontaneous representations of their patterns of language use and their linked ethnicities.

Films, TV and radio

The comments by the Blackhill youth about the presence and influence in their lives of Hindi films, for the most part confirmed Gillespie's research findings on the same topic in Southall (Gillespie, 1995), in a number of respects. Gillespie reported that girls were far more attached to these films than boys, used them as an opportunity to improve their understanding of Hindi language, and were interested in the romance driven by the song, dance and stars of the films which the boys rejected in favour of action. She found that the boys were more likely than the girls to be intolerant of the lack of complex plots and detailed cinematography in Hindi movies. According to Gillespie, the boys were far more committed to the 'heightened realism' of western film conventions which they contrast unfavourably with the 'ludicrously unrealistic action and fight sequences in Hindi films' (Gillespie, 1995: 86).

Most of the Blackhill youth said that they had seen these films on a fairly regular basis either as avid consumers or in passing because someone else in their household was watching. For the latter group the films formed merely a routine backdrop to their everyday lives. Only one or two of the youth mentioned going out of the home to cinemas to watch the films. In my research data, too, there is some evidence to suggest a gender differentiation with regard to the consumption of Hindi films. Blackhill girls appeared much more likely to declare themselves unambiguously as fans who wholeheartedly enjoyed the films. Manika confirms that she and her female school friends, 'watch a lot of Hindi films'. Diya concurs, 'I always watch Hindi films' and adds the importance of language in this choice, drawing at the same time a gendered contrast,

> in my house yeah it's like it's usually all the girls that watch all the Hindi films and the boys it's no[?] like they rather prefer watching English films it's just that they don't watch it that much I know it might be because they don't understand it that much or they're not interested in i[?]
>
> (Diya (f) Gujarati Hindu)

Even when they acknowledged the shortcomings and naiveties of the genre, Blackhill girls were far more willing to enthusiastically accept them for what they were. Punamdeep, for instance, first criticises Hindi films because of their failure to cope with realism and modernity then backtracks on her initial judgement,

> I think that is what makes some films a flop in Indian because no[?] a lo[?] of films have done that well.

> do you know right I think modernising isn't always the answer ... bu[?] I I don't like it when they modernise it too much ... it's really nice to have a really classical film
>
> (Punamdeep (f) Panjabi Sikh)

By contrast, a significant number of Blackhill boys not only said that they did not watch Hindi films or that if they did it was not by enthusiastic choice, but were often contemptuous of them; particularly the production values of these films.[13] It sometimes seemed as if the films symbolically stood as the feminine 'other' to the kinds of masculinity which they imagined for themselves, at least in fantasy. Hindi films were depicted as what sisters, mothers, aunties, grandmothers and female cousins paid attention to. Indeed, Nashita said she believed many boys were frightened to watch for fear of being ridiculed as girly or gay, 'I think they probably feel too scared to watch films their mates would probably take the piss'. These boys compared the films unfavourably to what they called 'English' films. By 'English' they were clearly referring to Hollywood films.[14] Their complaints against the Hindi films seemed to be centred on their failure to be convincingly 'realistic' within a strictly naturalistic narrative frame,

> some things like people crash into walls and they break the brick things down I I think jus- that's i- too much i- looks i[?] looks silly or cars go- going into brick massive thick walls and they break the wall down and all tha[?] ... they punch one person and he flies abou[?] one hundred metres
>
> (Amod (m) Gujarati Hindu)

Of particular interest to them were the action sequences whose execution they especially admired in Hollywood films,

> I've got interests like my uncle has in English films action and that ... we think that Indian films comparing to English films are not good because it's just their way of like special effects is kind of fake and that and then my sister she don't really care it's just like she likes the actresses
>
> (Amar (m) Panjabi Hindu)

In their eager consumption of Hollywood films, Blackhill boys showed themselves to be ready recruits to the preferred kinds of masculinity shaped by Hollywood and exported to willing male youth globally. Additionally, the Blackhill boys appeared to be particularly attracted by the kinds of masculinity projected by young black American, mainly working class, males. They made regular reference to the language used by such black males and said that they had integrated expressions used by them as a valued element of their own everyday speech with each other.

Meanwhile, those of the Blackhill youth, whether girls or boys, who *did* watch Hindi films, saw them not only as sources of pleasure, but also as a means of consolidating or even developing their understanding of Hindi language which could be utilised in other areas of their lives. For them the films were also instructional in another sense. Their formulaic depiction of boy-girl relationships as a major and legitimate source of conflict between feuding families, kept alive for the Blackhill youth the notion of certain residual traditional patterns of ethnic and cultural practice. Notwithstanding the stance of the minority, the Blackhill youth as a whole, like other British teenagers, were attracted, to and actively consumed, Hollywood films. They were often eager to refer by name to influences like *The Terminator, Pulp Fiction, Reservoir Dogs* and *Titanic*. On the other hand, in this, as in the case of music, what is distinctive in their practices is that, unlike other British teenagers, the backdrop to their routine everyday lives, inescapably also included Hindi films, regardless of the degree of any given individual's allegiance to these films. Consequently, an integral part of the ethnic and cultural experience of the Blackhill youth embraced the shared global diaspora sensibilities involved in their consumption of such films. This kind of sensibility was also shaped by their shared consumption of TV and Radio, although, as already stated, references to these media dimensions of culture were far less evident.

One speculative interpretation of the reason why the Blackhill youth made relatively infrequent reference to TV and radio is that my research fieldwork predated the main explosion in digital media which occurred at the very end of the 1990s and much more significantly after the turn of the new century.[15] This expansion has generated a major increase in the numbers of cable and satellite TV channels and specialist radio stations and with it the greater availability of broadcasting in languages other than English together with the generation of a greater intensity of disaporic ethnically specific contact, information and consumption. At the time of my research fieldwork in 1997 this phenomenon had not matured and on the whole references to TV consumption followed the pattern of Gillespie's findings (Gillespie 1995), which focused on programmes like the Soaps which were popular with the generality of the British population. Consequently, Blackhill youth, especially the girls, referred to their dedicated consumption of mainstream soap operas of the time on British TV, like *Neighbours, Home and Away, Eastenders, Coronation Street* and *Brookside*, as well as popular American TV drama series like *ER* and *The X-Files*.

In addition, the references that the Blackhill youth made to their interactions with popular culture where these concerned music, films, TV and radio sometimes made explicit links between the language they themselves use and generate, and the language they have encountered through these media sources. They provided examples of the symbiotic relationship involved, identifying London English, African American Vernacular English and South Asian languages as linguistic elements absorbed through TV programmes as particularly prominent in their lives. Finally, a significant number of the Blackhill youth referred to the presence in their lives of Zee TV.[16] Their awareness of Zee TV took a variety of forms. One seemed to be their perception that their parents and older relatives regularly watched programmes broadcast in South Asian languages which brought, for instance, news from the Indian subcontinent directly into their homes. Thus this TV station played an important role for some Blackhill youth in the consolidation and naturalisation of the kinds of diasporic link, involving language and culture, discussed in Chapter 6.[17] The youth tended to discuss their own specific relationship with Zee TV as being based on the viewing of popular music programmes. Several mentioned that they kept a regular eye on a Hindi Top Ten music chart programme on the channel. As elsewhere in their experience their declared linguistic deficiencies in South Asian languages were a factor in mediating their degree of interest and participation in these outlets. Reflecting a pattern already described, for those whose families possessed Zee TV, the channel constituted a familiar background presence rather than an exciting resource, especially where the broadcasts in South Asian languages were concerned. A somewhat parallel situation also seemed to exist with respect to radio stations specifically targetting Britain's South Asian populations.

The Blackhill youth made very few references to any influence of radio in their lives. There is evidence that those who made a point of emphasising their taste for pop chart music may well have listened regularly to mass popular music stations like Radio 1 and Capital Radio.[18] Surprisingly, none of the youth said that they listened regularly to pirate radio music stations which at the time were extremely prominent in London and certainly were strongly supported by working class black youth of Caribbean descent. Few of the Blackhill youth seemed even to be aware of the existence of these radio stations. On the other hand many of the young people did mention the routine background daily presence in their lives of Sunrise Radio broadcasts.[19] They generally claimed that it was their parents or other older relatives who were the principal consumers of Sunrise Radio, and thought that they were interested mainly in current affairs and news programmes broadcast in South Asian languages. For family elders these broadcasts seemed to be a key instrument for the maintenance of real and imagined local and diaspora communities. For the Blackhill youth, themselves, the broadcasts were an unremarkable subtextual backdrop to their everyday lives but at the same time a constant low key reminder of their own connection with the putative real and imagined local and diaspora communities, and a source for the keeping alive of the residually traditional in their ethnic and cultural environment.

Conclusion

This chapter has briefly outlined some of the ways in which popular culture in the form of music, films, TV and radio plays a part in the formation of the ethnicities and cultures of the Blackhill youth through the choices, allegiances and disavowals involved in the development of their tastes. Following a continuing thread running through the book, an attempt has been made to trace the conspicuous presence of questions of language in the shaping and positioning of these tastes. I have also emphasised the synthesis of the typically British adolescent nature of these tastes with the markedly South Asian, judging that for the most part in each case the British inflection is dominant, and this is a judgment which has been clear at every stage of the book. The argument is not that the youth live this experience in terms of a struggle between the old and the new, the traditional and the modern. Rather it has been argued that all these elements are potentially available at all times to the youth in their routine consumption of popular culture in the flow of everyday life. More precisely, the Blackhill youth are very similar to other British youth in their popular cultural tastes, except that they have available to them at most times sonic and visual backdrops not normally readily available to other formations of British youth affiliated to other ethnic groups including white British ones. As has been seen, these sonic and visual backdrops are provided by those elements of music, film, TV and radio which connect with the circulating migrations and cultural flows of the global South Asian diaspora. Care has been taken to pay particularly close analytical attention to how the Blackhill youth themselves represent their popular cultural tastes even when these responses might at first sight appear to be unromantic or commonplace rather than spectacular. This chapter has also demonstrated how important it is, with regard to popular cultural tastes, as with other cultural phenomena, to be guided by an anti-essentialist perspective. Without it the possibility of seeing the distinctions between the eclecticism of some Blackhill youth, the enthusiasms of others and the relative indifference of others still in their relationship with popular culture, would have been far more difficult.

8
What is a Brasian?

Introduction

Drawing on cultural studies, as well as sociolinguistic and sociological perspectives, this book has identified the emergence of a new and distinctive kind of social and cultural formation amongst young people in Britain of South Asian descent. I recognise at once that the grouping I have studied is not the only type of social and cultural formation discernible among young people of South Asian descent in Britain. The profile of the Blackhill youth is, for instance, heavily weighted in the direction of ethnicities related to an origin in India. There are, of course, other formations in Britain which, had they been studied, would have been strongly inflected towards South Asian ethnicities with origins in Pakistan or Bangladesh. Nevertheless, I am confident that other researchers will find similar forces at work amongst young people of Pakistani and Bangladeshi descent, as those I have found amongst the Blackhill youth. On the other hand, it is certainly the case that in all three of these groups with South Asian connections, there are other tendencies and formations in which the retention and reproduction of traditional cultural stances and practices are very strong, whether related to language, religion or cultural tastes. However, it is the attitudes and behaviours of the latter collectivities which have received the overwhelming proportion of the attention from discourses circulating in government, media, academia, and among the wider public. This book, by contrast, has been about the large, significant, but consistently overlooked formation which I have chosen to name as *Brasian*.

This formation empirically illustrated by the self-representations of the boys and girls of the Blackhill youth in West London in the late 1990s is one I want to label as *Brasian*, for reasons which this chapter will explain. I have arrived at this term as a result of trying to meet challenges posed by Stuart Hall's influential, and linked, theoretical propositions, 'new ethnicities' and 'cultures of hybridity'. In particular, the book has demonstrated what these theoretical constructs might mean and look like at the level of empirical realisation. Secondly, it has shown what the ethnicities of a group of visible minority youth might be like when the research emphasis focuses on the routine, the ordinary and the everyday. Another important consideration foregrounded is the illustration of how the understanding of ethnicity is enriched and clarified when careful and close attention is paid to how ethnic configurations might be structured when reliance on the visual is complemented or partially displaced by a concentration on the aural; in other words when ethnicity is coded through sound as well as through the visual. It is for this reason amongst others that I have placed so much emphasis on listening so closely to the voices of the Blackhill youth. Additionally, the reference to auditory codes has been developed in two important ways. Firstly, listening closely to the informants' voices has facilitated the revelation that the Blackhill youth's ethnic positioning is decisively founded on a bedrock of London Britishness marked by the specifically London English phonological, grammatical, lexical and idiomatic contours of their speech. Secondly, close 'listening' has made it possible to present analytic observations rigorously grounded on the representations offered by the Blackhill youth themselves in rich empirical detail; this, rather than the perhaps more customary practice of using informants' voices and self-representations as no more than an occasional interjection in the analyst's strong and previously established unequivocal categorisations. The research data and analysis in this book has enabled a refinement of the implication of dichotomy inherent in the term 'new' in 'new ethnicities', and the actually stated dichotomy in Hall's concept of 'translation' (Hall, 1992a), which generated his notion of 'cultures of hybridity'; and which appeared again in the title of one of his heavily cited articles, 'Old and new identities, old and new ethnicities' (Hall, 1991). More precisely, the sense of binary opposites in the new versus old dichotomy, and the sense of separate and clearly bounded cultures in the notion of 'translation' are limitations which I have attempted to transcend. This has been achieved, principally, by utilising Raymond Williams' indicative theoretical formulations referring to the constant co-presence in culture of residual, emergent and dominant elements. It is specifically the constant co-presence of residual traditional elements *and* newer emergent elements in the flow of their everyday lives which helps to mark the Blackhill youth as *Brasians*. One element does not erase another, but at any particular moment one or another might well be more accentuated. Before commenting further on the emergence of *Brasian* identities, it is worth clarifying and summarising the processes which bring them about.

New ethnicities and language use

This book has taken Hall's 'new ethnicities' and 'cultures of hybridity' as points of departure, and deliberately treated them as givens; sources of stimulation and inspiration, and has eschewed the opportunity to enter into an extended discussion of the nature of ethnicity and hybridity as general concepts. What interested me more was the discovery in my research data of a picture far more complex than the notion of new ethnicities versus old ethnicities, or of new cultures of hybridity as opposed to traditional, supposedly static and homogeneous cultures. The density of the empirical complexity encountered was amply demonstrated in Chapter 4, and extended and further deepened in Chapters 5, 6 and 7. These chapters established how new ethnicities and cultures of hybridity were linked to dimensions involving language, communities of practice, and the development of popular cultural tastes. Taking the language dimension first, I have demonstrated that while in every area of their lives the Blackhill youth evidenced their fundamental Britishness, this Britishness was anchored and embodied in a local specificity as represented in the Londonness of their patterns of language use. As Gunew, has commented, 'language remains the most portable of accessories one which has carved out a corporeal space' (Gunew, 2003: 41); in the case of the Blackhill youth one accessory which they carry at all times, particularly in their embodied phonology is their Londonness. And yet this embodiment of the local is also at all times deeply intertwined with a routine interaction with the globally diasporic in language in two forms. One form, suggestive of inherited tradition (for instance Panjabi, Gujarati, Hindi and Urdu), the other indicating the recently emergent (for instance Upspeak and other global teenage language forms), or the gradually appropriated (for instance Jamaican Creole or African American Vernacular English).

Overall, the linguistic dimension of the 'new ethnicities' and 'cultures of hybridity' described in this book, is constituted in varying intricate combinations of these very different linguistic elements in ways which were illustrated particularly sharply in Chapter 5. However, these 'new ethnicities' and 'cultures of hybridity' are not consituted in and through patterns of language use alone. Chapter 6 has shown how these patterns of language use are subtly linked with interlocking communities of practice which can be both lived and imagined; which can be both peer (same-age) related or cross-generational; which can be both profoundly local in a London British sense and at the same time inescapably connected with diasporically inscribed global formations. Such diasporic communities of practice are not necessarily primarily constituted in and around language practices as such, although these may well play a significant part. They are also, for instance, constructed around widely shared experiences of identification with, and participation in, religious observance, rituals, festivals, and trips to parental and grandparental homelands. Participation in voluntary community education efforts intended to secure the maintenance of traditional patterns of language use, historical knowledge and cultural practices may well also be involved. The nature of these communities of practice makes them some of the prime sites in which the workings of the residual/traditional, the emergent and the dominant in cultural practices can be observed in routine co-occurrence. It is also important to emphasise that in refusing the old versus new dichotomy in the analysis of ethnicities, I am arguing that the Blackhill youth, whether or not they were enthusiastic or lukewarm participants in communities of practice which are marked by traces of the old or the traditional in culture, showed no overt or strong signs of rejection or complete disavowal of these practices. They are active participants in, and co-constructors of, communities of practice which are dominated by their British inflections *at the same time as* incorporating elements drawn from, cultural practices symbolically associated with the residual/traditional originating from the global South Asian diasporas. Such practices, for example religious ones, may in turn be relatively dominant and prominent, or relatively backgrounded at any given moment or in any given context. Cross-cutting these intersecting dimensions of language and communities of cultural practices, is a third dimension concerned with the formation of popular cultural tastes.

   Again, here, the Blackhill youth representations conflict with perhaps more conventional accounts in which the formation of popular cultural tastes is heavily associated with patterns of cultural consumption somewhat stereotypically linked to what are regarded as traditional 'Asian' forms like bhangra music or Hindi films. By contrast, the Blackhill youth represent themselves as inhabiting an environment in which the dominant patterns of popular cultural taste and practice to which they feel strongly affiliated are very similar to those of other British teenagers of their age, locality and social positioning; while at all times they have available to them, either in heightened prominent form, or in low-key background ways, the popular cultural products of the South Asian diaspora. Some of the intricacies of this relationship were strongly outlined in Chapter 7.

In sum, the 'new ethnicities' of the Blackhill youth can be characterised as follows. As far as language is concerned, English language is dominant in most circumstances and this can be seen most clearly in Chapters 3, 4 and 5; and within this the London English variant is the most commanding. However, languages like Panjabi, Gujarati, Hindi and Urdu, are ever-present, either as part of the background soundscape as they are routinely used by close relatives, or other individuals in the community, or foregrounded at specific moments in their own speech exhanges, particularly in communication with their grandparents, parents, older relatives or other community elders. On the other hand, although a variety of inherited languages other than English suffuse their everyday environment, the Blackhill youth's engagement with them in the dimension of literacy is particularly weak. Their declared severe deficiences in reading and writing the languages, first indicated in Chapter 3, are more marked than their admitted uncertainties in understanding and speaking them, and may be influenced by the difficulties they have encountered in coping with the additional scripts integral to Panjabi, Gujarati and Hindi/Urdu literacies. As British children, their everyday experience from the age of five to the age of 16 is dominated by the compulsory acquisition of Standard English literacy throughout every aspect of their school lives, which utilises for this purpose the Roman alphabet. Contrastingly, for the Blackhill youth, apart from brief spells at community language classses, focused encounters with the radically different scripts associated with Panjabi (Gurmukhi script), Gujarati (Devanagari script), Hindi (Sanskrit-influenced Devanagari script), Urdu (Arabic-Persian script), have been fleeting and intermittent. The nature of their orientation to languages like Panjabi, Gujarati, Hindi and Urdu, plays a significant role in the kinds of ethnicities and cultures of hybridity which they construct in a number of different domains. This applies whether these pertain to religion (Chapter 6), travels to global diaspora locations (Chapter 6), interaction with popular culture in the form of Hindi films, Hindi film song lyrics or Bhangra music lyrics (Chapter 7), or radio and TV broadcasts directed at 'Asian' populations (Chapter 7). Additionally, there is in the mix, the language of black youth – African American or London Caribbean, whether or not this is assumed or experienced vicariously.

Highlighting the salience of everyday language use in the formation and enactment of 'new ethnicities' and 'cultures of hybridity', represents, perhaps, an unusual intervention in debates on the nature of ethnicity in contemporary British contexts. One linguist, Edgar Schneider has drawn attention to three related research propositions amongst variationist sociolinguists: (1) 'Show me how you speak, and I'll tell you where you're from!' (2) 'Show me how you speak, and I'll tell you who you are and which group you belong to!' (3) 'Show me how you speak and I'll tell you who you want to be!' (Schneider, 2000: 359–61). All of these propositions in differing ways are pertinent to the importance of questions of language in understanding the composition of new ethnicities. However, my own formulation might better approximate to the more cautious, 'Show me how you speak, and share with me your representations of language use in your life, and I'll show you how your ethnicities are partially but significantly constituted!'. My argument is not that the Blackhill youth's new ethnicities are wholly constituted around their orientations to language, but rather that the constitution of these ethnicities is to be found in the densely entangled interrelationship between the young people's positionings on language and the intersecting communities of practice they inhabit, and the popular cultural tastes and practices with which they are involved.

The importance of the everyday

An important ingredient in the perception of emergent ethnicities is the angle of the researcher's gaze. In this book relentless empirical attention has been paid to the routine, everyday and unspectacular markings of ethnicity and culture. This contrasts with studies of youth, including visible minority youth, which concentrate on the practices of the spectacular minorities in a cohort of young people. This means that I have not taken up opportunities to skew the research in the direction of (a) any minorities who may have been members of transgressive groups like gangs or (b) vivid representations within families of relatively essentialised and homogenised traditional conservative cultural formations or (c) individuals like Amaljeet or Karwan who may have been prominent members of the tiny minority of cultural innovators and leaders within the popular cultural arena in their generation (Chapter 4). Overall, the analysis offers a glimpse of what 'new ethnicities' and 'cultures of hybridity' might look like from the perspective of a putative 'silent majority' of a section of visible minority youth of South Asian descent who are *ordinary*. In this, prime importance has been accorded to their voices; what they have to say about themselves and how they say it.

However, trying to empirically realise these ambitions presents a number of challenges. First of all, if, as Stuart Hall suggests, in relation to 'cultures of hybridity', 'there are more and more examples of them to be discovered' (Hall, 1992a: 310), and at the same time they are to be perceived with a rigorously anti-essentialist eye, how is the resulting empirical complexity and density to be conveyed to the reader? The problem becomes even more difficult when one considers that any genuine attempt at an anti-essentialist approach necessarily involves deferring definitive theoretical formulations and interpretive judgements on ethnicity until careful, elaborate and respectful attention has been paid to a dense description of the informants' representational accounts of their own ethnic and cultural worlds from *their own* points of view. As Geertz has stated in an extended discussion on the notion of 'thick description' in ethnography within anthropological traditions, one task is, 'setting down the meaning particular social actions have for the actors whose actions they are ...' (Geertz, 1993: 27). Geertz argues that anthropologists attempt to achieve this using data which, 'are really our own constructions of other people's constructions of what they and their compatriots are up to' (*ibid*.: 9). Further, he usefully adds, the researcher's data collection yields,

a multiplicity of complex conceptual structures, many of them superimposed upon or knotted into one another, which are at once strange, irregular, and inexplicit, and which he must contrive somehow first to grasp and then to render.

(*ibid*.: 10)

I first attempted to address these difficult problems in Chapter 4. There I invited the reader to become immersed in extended and thickly described informants' accounts of their own patterns of language use and how these interact with other everyday elements in the rich tapestry of their culturally and ethnically positioned lives. These descriptive accounts, or portraits as I called them, drawn from a variety of data sources, were intended to be relatively unmediated by analytic and interpretive interventions. They were meant to offer the reader a deep 'feel' for the nature of the kinds of social formation under investigation, prior to the making of strong and neat interpretive judgements, which perhaps constitute a more customary, and, I would argue, premature procedure. In presenting Chapter 4 in this way I also exercised caution with respect to the ontological status of the chapter. On the one hand it was clear that what was offered in the chapter were informants' representations, not accounts of a would-be transparent social reality. On the other hand I *do* claim that the repetition of regularities in independent individual representations of the same social context is a way of uncovering some form of structured social reality. As Geertz suggests in relation to some of his own research informants, 'setting them in the frame of their own banalities ... dissolves their opacity' (Geertz, 1993: 14). In my work, inviting the reader to 'feel' a structured reality, was justified by reference to Williams' notion of 'structures of feeling' in the description and analysis of cultural formations (Williams, 1977, 1992); and also to Schutz's delineations of the 'life-world' and 'the stock of knowledge' (Schutz, 1970; Ritzer, 1992). At the same time my claim to have portrayed a structured social formation in Chapter 4 is at all times held in check by a strong sense of the agency of the individual social actors portrayed, acknowledging the value of Thompson's challenging requirements (Thompson, 1968, 1978). As Geertz has again helpfully pointed out,

> Understanding a people's culture exposes their normalness without reducing their particularity ... The aim is to draw large conclusions from small, but very densely textured facts; to support broad assertions about the role of culture in the construction of collective life by engaging them exactly with complex specifics.
>
> (Geertz, 1993: 15, 28)

The portraits presented in Chapter 4 taken together with the analyses and interpretive commentaries offered in Chapters 5, 6 and 7, try to enact Geertz's requirements. It is in this process that it becomes possible to describe *Brasian* identities. That is to say a particular kind of cultural formation saturated with symbols of Britishness, but inflected in a variety of complex ways ranging across a number of customs, practices and dispositions drawn from the global South Asian diaspora, and related to specific communities, religions, linguistic groups and popular cultural forms.[1] Before returning, finally, to the nature of *Brasian* identities, I want to further draw out two other considerations important to the uncovering of these identities.

Thinking with the ears as well as the eyes

A research approach resting on a procedure which relies on paying close and detailed attention to informants' 'voices', whether directly through interviews and their self-made audio recordings or figuratively through their written accounts and completed questionnaire surveys, opens the path to a particular way of studying and understanding ethnicity. Typically, the study of ethnicity within British Cultural Studies or Sociology has concentrated on the understandings to be gained through the deployment of visual codes which inevitably lead to an unwavering focus on the fixities associated with racial phenotypes, notwithstanding anti-esentialist claims to constant fluidity and change. This book's approach, by contrast, demonstrates the possibilities for expanded understandings of ethnicity by suggesting what can be achieved by, as it were, 'thinking with the ears' (Bull and Back, 2003), rather than the more customary 'thinking with the eyes'. As Bull and Back have powerfully commented,

> In the hierarchy of the senses, the epistemological status of hearing has come a poor second to that of vision ... The reduction of knowledge to the visual has placed serious limitations on our ability to grasp the meanings attached to much social behaviour ... . Thinking with our ears offers an opportunity to augment our critical imaginations, to comprehend our world and our encounters with it according to multiple registers of feeling.
>
> (Bull and Back, 2003: 1–2)

As I have alluded, the consequence of taking up such perspectives, is the paying of explicit attention not only to *what* informants say, but also to *how* they say it. This clearly has some ontological implications. *What* they say operates as representation not reality; *how* they say it has strong claims to the real. The approach I have adopted suggests that studies of ethnicity and culture in British contexts can no longer be considered adequate without explicit acknowledgement of the importance of both the actual as well as the claimed patterns of language use of ordinary social actors in everyday contexts. As Chapter 5 noted, talking and/or listening to the talk of others, occupies most of the waking hours of most ordinary human beings worldwide. How then can any adequate account of the ethnicities or cultures of any social group reasonably ignore how they use or claim to use language? Giving even modest attention to how the Blackhill youth talk allows one to see beyond the distractions of racial phenotypes, and religious or cultural labels, to perceive the central seam of their Britishness; more specifically the Londonness running through their linguistic and cultural practices. The embodiment of their Londonness through the phonology, but also the grammar, idiom and lexis of London English was particularly emphasised in Chapter 5. It was also further underlined elsewhere in the book whenever the speech of individual members of the Blackhill youth is directly quoted, by the device of marking the most commonly occurring signifiers of their London speech – their extensive T–glottalling. At the same time they are simultaneously linked through their routine, everyday

speech to general manifestations of pan-ethnic globalised teenage identities, by markers of speech such as 'Upspeak' or 'Australian Questioning
Intonation' and the use of 'like' with the verb to be as a quotative marker.
As ever, alongside all of these contemporary features of language are reten-
sions of the inherited South Asian and other languages.

The Past and the Present in the Present

To the extent that these noted speech characteristics are what is most
marked about the Blackhill youth's speech, they might be said to be representative of new emergent elements in their ethnicities and 'cultures
of hybridity'. This view, though, is complicated by the question of what
might be regarded as dominant at any given moment. For the Blackhill
youth, while their London English and global teenage language use is
virtually ever-present, at any given moment other varieties of language
may appear dominant. For instance, Panjabi, Gujarati, Hindi or Urdu, as
representatives of the residual/traditional might achieve dominance at
given moments in family or community settings, just as Standard
English does continuously in the domain of schooling.

Raymond Williams' suggestion that cultural formations might best be
understood in terms of the synchronic and syncretic occurrence of the
residual, the emergent and the dominant, enables me to add another
element to this study of ethnicity in Britain. I propose a way of moving
beyond the implied dichotomy of old versus new in the study of ethnicity or even ethnicities. The 'new ethnicities' and 'cultures of hybridity'
of the Blackhill youth are best described not in terms of what is old in
opposition to what is new, but in terms of the synchronic and syncretic
occurrence of the emergent, residual and dominant. Thus, following the
title the anthropologist Maurice Bloch gave to one of his papers, I argue
that what can be seen is, 'The Past and the Present in The Present'
(Bloch, 1977). This tendency emerges, for example, whether the object
of study is language specifically (Chapters 3 and 5), family, religious or
general community cultural practices (Chapter 6), or popular cultural
tastes (Chapter 7). In each case the balance of forces favours general
underlying contemporary British derived practices; but practices inherited
from past traditions are also always present and available for use.

The emergence of Brasian identities

Finally, what can be more precisely said about what I have chosen to
call *Brasian* identities? Firstly, I recognise the existence of significant

specificities related to Sikh, Hindu and Muslim ethnicities and cultural spaces, both within and outside British geographical locations. I also recognise particularities related, for instance, to East African, Indian, Pakistani, Bangladeshi, Singaporean and Mauritian experiences, or to Panjabi, Gujarati, Hindi and Urdu linguistic environments. Nevertheless, in this book I have identified and traced the contours of a definite and distinct instance of an emergent cultural formation within a 'new ethnicities' and 'cultures of hybridity' frame. This formation relates to young people of South Asian descent born or brought up in Britain. The proposition is that a formation such as that represented in the Blackhill youth research be referred to broadly as constituting emergent *Brasian* identities, comprised of collections of Brasian ethnicities and cultures of hybridity.

I first encountered the label *Brasian* in the hyphenated form 'Br–Asian' in the work of Kalra and Kalra (1996). These authors claimed ownership of what they said they were proposing as a new term referring to the,

> complex subject positions of migrants and their offspring settled in Britain with links both imagined and material to South Asia. It is intended to be an open term, beginning the exploration of shifting identifications and representations.
>
> (Kalra and Kalra, 1996: 219)

They go on to critique the more familiar term 'British Asian' since it, 'essentializes both terms, as well as hierarchizing the former against the latter' (*ibid.*: 219). I concur with this judgement but suggest that perhaps the hyphenation of the term as Br–Asian achieves a similar effect. I therefore propose the fused term *Brasian* as a way of partly overcoming the implied essentialised dichotomy with its hint of 'hierarchization'. Kalra and Kalra's main focus is popular music, yet they see the term Br–Asian as having a wider utility as it,

> is intended both to be disruptive of the centre-margin relationship and to destabilize fixed notions of Asian identities, stressing their contingency on historical and spacial moments.
>
> (*ibid.*: 221)

This characterisation coincides quite closely with what I envisage as useful about *Brasian*, although my research with the Blackhill youth demonstrates a greater certainty than the Kalras and others that, across a range of practices, Britishness is primary. It must be reiterated with special emphasis that the proposition that there are emergent *Brasian* identities in urban locations like London is in no way to be read as merely a new homogenising, essentialist or even crypto-assimilationist label. What is being suggested, as I have extensively shown, is a dense and complexly interwoven enactment of ethnicities in the interstitial textures of every-day life. This book has gone out of its way to illustrate the openness, variability and unpredictability of the *Brasian* formulation. Having said this, whatever the specificities of particular South Asian ethnicities, and however densely configured these might be with patterns of Britishness, I nevertheless argue that *Brasian* holds good. This is because it captures the way that Britishness is always there, deeply rooted, especially in the embodied and therefore inescapable form of everyday language use. One small example might serve to illustrate the tenacity of these effects. In 2002 a number of British newspapers reported on the case of Shafiq Rasul, a 24-year-old of Pakistani descent from the West Midlands town of Tipton who had been accused of fighting with the Taliban in Afghanistan and was now detained by the Americans in Camp X–Ray in Cuba. Two reporters from the The Sunday Mirror were invited into his family home in order to speak to his mother and brothers and build up a portrait of him. The following are some salient extracts from their report:[2]

'Shafiq was born in West Bromwich in 1977 ... attended the Roman Catholic Sacred Heart Primary School ... has a broad Brummie accent ... interested in girls and nightclubs ... had several white girl-friends ... [often] talking on his mobile phone to women [once went] camping in Wales ... too scared to spend even one night in a tent he wanted to go to a bed and breakfast ... listening to gangsta rap ... following the fortunes of his favourite football team Liverpool[3] and showing off his designer clothes ... a small bookcase in his home con-taining books written in Punjabi and English ... [played in the] Tipton Muslim Community Centre football team ... the furthest he'd travelled before was on a Club 18–30 holiday to Benidorm the year before ... Shafiq Rasul was wearing his favourite top – A Ralph Lauren American stars and stripes jumper when he flew to Pakistan last October ... off to do a computer programming course at university in Lahore'.

Here, then, is a young man at a moment of perhaps ultimate disavowal of Britishness, who has Britishness inscribed in his body through his Brummie accent.[4] He has strong British affiliations represented through his attachments to, and experiences of, everyday cultural practices. Yet at the same time he retains very real diaspora connections and possibilities as well as continuing local muslim and Panjabi language connections. This is a *Brasian* identity. As argued above, it is a concept retaining openness, variablity and unpredictablity, but its contours can be both clearly discerned and imagined.

The soundness of the idea of *Brasian* identities would also appear to be strengthened by one other expression of the formulation that I have been able to find. This is a London-based British organisation, led by individuals of South Asian descent, which is known as Br–Asian Media Consultancy, and describes itself as, 'a Public Relations (PR) and Marketing consultancy that focuses on communicating with the British Asian audience, in particular the youth sector' (www.Brasian.com, 2003). One significant section of the Frequently Asked Questions area of this company's website, reads as follows,

'Aren't young Asians mainly into Bhangra and Bollywood?'
'British Asian youth and middle youth are into the same predominantly urban music and pastimes as the rest of the population'.

Both of the proponents of the label Br–Asian cited in the present chapter, reference popular cultural production, especially music, TV and film as arenas in which ready evidence of the emergence of this cultural formation is apparent. Neither is as emphatic as I am about the weighting in favour of the British dimension. Nevertheless, it is plausibly arguable that films such as *East is East, Bhaji on the Beach,* or *Bend it Like Beckham,* and British TV series like *Goodness Gracious Me* and *The Kumars at No. 42,* are highly suggestive markers from within expressive culture of a broad *Brasian* identity embracing overlapping *Brasian* ethnicities. There is also evidence that elements of the print media are, in their own way, attempting to grapple with the idea. One newspaper, published by Ashoka Publishing Ltd. from London in 2001, was called 'BRITasian'. A glossy magazine, publishing from London in 2003 and aimed at prosperous young professionals with Indian diaspora sensibilities and links, calls itself 'indobrit'.

The emergent *Brasian* identity represented by the Blackhill youth is also linked to an apparently emergent *Desi* identity in North America which is beginning to attract academic interest (Maira 1998, 1999; Dawson 2002). According to Maira,

Desi literally means native of a *desh* ("country") and in the context of South Asian diasporic communities in the United States is used as a colloquial term to refer to those of South Asian descent, invoking a pan-ethnic rather than nationally bounded category. In India, it is sometimes used more pejoratively to index a "country-bumpkin" sensibility.

(Maira, 1999: 55)

Indeed both Maira and Dawson indicate that a significant element of *Desi* culture is a selection of musical styles generated by young people of South Asian descent in Britain in the late 1980s and early 1990s. In fact the term desi is gaining popular ground amongst younger people of South Asian descent in the United Kingdom itself. The BBC digital radio station 1Xtra which describes itself as a home for 'new black music', houses the Panjabi Hit Squad's *Desi Beats* show; the BBC 2 television channel has broadcast an 'Asian arts and entertainment show' entitled *Desi DNA*; an entertainment newspaper aimed at young people is called *DesiXpress* (www.desiexpress.co.uk). These developments are another expression of the kinds of forces described throughout this book and which I have chosen to call *Brasian*. They express the growing felt necessity to link the governing reality of a local rooted British existence with the continuing affective pull of the global diaspora. It also expresses something else. Namely, the beginnings of a discernible drift among some young people of South Asian descent towards some sense of collective grouping around certain racialised points of 'Asian' unity; that is to say, the condition of being a brown skinned person of South Asian descent in Britain. After all, since 9/11 and more specifically since the London bombings of July 2005, the British police services have directed their stopping and searching activities at young men who look 'South Asian';[5] a practice which does not differentiate between Sikhs, Muslims and Hindus, or between Panjabi, Gujarati, or Hindi/Urdu speakers. These pressures towards a unity of racialised experience are reminiscent of those which occurred amongst young people of Caribbean descent more than 30 years ago.[6] Their parents had migrated to Britain from a wide variety of British colonial possessions in the Caribbean islands and Guyana in South America, with fierce and distinctive island loyalties. These allegiances were eventually substantially eroded as pressures from racially hostile forces in Britain forced the emergence of a relatively unified defensive African-Caribbean social formation dominated by its Jamaican component. This is not to claim that pressures towards unity represented by the *Brasian* formation will be anything like as swift to consolidate, nor as strong. The traditional linguistic, religious and cultural differences are probably too deeply rooted for that. Nevertheless, it is likely that *Brasian* identities *will* consolidate, becoming more entrenched and increeasingly powerful over time, challenging other more centrifugal forces. I suggest that the emergence of *Desi* identity and ethnicities is somewhat analagous to the *Brasian* identity and ethnicities I have sought to identify. Their co-existence supports my contention in Chapter 6 that the Blackhill youth are connected in both material and imagined ways to certain global diasporic communities of practice. Of course, the sense of self and social life described in this book could be dismissed as simply an instance of a classic adolescent liminal period, with the resumption of 'normal service' in the form of the reinstatement of traditional ethnic and cultural identity and practice occurring once adulthood arrives. I dispute this interpretation. Certainly, it is likely that there will be some movement in this direction during adulthood, at least rhetorically. However, in my view the processes reported by the Blackhill youth are too profound to be readily reversed, and in particular I see no prospect of the perceptible language shift being easily reversed in any mass significant way.

To sum up then, two general questions remain. Firstly, how representative are the Blackhill youth of Brasian identity as a whole? Secondly, to what extent is the Brasian identity paralleled in a more general way by similarly structured emergent cultural formations in other ethnic sub-groups elsewhere in Britain? On the first issue, it is clear that the Blackhill youth are just one tightly researched cultural formation; one particularly related to contemporary global diasporic and inherited historic links tied in one way or another to India. I would expect to find, under the broad canvas of *Brasian* identity, cultural formations of youth with similar contours to those of the Blackhill youth, except with contemporary connections and inheritances linked with, for example, Pakistan (Qureshi and Moores, 1999; Saeed *et al.*, 1999) or Bangladesh (Alexander, 2000; Desai 2000). I would also expect to find other cultural formations of *Brasian* youth who are not so strongly marked by Britishness, who *do* proficiently understand, speak, read and write their inherited community languages, who have a strong religious allegiance accompanied by informed practice. These youth also retain an active and enjoyed identification and physical contact with parental and grandparental homelands, and strongly support the conservative maintenance of traditional South Asian norms and ideals of cultural practice in their communities in Britain. It would seem to me that there is ample scope here for further research, particularly, I would suggest, research conducted by people who are relative ethnic and community insiders, with competence in community languages and lifelong experience of the cultual practices and experiences of their own British-born youthful generation. The other speculation worth putting forward in passing, is that social formations resembling the *Brasian* ones are likely amongst other visible minority youth in Britain who are members of migrant families. Pang (1999) with reference to youth of Chinese descent in London provides an illustrative research example, but other examples are awaiting similar research among, for example, youth of say Somali or Kurdish descent.

Bulmer and Solomos (1998), referring to Gilroy's reminder about the urgent need to transcend the analytic category of race and thereby to think afresh about anti-racist ideas and policies, stated the need to, 'provoke reflection about how to reconceptualize the phenomena of ethnicity and race' (*ibid.*: 835). This book has tried hard to provoke reflection on these matters. As Hanif Kureishi has lamented, about the experience of visible minority young people in Britain in his youth, 'I mean the thing about race is what it does to you is that when you (sic) when somebody sees you they have ideas about you they have a lot of ideas about you that you probably don't have about them and that was really shocking' (Kureishi, 2003). It is to be hoped that this book, in its portrayal of the Blackhill youth, has made a small contribution to the slowing down, unsettling and disruption of such assumptions.

Appendices

Appendix A: Profile of the Blackhill youth

Name	Sex	Main family language besides English	Family religious affiliation
Amaljeet	m	Panjabi	Sikh
Amar	m	Panjabi	Hindu
Amod	m	Gujarati	Hindu
Amrita	f	Panjabi	Sikh
Bahiyaa	f	Panjabi	Hindu
Dhrishaj	m	Panjabi	Sikh
Diya	f	Gujarati	Hindu
Gurleetaa	f	Panjabi	Sikh
Gurshanti	f	Panjabi	Sikh
Japdev	m	Panjabi	Sikh
Jasjoti	f	Panjabi	Sikh
Julie	f	Swahili	Christian/Catholic
Karwan	m	Kurdish	Muslim
Keshav	m	Gujarati	Hindu
Manika	f	Gujarati	Hindu
Narjot	m	Panjabi	Sikh
Nashita	f	Gujarati	Hindu
Neetaa	f	Panjabi	Sikh
Patwant	m	Panjabi	Sikh
Premila	f	Gujarati	Hindu
Punamdeep	f	Panjabi	Sikh
Rishab	m	Panjabi	Hindu
Sachdev	m	Panjabi	Sikh
Sahima	f	Gujarati	Hindu
Sarah	f	Panjabi	Christian
Shanice	f	Jamaican Creole	Christian
Shariqah	f	Urdu	Muslim
Suhir	f	French Creole	Muslim
Sumandev	m	Panjabi	Sikh
Vishnu	m	Gujarati	Hindu

Appendix B: Blackhill youth – parents' jobs

Name	Sex	Mother's job	Father's job
Amaljeet	m	chef	builder
Amar	m	office worker	post office parcels & letters delivery
Amod	m	credit control manager	sales director electrical retailer
Amrita	f	housewife/unemployed	factory supervisor
Bahiyaa	f	Housewife	BT telephone engineer
Dhrishaj	m	factory worker	warehouse operative
Diya	f	housewife	post office worker
Gurleetaa	f		disabled
Gurshanti	f	building society clerk	airline ground crew worker
Japdev	m	catering worker	bakery worker
Jasjoti	f	hospital secretary	airline ground crew worker
Julie	f	unemployed	motor mechanic
Karwan	m	information not available	information not available
Keshav	m	primary school teacher	mechanical engineer
Manika	f	housewife	computer engineer
Narjot	m	nurse	psychiatric nurse
Nashita	f	factory worker	office accounts clerk
Neetaa	f	school dinner lady	construction engineer
Patwant	m	admin/secretary	worker with homeless
Premila	f	housewife	motor mechanic
Punamdeep	f	housewife (former factory worker)	quality controller
Rishab	m	information not available	bus driver
Sachdev	m	information not available	information not available
Sahima	f	biscuit packer	credit controller
Sarah	f	nurse	driving instructor
Shanice	f	factory worker	car exhaust fitter
Shariqah	f	care assistant	airline fork lift driver
Suhir	f	information not available	information not available
Sumandev	m	package labeller	printer
Vishnu	m	unemployed factory worker	unemployed factory worker

Appendix C: Blackhill School ethnic and linguistic monitoring data

Pupil number by ethnic origin*

Ethnic Origin	Total Number	%
Any other group	58	4.4
Bangladeshi	6	0.5
Black-African	37	2.8
Black-Caribbean	43	3.2
Black-Other	24	1.8
Chinese	3	0.2
Indian	902	67.9
Pakistani	107	8.0
Unclassified	14	1
White	134	10

Pupil number by mother tongue

Mother Tongue	Total Number	%
Bengali	12	0.9
Cantonese	2	0.5
English	264	19.9
Gujarati	149	11.2
Hindi	49	3.7
Italian	8	0.6
Other	86	6.5
Panjabi	653	49.2
Turkish	2	0.15
Unclassified	23	1.7
Urdu	80	6

* The figures in this appendix are for the academic year in which the Blackhill youth entered Blackhill School.

Notes

1 Introduction

1 In 2006 these young people will be 24 years old.
2 Throughout the book, for ease of reference, I will refer to my research informants by the collective label 'the Blackhill Youth' and their school as Blackhill
   School. These are pseudonyms in line with undertakings of confidentiality
   which I gave to the research participants and to their school 'gatekeepers'.
3 At a number of points I refer to 'visible' ethnic minorities. This is to indicate
   ethnic groups marked by skin colour – black or brown – in opposition to
   dominant British discourses which use terms like 'ethnic' or 'ethnicity' as a
   coded way of referring to black and brown people alone, while retaining white
   people as an unmarked norm, and thus, by implication, without ethnicity.
4 Linguistic Minorities Project 1985 *The Other Languages of England*. London:
   Routledge and Kegan Paul.
5 I am indebted to Les Back for this phrase.

2 Researching Ethnicities and Cultures

1. CCCS refers to the renowned Centre for Contemporary Cultural Studies at
    Birmingham University which was founded by Richard Hoggart.
2. Ali (2003) and the present volume represent other examples. Hall's 'New
    Ethnicities' theoretical formulation remains one of the most influential
    anti-essentialist formulations on 'race' and ethnicity to have emerged from
    the British Cultural Studies tradition and its reach has extended far beyond
    this sphere.
3. Blackhill is a pseudonym in line with undertakings of confidentiality I
    volunteered when seeking permission to research at the school.
4. According to Baumann the population of Southall in the 1991 National
    Census was 'Indian' (50%), 'Pakistani' (7%), 'Other Asian' (3%), 'White'
    (30%), 'Black-Caribbean' (5%), 'Other categories' (5%).
5. In 1988 the Conservative Government legislated to allow schools to become
    Grant Maintained by opting out of Local Education Authority control after a
    ballot of parents. This enabled GM schools to control their finances and
    development. They remained as comprehensive schools but with a small
    margin of control over their intake.
6. Approximately 19 hours of recorded interview data in total.
7. My perception of typical approaches to linguistic diversity teaching was
    gained from many years of experience of visiting classrooms across London
    and of working with teachers in In-Service Training contexts.
8. See Goulbourne, 1998: 25–49, for a brief account of this process.
9. See Brah, in Back and Solomos (eds) 2000: 431–446, for a relatively minor
    but deeply felt example.

3   Language Use and Ethnicity: Mapping the Terrain

1. The language whose current official designation is Panjabi was overwhelmingly written as 'Punjabi', while the current official label Gujarati was rendered variously as 'Gujrati' and 'Gujerati' as well as 'Gujarati'. 'Persian' was used where perhaps it is in contemporary terms more usual to see the term Farsi. There is some suggestion that the variations may be connected with older, often colonial, versions of the spellings. For example, according to Dalby (1998: 486) 'Punjab is an old-fashioned Anglo-Indian spelling of the word' [Panjab], and White (1991: 232) writes of 'the Anglicized term "Persian" which in English denotes Farsi'.
2. It should be noted that the 'experts' in the Linguistic Minorities Project were using the spelling 'Gujerati' as late as the mid-1980s (Linguistic Minorities Project 1985).
3. Space does not permit a detailed discussion of the relative meanings of the terms 'ethnicity' and 'identity'. In this book I have used 'ethnicity' to suggest a collection of fluid practices and allegiancies in which individuals are engaged. I use 'identity' to imply relatively stable perceived positionings of alleged attributes which individuals claim during moments of reflection and from which they often appear to draw some comfort.
4. This reference is evidently to the kinds of Jamaican Creole language use associated with Rastafarians and globally circulated through the widespread popularity of reggae music.

4   New Ethnicities As Lived Experience

1. My intention to present their accounts of their cultural experience in their own voices as assiduously and copiously as space allows does, of course, raise questions of the politics of transcription. A number of authors (Roberts, 1997; Lapadat, 2000; Bucholtz, 2000) have commented on the paradox that while transcription is integral to the qualitative analysis of language data and is widely used in social research, the theoretical and methodological issues it raises have received very little attention. According to Roberts, 'all transcription is representation, and there is no natural or objective way in which talk can be written' (Roberts, 1997: 168). As she sees it transcription involves an inevitable tension between accuracy, readability and the politics of representation. I decided on the selective use of phonetic linguistic symbols to indicate aspects of the informants' speech which I particularly wanted to highlight. In these cases I did not offer a fully phonetic transcription, but merely drew attention to the salient feature by bracketing it. For example where I wanted to emphasise the T – glottalling characteristic of London speech I did so by inserting the relevant phonetic symbol in the following manner /bu[ʔ]er/ (/bʌʔə/) for /butter/ to indicate the non pronunciation of the /t/ sound in the middle or at the end of words, which is a regular feature of classsic working class London speech. I also decided to include all the marked pauses, ums and ers, sighing, laughter and giggles as well as the instances of overlapping and latched speech because I thought these might be revealing of uncertainties, discomfort, intense engagement or enthusiasm when particular topics were being discussed. I also dispensed

with the punctuation conventions typical of written discourse so as to force attention to the quality of oral interactional discourse which typically does not present itself in well-constructed sentences, as in written language. In these senses my presentation of the informants' spoken accounts is conscious, deliberate and driven by explicit ideological and theoretical purposes.

2. Person knowledgeable about Sikh teachings.
3. Key Sikh religious text.
4. A sword – one of the 5 K'-s which are key symbolic markers of Sikhism.
5. See Rampton (1995) for some of the interactional processes involved in this kind of phenomenon.
6. The dhol drum is a key instrument used in the production of bhangra, a traditional music of the Punjab, India.
7. Moesha was a US TV situation comedy/drama which ran from 1996–2001, chronicling the life of a black teenager living in an area of Los Angeles. The lead part was taken by a young woman named Brandy who had a parallel career as a pop/r&b singer.
8. The use of a rising tone at the end of a phrase implying a question when no question is intended, sometimes referred to in the linguistics literature as uptalk or upspeak or Australian Questioning Intonation.
9. Pind is the Panjabi word for village.
10. Though Karwan is not from a South Asian background, the milieu he inhabits, including his friendship group, is dominated by South Asian influences. His experience overlaps with that of his Blackhill peers in two other ways. First, he shares with them the experience of being brought up in London in a migrant family. Seccond, as I suggest more fully in Chapter 8, the forces producing 'new ethnicities' and new 'cultures of hybridity' apply, too, to ethnic formations other than those of South Asian descent in Britain.
11. // indicates overlapping speech.
12. (.) indicates a short but noticeable pause.
13. = indicates latched speech.
14. At this point when speaking about Jamaica and the Caribbean there was a marked shift in his pronunciation towards the Caribbean Creole phonological pattern of pronouncing /the/ as /de/.
15. the use of the double colon (::) indicates that the preceding sound is elongated.
16. A popular British TV comedy show on Channel 4 which was based around a cast of black people of mainly Caribbean descent living in London. Porkpie was the nickname of one of the popular characters in the show.
17. He pronounced the word cool without the / l /sound but with a hint of the / w /sound to produce /coow (ku:w)/ in a way characteristic of working class London speech.
18. Originally Hindu annual festival of light celebrated throughout the worldwide Indian diaspora in October/November each year.
19. A nine-night Hindu autumn celebration attended in family groups in which girls in particular particpate in organised programmes of traditional dance.
20. A fasting ritual in June/July observed by female Gujaratis involving abstinence from salt.
21. ... indicates ellipsis – the omission of sections of text.
22. India's first Hindi satellite channel, launched in 1992.

23. Neighbours and Home and Away are soap operas produced in Australia which are highly popular in the UK. Eastenders is one of the most popular soap operas produced in Britain. It purports to portray life in London's East End.
24. ER is an American TV drama series set in a hospital accident and emergency unit. The X-Files is a US produced television science fiction drama series.
25. Independent station originally launched in 1989 to broadcast to West London's Asian community later expanded its reach by other franchises around Britain and more recently by inclusion in satellite TV packages.
26. London commercial radio station specialising in pop music, with an increasing national reach built by acquisitions and franchises.
27. Britain's first and only truly national pop music station, launched in 1967.
28. London radio station which began as a pirate becoming legal in 1990 and specialising in dance music.
29. Hindu religious scholar.
30. Bhagavad Gita one of the most well-known of the Hindu scriptures.
31. Major Hindu festival celebrated usually in November and sometimes known as the 'festival of lights'.
32. Ruislip is another local district to the west of London.
33. See James (1998) for a popular narrative history account, and Visram (2002) for an 'Asian' view of the historical relationship in Britain itself.
34. See *The Independent* newspaper 23 March 2000 for a vivid example from the then British Home Secretary Jack Straw in a story headed 'Straw: Families should adopt Asian values'.
35. Section 11 of the Local Government Act 1966. Since 1999 this funding has come under the heading of the Ethnic Minorities and Travellers Achievement Grant (EMTAG) or the Ethnic Minorities Achievement Grant (EMAG).
36. The Office for Standards in Education is a British government agency charged with the responsibility of inspecting schools and publishing the results in the form of public reports.

5 How You Talk Is Who You Are

1. I am indebted to Les Back for this summarising phrase.
2. It is important to emphasise that this book does not in any way claim to present an extended discussion of the complex matter of what Britishness is. Rather, it argues that in so far as Britishness is rooted in the everyday cultural practices of the peoples who inhabit Britain – as a geographical location – the Blackhill youth are an intimately integral part of it. For an interesting and detailed treatment of some aspects of the question, see Kumar (2003).
3. The survey data analysed in Chapter 3, are offered as representations of reality. The informants' self-made recordings of language use in their lives, offer a mixture of representation and 'reality' in so far as they also contain relatively involuntary phonological and grammatical features in the speech of those heard on these recordings.
4. A sociolinguistic analysis of this kind is promised by an ongoing research project led by Kerswill and Cheshire (2004–07).
5. In the earlier formulation the term 'local multi-racial vernacular' is used.
6. I have chosen not to concentrate as much on London specific lexical items in the speech of the Blackhill youth, although these, too, were copious. In

naturally occurring speech, the selection of lexical items is generally more susceptible to conscious control than phonological or grammatical items.

7. In London speech it is common for the /t/ sound in words such as 'butter' and 'not' to be ommitted so that they are ariculated as /bu[ʔ]er/ (bʌʔə) and /no[ʔ]/ (nɒʔ).

8. During the transcription process I noted not all occurrences of T – glottalling, but simply those which sounded marked and markedly London in their quality. A simple numerical count of 20 of the interview recordings yielded 3541 such occurrences.

9. In this chapter and the remaining chapters in the book the claimed linguistic, religious and ethnic affiliations of the informants are included with their direct quotations as a deliberate device to remind the reader at all times of the claims that the phenomena described are indicative of a broad social formation dominated by young people of South Asian descent, transcending the particularities of any one narrowly drawn ethnic grouping. The (m) and (f) following the quotes indicate male and female respectively.

10. In other words θ is the linguistic symbol expressing the voiceless /th/ sound in speech as in a word like *three*, and ð expresses the voiced /th/ sound as in a word like *mother*.

11. COLT (the Bergen Corpus of London Teenage Language) as the corpus is called, is strong on the facts of the linguistic characteristics exhibited by London teenagers, but is much less surefooted in the ethnographic interpretation of the provenance of these usages particularly where ethnic minority teenagers are concerned. This may be because the scholars involved are Corpus Linguists operating from the Department of English at the University of Bergen in Norway.

12. It was noticeable that a number of the Blackhill youth articulated the tag as /ennit/ as opposed to /innit/. The origin of this usage is not clear but may well be Southall-specific.

13. For historical reasons too complex to pursue here, it has been more common for elders of Caribbean descent to regard Creole language speech addressed to them by youngsters as a mark of a lack of respect, even insolence. I am aware that in many black families of West African descent in Britain it is common for younger members to routinely address elders in linguistically respectful ways similar to those outlined by the Blackhill youth.

14. It is probably highly significant that speakers of Panjabi, Hindi/Urdu and Gujarati routinely add the suffix /ji/ to utterances as a linguistic token emphasising respect or additional respect (Bhardwaj and Wells, 1989: 13; Bhardwaj, 1995: 23; Dave, 1995: 50).

15. The use of the double colon (::) indicates significant elongation of the preceding vowel.

16. Journalistic and academic anecdote in the UK has attributed the spread of this speech feature to British youth to the influence of the popular Australian TV soap operas Neighbours and Home and Away. It is interesting, then, to note that Gillespie (1995), in her research on Southall youth, describes them as avid watchers of Neighbours and devotes a whole chapter to the topic. In the Southall Youth Survey (1989–90), which her research shared with Gerd Baumann, Gillespie (1995: 217) reports that 67 per cent of her sample watched Neighbours every week and 20 per cent watched *Home and Away*.

17. ↑ This inserted symbol indicates that the preceding highlighted phrase was articulated with a rising tone as if accompanying a question rather than the statement which was in fact being made.
18. A calque is a loan-translation or borrowing in which a word or phrase from one language is translated literally word for word into another language to form a new word or phrase there.
19. The colloquialism 'she goes ...' was also strongly visible in Blackhill youth speech.
20. I have not focused on the markedly London nature of a significant amount of the lexical choices of the Blackhill youth 'bunk off' (play truant), 'leg it' (run away, run quickly), 'slag off' (insult, defame). The youth showed a sharp awareness that these and many other usages were ones they might consciously seek to control, especially, according to them, in the presence of teachers.

6 'My Culture', 'My Language', 'My Religion': Communities, Practices and Diasporas

1. Often the proprietary pronouns 'your' and 'our' were used to utter phrases like 'it's good to like be able to read and write in your own language' (Manika, interview), or to refer to 'our language'.
2. As we saw in Chapter 4, Karwan was a notable exception in that he had attended such classes for six years and had no serious complaint against having done so. There were also a very small number of the Blackhill youth who had never attended these classes.
3. // indicates overlapping speech.
4. Edwards (1986) found a similar phenomenon with Caribbean descended youth with respect to the retention of Jamaican Creole language use in the English Midlands in the 1980s. In her research boys were more likely to insert tokens of Jamaican Creole into their English language speech as symbolic markers while girls who did this less, were far more competent speakers of the language at the level of being able to sustain prolonged conversation in it. Sebba (1993), though not so gender specific, found something similar in his research.
5. In Panjabi, /*tuseen*/ the plural form of 'you' is used to show politeness and respect while /*tu*/, the singular form of you, is used to indicate intimacy or even disrespect. Dhrishaj went on to draw a careful comparison with the distinction between /*du*/ the informal form of 'you' in German and /*siezen*/ the most formal and respectful version of 'you' in that language.
6. Hindi language.
7. Although the focus of the present study can be expressed in such terms, these young people needed to negotiate constantly in intricate and often overlapping ways with other local ethnicities with different inflections, such as London Jamaican, London white working class, Somalian and so on.
8. Tupac Shakur a Brooklyn-born rapper, extremely popular and influential with black British youth to this day despite his early violent death in 1996 at the age of 25.
9. The highly developed forms of these rituals is well attested in the sociolinguistic literature. See, for example, Labov (1972), Smitherman (1977) and

Morgan (1998). Hewitt (1986), though, is careful to state that he found in his research no evidence of cussing and abuse rituals having such highly developed and sophisticated systems and this accorded with the evidence emerging from my own research evidence from the Blackhill youth.

10. The expression 'seen' as an affirmation of mutual understanding or being on the same wavelength as an interlocutor emerged from Jamaican Rastafarian speech in the 1970s to become a linguistic symbol of solidarity among many Caribbean-descended youth globally. For this and an extended discussion on the nature and influence of Rastafarian language in general, see Pollard (2000).

11. A popular Hollywood film released in 1993 centred on the story of a Jamaican bobsled team competing in the 1988 US Olympics.

12. ↑ indicates that the preceding word is spoken with a rising intonation.

13. One exception was Karwan who, as indicated in Chapter 4, said he had acquired significant proficiency in speaking Jamaican Creole from close involvement with a Creole speaking Jamaican family in South London during his childhood. Another was Shanice who described her regular encounters with her grandfather's Jamaican Creole speech.

14. Reminiscent again of Hewitt's 1992 formulations 'local multi-ethnic vernacular' or 'community English'.

15. The out of class use of German was also noted by Rampton (1999, 2002) in research also conducted at Blackhill School.

16. Occasional mention was made of some texts being available in English translation.

17. (.) indicates a significant pause.

18. It should also be remembered that a number of the Blackhill youth stated that their parents belonged to different faiths.

19. The two most regular examples of 'mixed marriages' in British social discourses have been with reference to marital unions between black and white people, especially black men and white women, and between Catholics and Protestants in Northern Ireland. Most of the 'mixed marriages' between black and white have taken place routinely and unremarked between ordinary people, but for a high-society, high-profile example see Dutfield (1990), on the public and political scandal in the late 1940s caused by the marriage of Seretse Khama a black political leader from Botswana and Ruth Williams, a middle class white British woman.

20. See *The Independent* newspaper 23 March 2000 for a vivid example from the then British Home Secretary Jack Straw in a story headed, 'Straw: Families should adopt Asian values'.

21. Seven out of the 30 Blackhill youth mentioned in conversation that their parents were separated or divorced. There may have been more but all these revelations emerged unprompted and I chose not to explore them further nor to enquire on this issue with those who did not spontaneously mention it.

22. Associated with the Hindu, Sikh and Muslim religions respectively.

23. While the 2001 UK national census (http://www.statistics.gov.uk) showed that 36 million people (nearly 70%) described themselves as White and Christian, other research (Matheson and Summerfield, 2000), has shown that active Church membership in the main Christian churches declined by almost a third between 1970 and 1990 from 9.3 million to 6.6 million.

24. The broader term Asia is here to accommodate individuals whose parents originated from countries like Malaysia and Singapore.
25. One informant also talked about young cousins from Austria who were German speakers and consequent constraints on communication between them.
26. Geordie is the popular label for natives of the Newcastle area and the vernacular English speech associated with them.
27. // indicates overlapping speech.
28. (..) indicates a lengthy pause.

7 Popular Culture, Ethnicities and Tastes

1. At the time that the research was being conducted the term 'Bollywood' was not as popular in common parlance as a label for Hindi language films as it was to subsequently become, particularly for outsiders. The Blackhill youth called them Hindi films, presumably because they were in Hindi language.
2. A number of the Blackhill boys mentioned Bally Sagoo as a musical artist whose work exemplified this approach and whom they particularly admired. Sagoo grew up in Birmingham with mainly black friends and an intense engagement with reggae and a variety of black Anglo-American musical styles which he subsequently integrated with Hindi film music and other Indian music. The evolution of this kind of innovation has now reached a kind of reverse synthesis at the time of writing, with highly popular contemporary Anglo-American music stars like Madonna, Britney Spears and Craig David explicitly commissioning Bhangra and other Indian-influenced remixes of their work. One producer who has produced this kind of remix for all three is Rishi Rich, a West Londoner of South Asian descent.
3. When Amar says 'done by people here' I take him to be referring to people in Britain as opposed to people in India.
4. During the research Amaljeet compiled a tape of a range of music that he said he listened to and presented it to me, and this range of musical styles dominated the recordings he gave me.
5. It should nevertheless also be noted, that in the self-made audio recording representative of language use in his life, Karwan included a new Kurdish language song which he described as 'mainly political with slight (sic) romantic'.
6. I am aware that a section of South Asian-descended youth in Britain *have* developed these kinds of masculinities in practice and not only vicariously, as Alexander (2000) and Desai (2000), amongst others have begun to show.
7. Coolio is a rapper and hip hop artist originally from the Compton area of Los Angeles notorious for the prevalence of violent gangs. He had an enormous international hit in 1995 with the track *Gangsta's Paradise*.
8. Shanice, for instance, said that, apart from popular music she liked listening to classical music, especially when she was doing yoga.
9. JFM and Horizon were both pirate radio stations specialising in soul and funk music which operated in Britain in the 1980s. Robbie Vincent and Greg Edwards were DJs on legal radio stations in Britain specialising in soul music who became well-known in the 1980s.
10. Damage were a r&b group of five black British boys of Caribbean descent who had success in the British pop charts in the mid-1990s.

11. A P.A. performance refers to an appearance in which artists sing with live microphones to a backing track of their tunes. The absence of accompanying musicians allows record companies to mount extensive promotional tours relatively inexpensively. Using school tours as a niche promotional device with guaranteed captive audiences became popular in the British music industry during the early 1990s; boy bands designed to excite teenage girls were typically involved.

12. Vishnu is referring to compilation albums on which all the tracks are recent pop chart hits.

13. It is important to emphasise, as always in this book, that these tendencies and dispositions are not intended to be taken as universal. A number of girls, like Shanice and others were equally scathing about the production values of Hindi movies.

14. It was noticeable that the Blackhill youth nearly always referred to Hollywood films as English films and Anglo-American popular music as English music. They seemed to use terms like Indian as a contrasting signifier. One would have expected them to talk about American or Hollywood films and American music or British music. So the term 'English' may be an emphatic reference to English *language* films and music. This may well be a necessary clarifying discourse strategy for the Blackhill youth in the highly complex multilingual environment which they inhabit. It could also be an indication of the ambivalence felt by many black and brown people who identify with the term British but distance themselves from the label English which carries connotations of white exclusivity.

15. See Ofcom's report (2004) on The Communications Market for one account of the rapid growth involved.

16. 'Zee TV is the most successful and popular Hindi and South Asian languages subscription television channel across South Asia, Europe, Africa and North America as well as parts of the Middle East and East Asia' (Dudrah, 2001: 269).

17. Dudrah (2001, 2002a), is particularly informative on the growing opportunities for the development of global South Asian diaspora identities and ethnicities provided by Zee TV.

18. Since this research was conducted the digital explosion has led to the introduction of radio stations or segments of stations aimed specifically at young people of South Asian descent and including a music element. BBC Asian network (http://www.bbc.co.uk/asiannetwork) and sections of BBC Radio 1XTRA (http://www.bbc.co.uk/1xtra) provide examples.

19. Sunrise Radio was described by Gillespie as claiming to be 'the eleventh largest commercial radio station in the UK and the most popular radio station in West London. It caters for a wide range of regional, linguistic and religious differences whilst attempting to maintain a broad-based appeal. News bulletins and current affairs programmes are transmitted in English, Punjabi, Hindi, Urdu and Gujarati. The primary emphasis is on news from the Indian subcontinent, local news stories and stories concerning "Asians" in Britain' (Gillespie, 1995: 99).

8   What is a Brasian?

1. This declaration has some importance given the long tradition in British political discourses of positioning people of South Asian descent as permanent

outsiders, often using questions of language as a key signifier. Following fighting in northern English towns in 2001 between youths of South Asian descent and the police and white racists, the then British Home Secretary David Blunkett made the following slippery statement: 'I have never said, or implied, that lack of fluency in English was in any way directly responsible for the disturbances in Bradford, Burnley and Oldham in the summer of 2001. However, speaking English enables parents to converse with their children in English, as well as in their historic mother tongue, at home and to participate in wider modern culture. It helps overcome the schizophrenia which bedevils generational relationships. In as many as 30% of Asian British households, according to the recent citizenship survey, English is not spoken at home. But let us be clear that lack of English fluency did not cause the riots' (Blunkett, 2002: 77).

2. *The Sunday Mirror* newspaper story (3 February 2002) headlined 'The West at War: Club 18–30 to Camp Hell' by Annabelle Steggles and Dominic Turnbull.

3. And indeed a report in *The Observer* newspaper (3 November 2002) claiming to quoting directly from a letter which he'd written to his family from the prison camp in Cuba says that his letter included the phrase 'Let me know the football scores …'.

4. Brummie is an informal term referring to people in England who come from Birmingham – a major city in the English Midlands – and its surrounding areas, and to the variety of English they speak.

5. For example, an article by Vikram Dodd in *The Guardian* newspaper (17 August 2005) headlined 'Asian men targeted in stop and search', states 'The use of counter-terrorism stop and search powers has increased sevenfold since the July 7 attacks on Britain, with Asian people bearing the brunt of the increase. … People of Asian appearance were five times more likely to be stopped and searched than white people, according to the latest figures compiled by British Transport Police. None of the stops has resulted in a terrorism charge the force said.'

6. See James (1993) for an account of this process.

Bibliography

Alexander, C.E. 1996 *The Art of Being Black: The Creation of Black British Youth Identities*. Oxford: Clarendon Press.

Alexander, C.E. 2000 *The Asian Gang: Ethnicity, Identity, Masculinity*. Oxford: Berg.

Algeo, J. and Algeo, A. 1994 *Among the New Words. American Speech*, Vol. 69, No. 2, Summer, pp. 177–86.

Ali, S. 2003 *Mixed-Race, Post-Race: Gender, New Ethnicities and Cultural Practices*. Oxford and New York: Berg.

Anwar, M. 1998 *Between Cultures: Continuity and Change in the Lives of Young Asians*. London: Routledge.

Atkinson, P. and Coffey, A. 2002 'Revisiting the relationship between participant observation and interviewing'. In J.F. Gubrium and J.A. Holstein (eds) *Handbook of Interview Research*. Thousand Oaks, CA: Sage.

Back, L. 1996 *New Ethnicities and Urban Culture: Racisms and Multiculture in Young Lives*. London: UCL Press.

Baker, P. and Eversley, J. (eds) 2000 *Multilingual Capital*. London: Battlebridge Publications.

Banerjea, K. and Banerjea, P. 1996 'Psyche and soul: a view from the "South". In S. Sharma, J. Hutnyk and A. Sharma (eds) *Dis-Orienting Rhythms: The Politics of the New Asian Dance Music*. pp. 105–24. London: Zed Books.

Banerjea, K. 1998 'Sonic diaspora and its dissident footfalls'. *Postcolonial Studies*, Vol. 1, No. 3, pp. 389–400.

Banerjea, K. 2000 'Sounds of whose underground?: The fine tuning of diaspora in an age of mechanical reproduction'. *Theory, Culture and Society*, Vol. 17, No. 3, pp. 64–79.

Banerji, S. 1988 'Ghazals to bhangra in Great Britain'. *Popular Music*, Vol. 7, No. 2, pp. 207–14.

Baumann, G. 1990 'The Re-Invention of bhangra. Social change and aesthetic shifts in a Punjabi music in Britain'. *World Music*, Vol. 32, No. 2, pp. 81–95.

Baumann, G. 1996 *Contesting Culture: Discourses of Identity in Multi-ethnic London*. Cambridge: Cambridge University Press.

Becker, H. 2001 'Georges Perec's experiments in social description'. *Ethnography*, Vol. 2, No. 1, pp. 63–76.

Bennett, A. 1997 'Bhangra in Newcastle: music, ethnic identity and the role of local knowledge'. *Innovation: The European Journal of Social Sciences*, Vol. 10, No. 1, March, pp. 107–17.

Berrington, A. 1996 'Marriage Patterns and Inter-ethnic Unions'. In D. Coleman and J. Salt (eds) *Ethnicity in the 1991 Census*, Volume one, pp. 178–212. London: HMSO.

Best, J. 1989 *Images of issues*. Hawthorne, NY: Aldine de Gruyter.

Bhabha, H. 1994 *The Location of Culture*. London: Routledge.

Bhardwaj, M. and Wells, G. 1989 *Hindi Urdu Bol Chaal: A Beginners' Course in Spoken Hindi and Urdu on BBC Television*. London: BBC Books.

Bhardwaj, M. 1995 *Colloquial Panjabi: A Complete Language Course*. London: Routledge.

Bhatti, G. 1999 *Asian Children at Home and at School: An Ethnographic Study*. London: Routledge.

Bloch, M. 1977 'The past and the present in the present'. *Man*, New Series, Vol. 12, No. 2, August,. pp. 278–92.

Bloome, D. and Green, J. 1996 'Ethnography and ethnographers of and in education: a situated perspective'. In J. Flood, S. Brice–Heath and D. Lapp (eds.) *A Handbook for Literacy Educators*. New York: Macmillan.

Blunkett, D. 2002 'Integration with diversity: globalisation and the renewal of democracy and civil society'. In P. Griffith and M. Leonard (eds) *Reclaiming Britishness*. pp. 65–77. London: The Foreign Policy Centre.

Blyth, C. Recktenwald, S. and Wang, J. 1990 'I'm like "say what?!"': A new quotative in American oral narrative'. *American Speech*, Vol. 65, No. 3, pp. 215–27.

Booth, G. 2000 'Religion, gossip, narrative conventions and the construction of meaning in Hindi films songs'. *Popular Music*, Vol. 19, No. 2, pp. 125–45.

Bourdieu, P. *et al.* 1999 *The Weight of the World: Social Suffering in Contemporary Society*. Cambridge: Polity Press.

Brah, A. 1993 'Difference, diversity, differentiation'. Ch. 29. In L. Back and J. Solomos (eds) 2000 *Theories of Race and Racism: A Reader*. pp. 431–46. London: Routledge.

Brah, A. 1996 *Cartographies of Diaspora: Contesting Identities*. London: Routledge.

Bucholtz, M. 2000 'The politics of transcription'. *Journal of Pragmatics*, Vol. 32, pp. 1439–65.

Bull, M. and Back, L. (eds) 2003 *The Auditory Culture Reader*. Oxford: Berg.

Bullock Report 1975 *A Language for Life*. London: HMSO.

Bulmer, M. and Solomos, J. 1998 'Introduction: re-thinking ethnic and racial studies'. *Ethnic and Racial Studies*, Vol. 21, No. 5, September, pp. 819–37.

Carby, H.V. 1982a/1992 'Schooling in Babylon'. In CCCS (eds) 1982 *The Empire Strikes Back*. pp. 183–211. London: Routledge.

Carby, H.V. 1982b/1992 'White woman listen! Black feminism and the boundaries of sisterhood'. In CCCS (eds) 1982 *The Empire Strikes Back*. pp. 212–35. London: Routledge.

CCCS 1982/1992 *The Empire Strikes Back: Race and Racism in 70s Britain*. London: Routledge.

Cheshire, J., Edwards, V. and Whittle, P. 1993 'Non-standard English and dialect levelling'. In J. Milroy and L. Milroy (eds) *Real English: The Grammar of English Dialects in the British Isles*. pp. 53–96. London: Longman.

CILT 2001 *Speaking up for Languages: The European Year of Languages and the Promotion of Language Learning*. London: CILT.

Clarke, J., Critcher, C. and Johnson, R. 1979 *Working Class Culture: Studies in History and Theory*. London: Hutchinson.

Clifford, J. 1994 'Diasporas'. *Cultural Anthropology*, Vol. 9, No. 3, pp. 302–38.

Cohen, P. 1997 *Rethinking the Youth Question: Education, Labour and Cultural Studies*. Basingstoke, Hampshire: Macmillan Press.

Cohen, R. 1997 *Global Diasporas: An Introduction*. London: UCL Press.

Commonwealth Immigrants Advisory Committee 1964 cited in Tomlinson, S. 1983 *Ethnic Minorities in British Schools*. London: Heinemann Educational Books.

Dailey-O'Cain, J. 2000 'The sociolinguistic distribution of and attitudes toward focuser like and quotative like'. *Journal of Sociolinguistics*, Vol. 4, No. 1, pp. 60–80.

Dalby, A. 1998 *Dictionary of Languages*. London: Bloomsbury.

Dalrymple, T. 1998 'Can a liberal society tolerate eastern culture?' *New Statesman*, 23.10. 1998. pp. 28–9.

Dave, J. 1995 *Colloquial Gujarati: A Complete Language Course*. London: Routledge.

Dawson, A. 2002 'Desi remix: the plural dance cultures of New York's South Asian Diaspora'. *Jouvert: A Journal Of Postcolonial Studies*, Vol. 7, No. 1, http:// social.chass.ncsu.edu/jouvert/. Consulted 06. 02. 2003.

Deol, Singh, J. 2003 *Talk: Thought for the Day*. BBC Radio 4. 1.11.2003.

Desai, P. 2000 *Spaces of Identity, Cultures of Conflict: The Development of New British Asian Masculinities*. Unpublished PhD Thesis. Goldsmith's College, University of London.

Dingwall, R. 1997 'Accounts, interviews and observations'. In G. Miller and R. Dingwall (eds) *Context and Method in Qualitative Research*. London: Sage.

Douglas, M. 1986 *How Institutions Think*. Syracuse, NY: Syracuse University Press.

Dudrah, R.K. 2001 *British South Asian Identities and Popular Cultures of British Bhangra Music, Bollywood Films and Zee TV in Birmingham*. Unpublished PhD Thesis. University of Birmingham.

Dudrah, R.K. 2002(a) 'Zee TV – Europe and the construction of a pan-European South Asian identity'. *Contemporary South Asia*, Vol. 11, No. 2, pp. 163–81.

Dudrah, R.K. 2002(b) 'Drum "n" dhol: British bhangra music and disaporic South Asian identity formation'. *European Journal of Cultural Studies*, Vol. 5, No. 3, pp. 363–83.

Dutfield, M. 1990 *A Marriage of Inconvenience: The Persecution of Ruth and Seretse Khama*. London: Unwin Hyman.

Edwards, V. 1986 *Language in a Black Community*. Clevedon, Avon: Multilingual Matters.

Egharevba, I. 2001 'Researching an-"other" minority ethnic community: reflections of a black female researcher on the intersections of race, gender and other power positions on the research process'. *International Journal of Social Research Methodology*, Vol. 4, No. 3, pp. 225–41.

Fasold, R. 1987 *The Sociolinguistics of Society*. Oxford: Blackwell.

Ferrara, K. and Bell, B. 1995 'Sociolinguistic variation and discourse function of constructed dialogue introducers: the case of be + like'. *American Speech*, Vol. 70, No. 3, pp. 265–90.

Fishman, J. 1964 'Language maintenance and language shift as fields of inquiry'. *Linguistics*, Vol. 9, pp. 32–70.

Fishman, J. 1989 *Language & Ethnicity in Minority Sociolinguistic Perspective*. Clevedon, Avon: Multilingual Matters.

Foulkes, P. and Docherty, G. (eds) 1999 *Urban Voices: Accent Studies in the British Isles*. London: Arnold.

Frosh, S., Phoenix, A. and Pattman, R. 2002 *Young Masculinities: Understanding Boys in Contemporary Society*. Basingstoke, Hampshire: Palgrave.

Geertz, C. 1993 *The Interpretation of Cultures*. London: Fontana Press.

Gillespie, M. 1995 *Television, Ethnicity and Cultural Change*. London: Routledge.

Gilroy, P. 1987 *'There Ain't No Black in the Union Jack': The Cultural Politics of Race and Nation*. London: Routledge.

Gilroy, P. 1993a *The Black Atlantic: Modernity and Double Consciousness*. London: Verso.

Gilroy, P. 1993b *Small Acts: Thoughts on the Politics of Black Cultures*. London: Serpent's Tail.

Gilroy, P. 2001 *Between Camps: Nations, Cultures and the Allure of Race*. London: Penguin Books.

Goulbourne, H. 1998 *Race Relations in Britain Since 1945*. Basingstoke, Hampshire: Macmillan Press Ltd.

Gubrium, J. 1993 'For a cautious naturalism'. In J. Holstein and G. Miller (eds) *Reconsidering Social Constructionism: Debates in Social Problems Theory*. pp. 89–101. Hawthorne, NY: Aldine de Gruyter.

Gubrium, J.F. and Holstein, J.A. 2002 'Introduction'. In J.F. Gubrium and J.A. Holstein (eds) *Handbook of Interview Research*. Thousand Oaks, CA: Sage.

Gunew, S. 2003 'The home of language: a pedagogy of the stammer'. In S. Ahmed, C. Castañeda, A-M. Fortier and M. Sheller (eds) *Uprootings/Regroundings: Questions of Home and Migration*. pp. 41–58. Oxford: Berg.

Guy, G., Horvath, B., Vonwiller, J., Daisley, E. and Rogers, I. *1986* 'An intonational change in progress in Australian English'. *Language in Society*, Vol. 15, pp. 23–51.

Hall, K.D. 2002 *Lives in Translation: Sikh Youth as British Citizens*, PA. Philadelphia: University of Pennsylvania Press.

Hall, S. and Jefferson, T. (eds) 1976 *Resistance Through Rituals: Youth Subcultures in Post-war Britain*. London: HarperCollins Academic.

Hall, S. 1981 'Cultural studies: two paradigms'. In T. Bennett et al. (eds) *Culture, Ideology and Social Process*. pp. 19–37. Milton Keynes: Open University Press.

Hall, S. 1988 'New ethnicities'. In A. Rattansi and J. Donald (eds) 1992 *'Race', Culture & Difference*. pp. 252–59. London: Sage/Open University.

Hall, S. 1989 'Politics and letters'. Ch. 3, pp. 54–66. In T. Eagleton (ed.) 1989 *Raymond Williams: Critical Perspectives*. Cambridge: Polity Press.

Hall, S. 1990 'Cultural identity and diaspora'. In J. Rutherford (ed.) *Identity: Community, Culture, Difference*. pp. 222–37. London: Lawrence & Wishart.

Hall, S. 1991 'Old and new identities, old and new ethnicities'. In A. King (ed.) *Culture, Globalization and the World System*. pp. 41–68. London: Macmillan.

Hall, S. 1992 'The question of cultural identity'. In S. Hall, D. Held and T. McGrew (eds) *Modernity and its Futures*. pp. 273–316. Cambridge: Polity Press.

Hall, S. 1996 'Cultural identity and cinematic representation'. In H. Baker, M. Diawara and R. Lindeborg (eds) *Black British Cultural Studies: A Reader*. pp. 210–22. Chicago, IL and London: University of Chicago Press.

Hall, S., Critcher, C., Jefferson, T., Clarke and Roberts, B. 1978 *Policing the Crisis: Mugging, The State, and Law and Order*. London: Macmillan.

Hammersley, M. 2003 'Recent radical criticism of interview studies: any implications for the sociology of education?'. *British Journal of Sociology of Education*, Vol. 24, No. 1, pp. 119–26.

Harris, R. and Billington, R. (eds) 1987 *West African Students, Language and Education* [video]. London: ILEA.

Harris, R. and Savitzky F. (eds) 1988 *My Personal Language History*. London: New Beacon Books.

Harris, R. and Savitzky, F. (eds) 1985 *Afro-Caribbean Language Issues: Some Student Views* [video]. London: ILEA.

Harris, R. 1996 'Openings, absences and omissions: aspects of the treatment of "race" and ethnicity in British Cultural Studies'. *Cultural Studies*, Vol. 10, No. 2, pp. 334–44.

Harris, R. 1997 'Romantic bilingualism: time for a change?' In C. Cable and C. Leung (eds) *English as an Additional Language: Changing Perspectives*. Watford: NALDIC.

Harris, R. Schwab, I. and Whitman, L. (eds) 1990 *Language and Power*. London: Harcourt Brace Jovanovich/Harper Collins.

Hebdige, D. 1979 *Subculture: The Meaning of Style*. London: Methuen.

Hebdige, D. 1987/1990 *Cut 'N' Mix: Culture, Identity and Caribbean Music*. London: Routledge.

Hewiit, R. 1989 'A sociolinguistic view of urban adolescent relations'. Paper at the conference: *Everyday Life, Cultural Production and Race*, Institute of Cultural Sociology, University of Copenhagen.

Hewitt, R. 1986 *White Talk Black Talk: Inter-racial Friendship and Communication Among Adolescents*. Cambridge: Cambridge University Press.

Hewitt, R. 1992 'Language, youth and the destabilisation of ethnicity'. In C. Palmgren, K. Lovgren and G. Bolin (eds) *Ethnicity and Youth Culture*, pp. 27–41. Stockholm: Stockholm University.

Highmore, B. (ed.) 2002 *The Everyday Life Reader. Introduction: Questioning everyday life*. London and New York: Routledge.

Holstein, J. and Gubrium, J. 1998 'Phenomenology, ethnomethodology, and interpretive Practice'. In N. Denzin and Y. Lincoln (eds) *Strategies of Qualitative Inquiry*. Volume two. *Handbook of Qualitative Research*. pp. 137–57. London: Sage.

Hughes, A. and Trudgill, P. 1996 *English Accents and Dialects: An Introduction to Social and Regional Varieties of English in the British Isles*. Third edition. London: Arnold.

Huq, R. 1996 'Asian kool?: bhangra and beyond'. In S. Sharma, J. Hutnyk and A. Sharma (eds) *Dis-Orienting Rhythms: The Politics of the New Asian Dance Music*. pp. 61–80. London: Zed Books.

Huq, R. 1999 *Too Much Too Young: British Youth Culture in the 1990s*. Unpublished PhD Thesis. University of East London.

Hutnyk, J. 2000 *Critique of Exotica: Music, Politics and the Culture Industry*. London: Pluto Press.

James, W. 1993 'Migration, racism and identity formation: the Caribbean experience in britain'. In W. James and C. Harris (eds) *Inside Babylon: The Caribbean Diaspora in Britain*, pp. 231–87. London: Verso.

James, L. 1998 *Raj: The Making and Unmaking of British India*. New York: St Martins Press.

Jones, S. 1988 *Black Culture, White Youth: The Reggae Tradition from JA to UK*. Basingstoke: Macmillan Education.

Kalra, R.K. and Kalra, V.S. 1996 'New paths for South Asian identity and musical creativity'. In S. Sharma, J. Hutnyk and A. Sharma (eds) *Dis-Orienting Rhythms: The Politics of the New Asian Dance Music*. London: Zed Books.

Kalra, V.S. 2000 'Vilayeti rhythms: beyond bhangra's emblematic status to a translation of lyrical texts'. *Theory, Culture & Society*, Vol. 17, No. 3, pp. 80–102.

Kerswill, P. and Cheshire, J. 2004–07 'Linguistic innovators: the English of adolescents in London'. ESRC Grant Number RES-000-23-0680. Swindon: Economic and Social Research Council.

Khan, Z. 2000 'Muslim presence in Europe: the British dimension – identity, integration and community activism'. *Current Sociology*, Vol. 48, No. 4, pp. 29–43, October.

Kumar, K. 2003 *The Making of English National Identity*. Cambridge: Cambridge University Press.

Kureishi, H. 2003, January. BBC World Service Programme World Book Club. Talking about Bhuddha of Suburbia.

Labov, W. 1972 'Rules for ritual insults'. In (ed.) *Language in the Inner City: Studies in the Black English Vernacular*. pp. 297–353. Oxford: Basil Blackwell.

Lakhani, S.S. 2000 *Integration/Exclusion?: Young British Asians and the Politics of Ethnicity*. Unpublished PhD Thesis, King's College, University of London.

Lapadat, J.C. 2000 'Problematizing transcription: purpose, paradigm and quality'. *International Journal of Social Research Methodology*, Vol. 3, No. 3, pp. 203–19.

Linguistic Minorities Project. 1983 *Linguistic Minorities in England*. London: Institute of Education, University of London.

Linguistic Minorities Project. 1985 *The Other Languages of England*. London: Routledge and Kegan Paul.

Mac an Ghaill, M. 1988 *Young, Gifted and Black*. Milton Keynes: Open University Press.

Macaulay, R. 2001 'You're like "why not?" The quotative expressions of Glasgow adolescents'. *Journal of Sociolinguistics*, Vol. 5, No. 1, pp. 3–21.

Maira, S. 1998 'Desis reprazent: bhangra remix and hip hop in New York City'. *Postcolonial Studies*, Vol. 1, No. 3, pp. 357–70.

Maira, S. 1999 'Identity dub: the paradoxes of an Indian American Youth Subculture (New York Mix)'. *Cultural Anthropology*, Vol. 14, No. 1, pp. 29–60.

Malmkjaer, K. (ed.) 1995 *The Linguistics Encyclopedia*. London: Routledge.

Marre, J. and Charlton, H. 1985 *Beats of the Heart: Popular Music of the World*. New York: Pantheon Books.

Matheson, J. and Summerfield, C. (eds) *2000 Social Trends 30*. London: The Stationery Office.

Matthews, W. 1938 *Cockney Past and Present*. London: George Routledge.

McArthur, T. (ed.) 1992 *The Oxford Companion to the English Language*. Oxford: Oxford University Press.

McRobbie, A. and Garber, J. 1976 'Girls and Subcultures'. In Hall, S. and Jefferson, T. (eds.) *Resistance Through Rituals: Youth Subcultures in Post-war Britain*. pp. 209–222. London: HarperCollinsAcademic.

McRobbie, A. 1978 'Working class girls and the culture of femininity'. In Womens' Studies Group (CCCS) (eds) *Women Take Issue: Aspects of Women's Subordination*. pp. 96–108. London: Hutchinson.

McRobbie, A. 1980 'Settling accounts with subculture: a feminist critique'. In Screen Education, Spring 1980, no. 39. Reprinted in McRobbie, A. 1991 *Feminism and Youth Culture: From Jackie to Just Seventeen*, pp. 16–34. London: Macmillan.

McRobbie, A. 1992 'Post-Marxism and cultural studies: a post-script'. In L. Grossberg, C. Nelson and P.A. Treichler (eds) *Cultural Studies*, New York and London: Routledge.

Mercer, K. 1994 *Welcome to the Jungle: New Positions in Black Cultural Studies*. London: Routledge.

Mercer, K. 2000 'A sociography of diaspora'. In P. Gilroy, L. Grossberg and A. McRobbie (eds) *Without Guarantees: In Honour of Stuart Hall*, pp. 233–44. London: Verso.

Milroy, J., Milroy, L., Hartley, S. and Walshaw, D. 1994 'Glottal stops and Tyneside glottalization: competing patterns of variation and change in British English'. *Language Variation and Change*, Vol. 6, 327–57.

Mirza, H. 1992 *Young, female and black*. London: Routledge.

Modood, T. and Berthoud, R. 1997 *Ethnic Minorities in Britain: Diversity and Disadvantage*. London: Policy Studies Institute.

Morgan, M. 1998 'More than a mood or an attitude: discourse and verbal genres in African-American culture'. In S. Mufwene, J. Rickford, G. Bailey and J. Baugh (eds) *African-American English: Structure, History and Use*, pp. 251–81. London: Routledge.

Nicholas, J. 1994 *Language Diversity Surveys as Agents of Change*. Clevedon, Avon: Multilingual Matters.

Nihalani, P., Tongue, R. and Hosali, P. 1979 *Indian and British English: A Handbook of Usage and Pronunciation*. Delhi: Oxford University Press.

Nuffield Foundation 2000 *Languages: The Next Generation (The Nuffield Languages Inquiry)*. London: The Nuffield Foundation.

Ofcom 2004 *The Communications Market 2004*. London: Ofcom.

Pang, K.K. 1999 *Towards British-Chinese Futures: A Social Geography of Second Generation Young Chinese people in London*. Unpublished PhD Thesis, Queen Mary and Westfield College, University of London.

Parmar, P. 1982/1992 'Gender, race and class: Asian women in resistance'. In CCCS (eds) 1982 *The Empire Strikes Back*. pp. 236–75. London: Routledge.

Patterson, S. 1963 *Dark Strangers*. London: Tavistock.

Peach, C. 1996 'Introduction'. In C. Peach (ed.) *Ethnicity in the 1991 Census*. Volume Two. pp. 1–24. London: HMSO.

Perec, G. 1999 *Approaches to What? In Species of Spaces and Other Pieces*. pp. 209–11. London: Penguin Books.

Pollard, V. 2000 *Dread Talk: The Language of Rastafari*. University of the West Indies, Jamaica: Canoe Press/Montreal: McGill-Queen's University Press.

Puwar, N. and Raghuram, P. (eds) 2003 *South Asian Women in the Diaspora*. Oxford: Berg.

Qureshi, K. and Moores, S. 1999 'Identity remix: tradition and translation in the lives of young Pakistani Scots'. *European Journal of Cultural Studies*, Vol. 2, No. 3, pp. 311–30.

Raj, D.S. 1997 *Shifting Culture in the Global Terrain: Cultural Identity Constructions amongst British Punjabi Hindus*. Unpublished PhD Thesis. Lucy Cavendish College, University of Cambridge.

Rampton, B. 1990 'Displacing the "Native Speaker": expertise, affiliation, and inheritance'. *ELT Journal*, Vol. 44, No. 2, pp. 97–101.

Rampton, B. 1995 *Crossing: Language and Ethnicity Among Adolescents*. London: Longman.

Rampton, B. 1999 'Inner London Deutsch and the animation of an instructed foreign language'. *Journal of Sociolinguistics*, Vol. 3, 480–504.

Rampton, B. 2002 'Ritual and foreign language practices at school'. *Language in Society*, Vol. 31, 491–525.

Ritzer, G. 1992 *Sociological Theory*. Singapore: McGraw-Hill, Inc.

Roberts, C. 1997 'The politics of transcription – transcribing talk: *issues of representation*'. *TESOL Quarterly*, Vol. 31, No. 1, pp. 167–72.

Roberts, P.A. 1988 *West Indians and Their Language*. Cambridge: Cambridge University Press.

Romaine, S. and Lange, D. 1991 'The use of like as a marker of reported speech and thought: a case of grammaticalization in progress'. *American Speech*, Vol. 66, No. 2, pp. 227–79.

Rosen, H. and Burgess, T. 1980 *Languages and Dialects of London School Children*. London: Ward Lock Educational.

Runnymede Trust 1997 *Islamophobia: A Challenge for Us All*. London: Runnymede Trust.

Saeed, A., Blain, N. and Forbes, D. 1999 'New ethnic and national questions in scotland: post-British identities among Glasgow Pakistani teenagers'. *Ethnic and Racial Studies*, Vol. 22, No 5, September, pp. 821–44.

Saxena, M. 1995 *A Sociolinguistic Study of Panjabi Hindus in Southall: Language Maintenance and Shift*. Unpublished PhD Thesis, York University.

Schneider, E.W. 2000 'From region to class to identity: "Show me how you speak, and I'll tell you who you are"?' *American Speech*, Vol. 75, No. 4, pp. 359–61.

Schutz, A. 1970 *Alfred Schutz on Phenomenology and Social Relations: Selected Writings*. H.R. Wagner (ed.). Chicago, IL: The University of Chicago Press.

Schwandt, Thomas. A. 1998 'Constructivist, interpretivist approaches to Human Inquiry'. In Denzin, N. and Lincoln, Y. (eds) *The Landscape of Qualitative Research:Theories and Issues. Handbook of Qualitative Research*, Vol. 1, pp. 221–59. London: Sage.

Sebba, M. 1993 *London Jamaican: Language Systems in Interaction*. London: Longman.

Sewell, T. 1997 *Black Masculinities and Schooling: How Black Boys Survive Modern Schooling*. Stoke on Trent, Staffordshire: Trentham Books.

Sharma, S., Hutnyk, J. and Sharma, A. (eds) 1996 *Dis-Orienting Rhythms: The Politics of the New Asian Dance Music*. London: Zed Books.

Silverman, D. 1997 'Towards an aesthetics of research'. In D. Silverman (ed.) *Qualitative Research: Theory, Method and Practice*. London: Sage.

Spivak, G.C. 1984 'Criticism, Feminism, and The Institution'. In S. Harasym (ed.) 1990 *The Postcolonial Critic: Interviews, Strategies, Dialogues*. London: Routledge.

Stenström, A–B., Andersen, G. and Hasund, I.K. 2002 *Trends in Teenage Talk: Corpus Compilation, Analysis and Findings*. Amsterdam/Philadelphia: John Benjamins Publishing Company.

Sutcliffe, D. 1982 *British Black English*. Oxford: Basil Blackwell.

Swann Report 1985 *Education for All*. London: HMSO.

Tagliamonte, S. and Hudson, R. 1999 'Be like et al. beyond America: the quotative system in British and Canadian youth'. *Journal of Sociolinguistics*, Vol. 3, No. 2, 147–72.

Tate, S.A. 2005 *Black Skins, Black Masks: Hybridity, Dialogism, Performativity*. Aldershot, Hampshire: Ashgate.

The Nationality, Immigration & Asylum Act 2002. London: The Stationery Office.

Thompson, E.P. 1968 *The Making of the English Working Class*. Harmondsworth, Middlesex: Penguin Books.

Thompson, E.P. 1978 *The Poverty of Theory & Other Essays*. London: Merlin Press.

Visram, R. 2002 *Asians in Britain: 400 Years of History*. London: Pluto Press.

Wardhaugh, R. 1992 *An Introduction to Sociolinguistics*. Oxford: Blackwell.

Wells, J.C. 1986 *Accents of English 2: The British Isles*. Cambridge: Cambridge University Press.

Wenger, E. 1998 *Communities of Practice: Learning, Meaning and Identity*. Cambridge: Cambridge University Press.

White, S.T. 1991 'The Farsi (Persian) speech community'. In S. Alladina and V. Edwards (eds) *Multilingualism in the British Isles: Africa, The Middle East & Asia*. pp. 231–38. London: Longman.

Williams, R .1958 *Culture and Society. 1780–1950*. London: Chatto and Windus.

Williams, R. 1980 *Problems in Materialism and Culture: Selected Essays*. London: Verso.

Williams, R. 1976/1983 *Keywords: A Vocabulary of Culture and Society*. London: Fontana Press.

Williams, R. 1977 *Marxism and Literature*. Oxford: Oxford University Press.

Williams, R. 1992 *The Long Revolution*. London: The Hogarth Press.

Willis, P. 1978 *Profane Culture*. London: Routledge and Kegan Paul.

Willis, P. 1977/1980 *Learning to Labour: How Working Class Kids Get Working Class Jobs*. Aldershot, Hampshire: Gower.

Women's Studies Group: Editorial Group 1978 'Women's Studies Group: trying to do feminist intellectual work'. In Womens' Studies Group (CCCS) (eds) *Women Take Issue: Aspects of Women's Subordination*. London: Hutchinson.

Index

208   *Index*